A DIRTY WAR

A Russian Reporter in Chechnya

ANNA POLITKOVSKAYA has been a special correspondent for the bi-weekly Russian newspaper *Novaya gazeta* (circulation 700,000) since 1999. After graduating from the Journalism Faculty of Moscow University in 1980, she worked first for the *Izvestiya* daily, and then, in the 1990s, for the *Megapolis Express* and *Obshchaya gazeta* weeklies. She has made social issues her subject: public mores, the defective judicial system, prison conditions, and the fate of orphans, the disabled and the country's many refugees and displaced persons. In January 2000 she was awarded the prestigious Golden Pen Award by the Russian Union of Journalists for her outspoken coverage of the new federal campaign in Chechnya.

JOHN CROWFOOT lived in Moscow from 1986 to 1999. In the early 1990s he worked with *Express Chronicle* human rights weekly and Vozvrashchenie publishers. Among his translations from the Russian are Vitaly Shentalinsky's *The KGB's Literary Archives*, Lev Razgon's *True Stories* and an anthology of women's memoirs of the Gulag, *Till My Tale is Told*. He is currently translating the memoirs of Emma Gerstein.

THOMAS DE WAAL reported on Russia and the Caucasus from 1993 to 1999 for the *Moscow Times*, *The Times*, the *Economist* and the BBC World Service. With Carlotta Gall, he won a James Cameron Prize for Outstanding Reporting for their book *Chechnya: A Small Victorious War* (1997). He is now based in London and working on a book about the Nagorny Karabakh conflict.

Anna Politkovskaya

A DIRTY WAR

A RUSSIAN REPORTER
IN CHECHNYA

Translated from the Russian and edited by
John Crowfoot
with an Introduction by
Thomas de Waal

THE HARVILL PRESS
LONDON

First published in *Novaya gazeta*

This edition first published in 2001 by
The Harvill Press
2 Aztec Row, Berners Road
London N1 0PW

www.harvill.com

1 3 5 7 9 8 6 4 2

© Anna Politkovskaya, 1999
English translation © John Crowfoot, 2001
Introduction © Thomas de Waal, 2001

Anna Politkovskaya asserts the moral right to be
identified as the author of this work

All maps by Reginald Piggott

A CIP catalogue record for this title is
available from the British Library

ISBN 1 86046 897 7

Designed and typeset in Scala at
Libanus Press, Marlborough, Wiltshire

Printed and bound in Great Britain by Butler & Tanner Ltd
at Selwood Printing, Burgess Hill

CONTENTS

PART THREE: RESTORING ORDER (May 2000–January 2001)

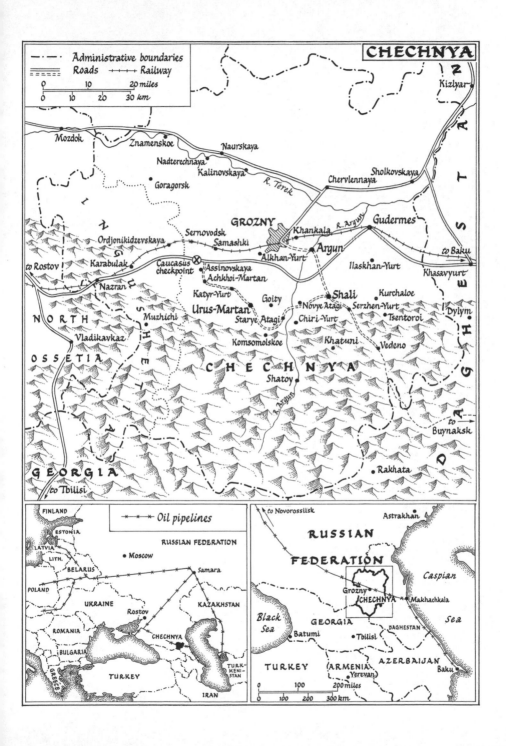

PREFACE

On 11 December 1994 Russian forces were sent into Chechnya "to restore the constitutional order" after three years of tension and uncertainty. "Why can't we carry out an operation in our country like the US did in Haiti?" demanded Kremlin hawk Oleg Lobov when warned of the possible consequences. Whether the attitudes of the war-party were shaped by contempt or historical ignorance, the use of force turned a minor distraction into a major conflict.

The Chechen fighters denied the federal authorities a rapid victory. The generals and politicians leading the campaign had to face the unaccustomed scrutiny of Russia's new media and parliament. A small but articulate minority in Moscow opposed the operation from the outset and mounting casualties extended public disaffection: a year later Boris Nemtsov, young governor of the Nizhny Novgorod Region, gathered a million signatures on a petition against the war. Finally, after 18 months of armed conflict and uneasy ceasefires, the stalemate was officially acknowledged.

Following Yeltsin's re-election as President of the Russian Federation (and a last outburst of fighting), an agreement was reached with Chechnya's leaders in August 1996. Federal troops were withdrawn, and a five-year moratorium imposed on any discussion of the republic's disputed status. The war had been a terrible and disturbing lesson for the reformers.

A mere ten years earlier the USSR was a nuclear superpower and serious rival to the West. The rapid dissolution of the Soviet bloc and the emergence of more than a dozen new states from the USSR was "in retrospect a remarkably non-violent process"[1] – only in Chechnya (and distant Tajikstan) did the transition result in war. The end of the fighting offered a new start, both to Russia and Chechnya. For a time it seemed that the brutal military campaign had been a singular lapse, one last appalling aberration in a momentous period of change that saw the end of the Cold War, the defeat of communism, and the beginning of market reforms in the old Soviet Union.

In January 1997 Aslan Maskhadov was chosen President of Chechnya in elections that international monitors agreed were free and fair. In May that year he met President Yeltsin and they signed a treaty that further confirmed the end of hostilities. Both sides seemed determined henceforth to resolve their differences by non-violent means. This commitment to democracy and diplomacy justified Russia's admission to the Council of Europe in 1996. In international eyes Chechnya remained within the Russian Federation, and was thus also regarded as part of a wider Europe.

However, others drew a different lesson from the first military campaign. If such an operation were repeated, the government was advised, the forces sent into Chechnya should be properly led and co-ordinated; and this time public opinion, the media and parliament would have to be effectively prepared and managed. When Anna Politkovskaya began reporting for the popular bi-weekly *Novaya gazeta* in summer 1999, Yeltsin was selecting a new prime minister. The little-known Vladimir Putin's candidacy benefited from a widespread feeling that the country needed firmer government, that the new business magnates, the so-called oligarchs, should be reined in and that the Federation's 89 restive regions and republics ought to be

1 John Keep, *Last of Empires: A History of the Soviet Union 1945–91*, (Oxford 1996).

brought back under control. With parliamentary elections soon to be held, a rapidly escalating sequence of events provided an opportunity for Yeltsin's protégé to give a dramatic demonstration of such firmness – fighting in Daghestan, terrorist explosions in Moscow and the second deployment of federal forces in Chechnya on 1 October 1999.

JOHN CROWFOOT

INTRODUCTION

In 1818 the tsarist general Alexei Yermolov founded a new fortress in the North Caucasus. He was stepping up his efforts to subdue the rebellious native peoples in the mountains to the south and he called the fortress Groznaya, meaning "Terrible" or "Formidable", as a token of his intent to intimidate them. How grimly appropriate then that the city of Grozny, the successor to that fortress, should now symbolise the terror that the Russian military can inflict in the modern age. Grozny, which once had a population of 400,000, is now barely a city at all. All its major buildings stand in ruins. It is modern Europe's most powerful symbol of what happens when politics fails and violence takes over.

The destruction wrought on Grozny makes even the damage to a battle-scarred town like Sarajevo seem light. Wandering through the streets after its ruination during the first Chechen war in 1994–6, it was hard to conceive how conventional weaponry had done so much harm. The centre of the city was reduced to rubble, with many of the inhabitants of these streets lying in mass graves. Ruins had been swept into tottering piles. Streets had become empty thoroughfares that ran between large areas of sky. If an occasional building had escaped the bombing, it was only a large windowless facade facing nowhere. It would have seemed more plausible to be told that the place had suffered a nuclear attack or some giant natural catastrophe.

The destruction of Grozny was both terrible and strange. Terrible, because of the wantonness and scale of the damage. Strange, because this destruction was ordered from Moscow with the stated aim of preserving Chechnya within the Russian Federation. Chechnya was Russia's equivalent of Northern Ireland within the United Kingdom or the Basque country in Spain – an unstable dissident region, some of whose citizens wanted to secede, some of whom wanted to stay in the larger country. Like both those places, it had a mixed population. The majority of the inhabitants of the centre of Grozny were Russians.

This turned out to be only the first round. In 1999–2000 even more devastation was inflicted on the city by artillery and bombers. Chechnya has now lost almost everything we associate with a modern state: government, economy, housing, power, healthcare. Chillingly, recent visitors also note a lack of men. Wandering through the devastated streets of what he called the "Hiroshima of the Caucasus" in September 2000, a British journalist found only women working on tiny efforts at rebuilding from the ruins: "The men are not simply demoralised: they have vanished – for some good reasons."[1] One reason was an order by the Russian military command to treat all Chechen males between the ages of 10 and 60 as potential fighters. Many were arrested and "filtered" into places like Chernokozovo, a former prison, turned into a "filtration camp". Chernokozovo was officially set up in order to unmask Chechen fighters, but was turned into a factory of torture and extortion against the Chechen male population. According to human rights researchers who interviewed survivors the Russian soldiers greeted new inmates with the words "Welcome to Hell".[2]

How did this hell come to pass? How did Chechnya end up obliterated by war? In answering these questions, it is important

1 Steve Crawshaw, "No Man's Land", *Independent*, 17 September 2000.
2 See Human Rights Watch "Welcome to Hell: Arbitrary Detention, Torture, and Extortion in Chechnya", October 2000 (www.hrw.org).

to remember that, although the conflict has deep historical roots, Chechnya's implosion was quite rapid. Ten years ago it was an unusual but by no means exotic southern region.

Three snapshots from my visits to Chechnya as a reporter over four and a half years, show its descent into the Inferno: I first visited Grozny in January 1994, eleven months before war broke out and a little more than two years after General Jokhar Dudayev proclaimed the republic independent of Moscow. Its freedom was only symbolic: direct flights operated from Moscow, Chechnya's borders with the rest of Russia were open and the currency was the rouble. Yet Grozny was already a bizarre place, where guns were traded in the bazaar and the silence of the night was punctuated by baying dogs and random shots. The project of Chechen independence had gone sour, and yet Grozny was still an imposing Russian city with broad boulevards, a university, shops and cafés.

Three years later in January 1997 this city had vanished. The university, the neo-classical Hotel Kavkaz, the presidential building had all been levelled by bombs. The human cost had been appalling, but a residual society had survived the war. Most of the Chechen population had retained their one-storey houses on the edge of the city. And the occasion was an optimistic one: after the Chechen victory and the Russian military withdrawal, the Chechens were holding elections, monitored by international observers. All the candidates advocated Chechen independence, but the long lines of voters were solidly behind the most pragmatic and apparently honest of them, the chief military commander Aslan Maskhadov.

Contrast these scenes to a year and a half later, the hot summer of June 1998 and my last visit to Grozny. Maskhadov had failed and peace had only brought new nightmares. The city had never been so forbidding and for the first time a foreigner had to fear for his safety in broad daylight. I had four guards with me all the time, to deter the kidnappers, who were Chechnya's most – its only – successful entrepreneurs. Hundreds of people, the majority of them Chechens, but also Russians and foreigners, were being held hostage. At the children's hospital, where staff had not been paid for months, the chief doctor told me about a growing tuberculosis epidemic. Almost the entire adult population was unemployed and insurgents opposed to President Maskhadov were growing more powerful.

This was the background to Moscow's second military intervention in the autumn of 1999, bringing yet more destruction, marauding and hatred. The second Chechen conflict is Anna Politkovskaya's subject in *A Dirty War*. Normal civilian lives are often overlooked by war correspondents in the heat of battle, but this is Politkovskaya's essential subject. By her careful reporting, the author becomes our Virgil, Dante's guide through the Inferno, a guide both to this apocalypse and to the attempts at ordinary life lived in its shadow.

This book is a work of immense courage. Politkovskaya risked the dangers of a partisan war, of army checkpoints and Chechen kidnap gangs. Finally, and most frighteningly, she was arrested, abused and threatened with death by some of the same soldiers she was investigating for atrocities. This is investigative reporting in the truest sense. She also has the capacity to remain human in the most inhuman of situations. She feels sympathy – and elicits *our* sympathy – for the victims of this conflict, however little their story. There is real pathos in the story of the Russian conscripts, misled into going to a war zone by being fuddled with alcohol and packed off in the middle of the night; or the poor villager whose only cow has been shot by a rabid Russian general using it for target practice. Of such little calamities is a great tragedy made.

Much has been misunderstood about the origins and nature of the Chechen conflict. Many of the categories commentators use to describe it are simply misleading. The war was not, as Moscow determined it in 1999, an "anti-terrorist operation": you do not flatten cities in anti-terrorist operations. It has never been an Islamic jihad – the Chechnya that initially fought for its independence in 1994 was, formally at least, a secular republic. Islam won more recruits during the war and afterwards, but it was more a new badge of identity than fuel for conflict. Equally, the politics of oil, despite many Western analyses, was always a secondary consideration. Chechnya was producing very little oil by the 1990s and the separatist regime in Grozny never interfered with the oil pipeline from the Caspian Sea that ran through Chechnya. In dozens of conversations with Russian officials about the origins of the 1994 war I do not remember the subject coming up once.

It is better to see the Chechen war within the particular history of the North Caucasus Region and the clumsy efforts made to integrate it into the Russian state. The region is both Russia and not Russia. The mountains, foothills and plains on the north side of the Caucasus contain a patchwork of small nationalities, which were incorporated into the Russian Empire only in the mid-nineteenth century. In the Soviet era they were divided into six – now seven – "autonomous republics", regions where some of the more populous nationalities were honoured with a higher symbolic status and a few token institutions. The common language and urban culture is Russian. Yet they were and remain a world away from the flat Slavic heartlands of Russia because of their mountainous geography, distinct ethnic traditions and the predominance of Islam over Christianity.

In the summer of 1999, when Anna Politkovskaya travelled to the region, the focus of anxiety was the easternmost republic, Daghestan. Daghestan forms a long sliver of mountains that falls down to a strip of coastline and then the Caspian Sea. Almost every valley is home to a new nationality and language; by one estimate there are 34 main ethnic groups in the republic. This has helped to make Islam a greater force than in Chechnya, indeed the republic's *lingua franca* used to be Arabic, as taught in the mosques (it is now Russian). Deeply divided within itself and heavily reliant on Moscow for economic subsidy, the region has remained, as it were, Russian by default and the idea of Daghestani independence has never carried weight.

Yet after the war in Chechnya ended in 1996, Daghestan began to fall apart. Radical Islam made headway among young men and many of them flocked to two villages, Karamakhi and Chabanmakhi, which declared themselves autonomous from the regional government. The republic's notoriously venal politicians resorted to violence to sort out their feuds and there were prominent victims in gangland-style bombings and shootings every week. Chechnya, de facto independent and next door, provided a haven and safe refuge for armed gangsters and militants on the run

On 7 August 1999 two Chechnya-based warlords moved across the mountains from Chechnya into Daghestan in a convoy of vehicles and armed men. They acted suddenly and their motives were unclear. One was Shamil Basayev, the most famous of the Chechen warriors of the first conflict. Basayev had become Russia's enemy number one after he led a raid deep into southern Russia in 1995 and took hundreds hostage in the town of Budyonnovsk. He had been allowed to escape back to Chechnya in return for the promise of peace negotiations. A year later he led the Chechen recapture of Grozny. Basayev is more radical than President Maskhadov and was seeking a new role for himself in post-war Chechnya. Equally, he was not a radical Islamist, merely a devout adherent of the *Naqshbandiya*, the local Chechen brand of Sufi Islam.

His comrade-in-arms was Emir Khattab, a frightening individual with long black Medusa-like locks. Khattab, the only non-Chechen to have fought with prominence in the first war, is a Bedu from Saudi Arabia. He fought with the mujahedin against the Soviets in Afghanistan and moved to Chechnya in 1995. A year later he led an operation that destroyed an entire Russian tank column high in the southern mountains. A video cassette of the attack – released no doubt to elicit more money from his Saudi sponsors and on sale in Grozny market – shows Khattab walking along a line of charred Russian corpses, yelling in triumph. After the war was over, Khattab stayed on in Chechnya and started a training camp for fighters.

The two warlords, together with a couple of thousand warriors, moved into three villages in the mountains. They said later they were responding to a call for help from Islamist allies in three mountain villages, but their broader goals are disputed. It seems unlikely that at this point Basayev and Khattab were anticipating a new war in Chechnya. A year before they had publicly proclaimed their desire to yoke Chechnya and Daghestan together into one Islamic republic. A union with Daghestan was probably their long-term ambition and any rebel movement in the North Caucasus needed Daghestani support to flourish; but in 1999 a union like this had no widespread public support and was little more than a slogan. (Indeed Basayev seemed to be aware of this. When I interviewed him in June 1998 the subject of Daghestan did not come up once, he talked only about Chechnya and Russia.) Another writer has called the fighters "Che Guevaras in turbans", men more interested in the overthrow of the pro-Russian corrupt order in Daghestan than in creating an Islamic state.[3] Just as important a spur for Basayev was his obsessive desire to continue the fight against the Russians in any manner possible; since 1996 he had lost status and purpose in Chechnya and had had an unsuccessful spell as the republic's prime minister. He remained a man in quest of martial glory as an end in itself.

Inevitably, this being the Caucasus, there are also suggestions of conspiracy. Some suspect that the Chechen incursion was deliberately provoked by someone in Moscow to justify a strong military response. The two men were invited into Daghestan by two criminalised politician brothers, the Khachilayevs, who had shadowy connections in Moscow (one of them has since been murdered). It was also an open secret in Chechnya that the telephones and the radical Islamic website used by the invaders had been paid for by the prominent Kremlin insider and business tycoon Boris Berezovsky – a man with long-standing business links in Chechnya and a murky political agenda in Moscow.

What needs no proof is that Basayev and Khattab's incursion into

3 Georgi M. Derluguian, "Che Guevaras in Turbans", *New Left Review*, September/ October 1999.

Daghestan was the cue for a momentous shift of power in Moscow: the entry on to the Russian political stage of a new strong man, the then head of the counterintelligence service or FSB, Vladimir Putin. Putin was named Russia's new Prime Minister on 9 August, two days after the first raid. He promptly flew down to Daghestan to take charge and ordered an escalation of the Russian response. Three weeks later he ordered an attack on the two separatist Islamic villages in the plains. Then a bomb, almost certainly planted by the rebels, tore apart a Russian army compound in the Daghestani town of Buinaksk; it killed 62 people. Further terrorist bomb attacks, their motive unexplained, killed more than 200 people in Moscow and southern Russia. They provided the background to a new intervention in Chechnya.

By marching into Daghestan, Basayev and Khattab had detonated a different kind of explosion in Russia's most fragile region. They also made a big miscalculation. They clearly believed that they could count on local support, but instead a flood of Daghestanis poured away from the mountains and there were demonstrations and rallies against the Chechen invaders. Thousands of Daghestanis appealed to the Russian authorities to give them weapons to fight the Chechens. The region was threatening to turn into a mini-Lebanon, a place with no central control, fought over by private armies.

It is crucial here to emphasise how different Daghestan and Chechnya are. There is no "domino effect" waiting to happen in the North Caucasus – or indeed elsewhere in Russia. Few Daghestanis have ever advocated secession from Russia. Chechnya was and remains very different, its attempt at independence a special case. This is because, in contrast to their other North Caucasian neighbours, the Chechens had two engines that propelled their movement for independence: both a political and economic base and a common memory of mass persecution. Of all the pieces in the mosaic of the North Caucasus, Chechnya alone had a productive economy, centred on its factories and oil refineries, and a large and homogeneous population (with around 800,000 Chechens in 1991). They also had a living recollection of mass trauma: they were the largest ethnic group in the Caucasus to be deported en masse by Stalin to Kazakhstan in 1944. Tens of thousands died on the way and Chechnya was abolished and erased from the map. The Chechens were allowed to return home only in 1957 after Nikita Khrushchev's Secret Speech denouncing Stalin, but even then were still second-class citizens in their own republic, subordinate to ethnic Russians.

In 1991 Chechnya gained a radical leader, General Dudayev, who was able to mobilise these grievances into a bid for independence. Dudayev made his dash for freedom in September 1991, when the whole architecture of the Soviet Union was breaking up. It was not a classical act of de-colonisation. Dudayev had been a patriotic Soviet general, who spoke Russian better than Chechen and was married to a Russian. He was an impulsive and difficult leader, who found it difficult to negotiate with Moscow – but sometimes offered very favourable terms for re-joining Russia.

The tragedy of Chechnya is that the 1994 war was completely avoidable. Dudayev was a poor negotiator. But, far more importantly, the administration in Moscow lacked any maturity and historical insight in their bargaining process with the Chechens. To achieve a peaceful settlement with Dudayev required a gesture of historic respect for what would have been the Chechens' first ever voluntary submission to a Russian state. The failure to meet this challenge was the biggest failure of Yeltsin's new Russia.

The men in the Kremlin also lacked the courage to do something else: to cut off the roots of the outlaw economy that had allowed Chechnya to flourish for three years – and they were in Moscow not Grozny.

The Chechens had always had an outlaw reputation. Even in the twentieth century, administration by Moscow was at best provisional. The American engineer George Burrell saw this in 1929, when the Soviet authorities were attempting forced collectivisation of Chechnya:

When we first went to Grozny we locked the doors and windows at night and were a little apprehensive about the fighting going on around us. We would see the soldiers going out fully equipped for a foray into the hills or the steppe, and see them coming back, tired after a seemingly hard campaign, bringing their dead and injured with them, for they by no means escaped unscathed. But the Army is too powerful for scattered bands of tribesmen or groups of villagers to contend with, hence as time passed less fighting occurred in the surrounding district.

The trouble would sometimes start when a Government agent went to a village to collect taxes, grain or cattle. He was occasionally roughly handled, or killed. Then retaliatory measures commenced and mayhap what was left of that village was little enough. Some motor cars in Grozny were punctured with bullet holes. Anybody in a motor car out on the steppe might be mistaken for the tribesmen's persecutors and a shot would come winging through the air. Several chauffeurs were killed while we were in Grozny, hence there were some localities not far from Grozny where foreign experts were forbidden to go.

The tribesmen, say the Chechens, are a proud race, not easy to coerce. Many of them dislike the Government on various counts. The men never did much work, allowing the women that privilege. Now an effort is being made to make them work. Furthermore, many are Mohammedans, difficult to persuade on religious matters, and do not take kindly to the Communistic form of religion, or to any change in their mode of living. The Government, they find, wants to change everything. They resent changes in their age-old customs – the blood-feud, harems and the sale of brides. The Mohammedans hopelessly see the passing of Islam as a force in Soviet Russia."[4]

There was an old Chechen tradition of the *abrek*, the noble bandit who resists authority. In the modern period he had a less glamorous descendant, the Chechen Mafioso. The generation of Chechens that grew up in exile in Kazakhstan was excluded from positions of authority in the Soviet system and men from this group formed one of the most feared criminal networks in Moscow. Even today, Chechen criminals have powerful influence in the Russian second-hand car business, oil pipelines and even the Moscow city administration. Naturally the existence between 1991 and 1994 of a "free economic zone" in the south outside the Kremlin's jurisdiction made their lives – and the lives of a lot of corrupt Russian politicians – a great deal easier.

Reading Politkovskaya's book, we are reminded that war did not close down the shadow economy in Russia and Chechnya. It merely changed the list of products for sale and raised the prices.

The fact that men make money out of war is a truism. In Chechnya this process has gone much further than usual and the pursuit of financial gain has distorted all other goals. Put simply, everything is up for sale. Politkovskaya records that Russian officers had allegedly taken over control of the backyard oil wells that were Chechnya's most lucrative asset. At the same time they were also alleged to be shipping metal out of the republic.[5]

This is only the tip of the iceberg. "I could buy a tank if I wanted to," a Chechen trader once told me with typical braggadocio, but he was exaggerating only a little. He had already bought automatic weapons, grenades and ammunition from Russian conscripts – weapons that were bound to be later turned on them or their comrades. Politkovskaya discovered evidence of the same practice in the latest conflict. The first chapter in this book is yet more

4 George A Burrell, *An American Engineer Looks at Russia*, Boston, 1932, pp.110–11.
5 This allegation was made by Ruslan Khasbulatov, the former speaker of the Russian parliament and a strong opponent of Chechen independence in a devastatingly critical article on Moscow's policies in *Nezavisimaya gazeta*, 29 December 2000.

grotesque, as she relates in effect how unidentified corpses became articles of commerce. Samuel Beckett – or nearer to home Nikolai Gogol – could not have dreamed up anything blacker.

The largest amounts of money to be earned in Chechnya came with the kidnapping business. The taking of hostages is an old practice in the North Caucasus, where many mountain tribesmen were in the habit of raiding Cossack settlements and traders in the plains. War, economic collapse and a plentiful supply of guns caused it to surge up again in Chechnya in 1997.

This time however it took on a very contemporary spin. Gangs armed themselves with four-wheel-drive vehicles and satellite phones. The kidnappers were exceptionally brutal, given to torturing their victims and despatching gruesome videotapes of their acts to the families involved. They used "intermediaries", often top-ranking Russian and local officials, who reputedly won large slices of any financial deal negotiated. And they extracted ransoms that were staggering by regional standards. In a region where salaries were at best a few dollars a month, kidnappers demanded – and received – millions of dollars in ransom fees. After several Russian magnates paid out this kind of money, shares in the kidnapping business rocketed.

At least some of the kidnappers have found favour with the Russian authorities. In a extraordinary twist to this tale, it was reported in the autumn of 2000 that the Russian domestic intelligence service, the FSB, was protecting Arbi Barayev, a ruthless Islamist, implicated in numerous kidnappings and the beheading of four Western telecom engineers in Chechnya in 1998. *Moscow News* reported that Barayev and two other prominent kidnappers, the Akhmadov brothers, had apparently switched sides and were helping the Russians. The three were living in their own houses and travelling freely across Chechnya in their own vehicles. None of them had been put on Russia's wanted list and the Akhmadovs were said to be in possession of FSB documents. If true, the implications of this are devastating: the Russian security services have been working with the very "bandits" in Chechnya they claimed to have come to disarm.[6]

The complexity and danger of Chechnya make it a difficult place for reporters. In the first war there were compensations. Russia and Chechnya were so anarchic that it was possible to drive into Chechnya with a hired driver and travel freely. The two sides were often extraordinarily close; I once took tea with the rebel Chechen vice-president – a man with an arrest warrant on his head in Moscow – less than a mile from a Russian checkpoint. And ordinary Chechen villagers were unfailingly warm and helpful to Western reporters. Most had no political affiliation, although almost all were full of hatred against the Russian invader. They took us in without a moment's thought, mindless of the risks and the expense of having guests during a war.

The Russian side was always more difficult. The generals never spoke to us, making exceptions only for a handful of faithful Russian correspondents. The information supplied by the Defence Ministry in Moscow was worse than useless. Only the lower ranks, miserable and badly informed, were accessible. They divided into two categories, the conscripts and the contract soldiers, known as *kontraktniki*. In the spring of 1996 I spent an hour with three conscripts in a guard-post in Grozny. They had one bed, a scrappy wood fire, and a cast-iron pan. One of them had scrawled on the wall in wavy chalk: *I want to go home!* I do not know if they ever got home before the Chechen fighters came back to Grozny three months later; I do know that if they were there they would have either surrendered or been slaughtered. We were more likely to meet the *kontraktniki* at checkpoints, where they were more ruthless at extracting bribes. They were often ex-criminals with tattoos along their arms and bandannas on their

6 Sanobar Shermatova, "The Secret War between Russian Intelligence Agencies in Chechnya", *Moscow News*, 8 August 2000.

heads, creatures more of gangland than a modern European army –
and no friends to journalists.

The latest war has posed a far bigger challenge to journalists. The
Chechen side has been simply shrouded in darkness, the risk of kidnap having made it too dangerous to report on. The brave reporters
that have managed to gain access to the Chechen leadership have done
so undercover and have had little contact with the local population.

By contrast, the Russian authorities have waged their information
war with much greater professionalism. In Moscow Valery Manilov,
deputy head of the General Staff, became the army's omnipresent
spokesman, spouting a stream of often contradictory statistics.[7] On
the ground generals, like the much-feared Vladimir Shamanov, turned
into media figures. On the strength of his public image, Shamanov
was elected governor of Ulyanovsk Region, the birthplace of Lenin,
after he was removed from his post.

The government has put tight controls on the media. Russian
journalists were routinely summoned for interviews in which they
were reminded of their patriotic duty in reporting the "anti-terrorist
operation". Strenuous efforts were made to keep foreign correspondents out of the combat zone altogether. Those who went there
without the proper accreditation risked being denied visas, while
Moscow-based correspondents were called to the Foreign Ministry
and reprimanded for their anti-Russian coverage.

The most important difference, however, came from within.
This time the military intervention in Chechnya had broad popular
support. The main reason for this was a wave of anger and revulsion
that followed a string of bomb explosions in Russian cities in
September 1999.

7 Eg Manilov's public calculation of Chechen rebel numbers ranged between 8,000
  and 26,000. His estimation of rebel losses ranged between 3,000 and 7,000. See
  Simon Saradzhyan, "General Manilov's 'Dead Souls' Math", Moscow Times, 25 July
  2000. He also stated that the total population of Chechnya in August 1999 was only
  300,000, although twice that number of Chechens had voted in the presidential
  election two years before.

The first tremor, on 4 September, came with the slaughter of Russian soldiers and their families in Buinaksk in Daghestan. Shocking as it was, this made little impact outside the North Caucasus. But then the whole country was traumatised. Two apartment blocks, seemingly chosen at random, were blown up in Moscow within a week. More than 200 people were killed in their beds. A fourth and final blast in the southern city of Volgodonsk killed 17 more people.

The explosions were terrifying acts of murder, all the more so because no warnings had been given and no responsibility claimed. The Russian authorities laid the blame on "Chechen terrorists" – only to get a stout denial from Shamil Basayev that he was involved.

The conspiracy theorists have again posed some challenging questions. How come Basayev was accused of randomly killing civilians in Moscow, when he had never targeted civilians before? And wasn't it true that the main beneficiary of the bombings was the new administration of Vladimir Putin? It is indeed strange, to say the least, that the explosions happened out of the blue when Chechnya was at peace – and then stopped again so suddenly. Fighting only broke out in Chechnya after the chain of explosions had ended.

Yet several extremist Islamic militants in the North Caucasus did also have both the means and the motive to stage revenge attacks on Russian cities. The trail here leads to Daghestan, more than to Chechnya. There is a clear circumstantial link between the slaughter at Buinaksk in Daghestan and the two militant Islamic villages in the same region, which were captured with great bloodshed by Russian forces only a few days before. In an interview at the time (in the Czech newspaper *Lidove Noviny*) Basayev acknowledged the connection: "I denounce terrorism, including state terrorism used by the Russian empire," he said. "The latest blast in Moscow is not our work, but the work of the Daghestanis. Russia has been openly terrorising Daghestan . . . What is the difference between someone letting a bomb go off in the centre of Moscow and injuring 10 to 20 children and the Russians dropping bombs from their aircraft over

Karamakhi and killing 10 to 20 children? Where is the difference?" Although denying personal involvement with the bombings, Basayev seemed to suggest he knew something about them.

To the Russian authorities, however, this was not simply a matter of unsubstantiated suspicions. Officials said they had evidence that linked the bombings to "international terrorism" in Chechnya and made the sensational accusation that the bombers are linked to the Afghanistan-based Saudi dissident, Osama Bin Laden, who is wanted by the United States for explosions in American embassies in East Africa.

The trouble with these very serious charges is the meagre scraps of evidence produced in support of them: a small group of foreign captives, a few brazen quotations from the Chechen war-lords and an Islamic website preaching holy war, www.kavkaz.org. Set against this are some good reasons to be sceptical in the absence of more concrete facts. The Islamic website was set up by the hard Islamic wing of the Chechen rebels with the explicit aim of attracting foreign support; their claims about an Islamic holy war can easily be interpreted as an opportunistic recruiting drive. The Russians have a vested interest in naming Osama Bin Laden, as that helps to blunt Washington's criticism of its conduct in Chechnya. Despite its talk of battalions of Islamic volunteers, the Russians have only been able to produce half a dozen foreigners taken captive out of the hundreds of Chechen fighters that have fallen into their hands. Most of these probably belong to the unit that Khattab brought to Chechnya in 1995. Even if more volunteers want to join the rebels – which seems a reasonable proposition – there are big logistical problems preventing them crossing two other countries, Georgia and Azerbaijan, and the Caucasus mountain range.

The enigma of the bombings has not yet been solved. In September 2000 the Russian authorities said they had arrested 63 people in connection with the attacks. Interestingly they said that most were of North Caucasian origin, but there were very few Chechens among them.

Literature rather than politics provides one possible key for unlocking these horrific events. In *The Devils* Dostoevsky portrays a group of terrorists so infiltrated by the secret police that it does not know which way it is looking. The tradition of the militant-turned-provocateur is a long one in Russia and takes in Father Gapon, the man who led the revolutionary workers on the Bloody Sunday march in St Petersburg in 1905 – and then turned out to have been working for the tsarist secret police. The same kind of suspicion has fallen on the Khachilayev brothers in Daghestan. So it should not be ruled out, bizarre as it sounds, that *both* Islamic militants *and* Russian provocateurs had a role to play in the bomb explosions.

None of this is to deny that Moscow faces a real dilemma in Chechnya – albeit one largely of its own making – and that it faces some very desperate and dangerous enemies, such as Basayev and Khattab. The devil is all in the detail. The campaign that Putin waged – and which helped to sweep him into the Russian presidency – made no fine distinctions between separatists and terrorists, political rebels and bandits. The Russian public was encouraged to identify all Chechens as enemies and an intense wave of xenophobia, cultivated from the top down, swept through the country.

The first victim of this was Chechnya's president, Aslan Maskhadov. Maskhadov had failed to bring order to Chechnya. He had tried to please everybody and lost a lot of credibility in the process. But he remained the legitimate leader of Chechnya, acknowledged as such by the Russian authorities after an election that was judged free and fair by international observers. In May 1997 President Yeltsin even received him in the Kremlin. To simply ignore him looked wilful and arrogant. But he too was now demonised, his repeated requests for meetings with Russian officials turned down. His envoy in Moscow, who had been attempting to negotiate, was arrested and jailed for allegedly carrying a pistol.

The official media fuelled the hysteria, portraying the conflict in deterministic good-and-evil terms. As Russian troops went into

Chechnya, the three main television channels went to reports by young fair-haired boys in their twenties, always in among the Russian armed forces; they talked about the successes of "our boys" against the "terrorists", while the Chechen rebels on the other side were never killed, always "destroyed".

On 21 October a volley of missiles butchered dozens of Chechen civilians in Grozny's Central Market. Russian television broadcast no pictures of the massacre, initially denied that it had happened at all, and then gave several contradictory accounts of how it had been the work of the Chechens themselves.

Few Russian media outlets had the courage to report the story objectively. The palm goes to a handful of Moscow newspapers, in particular the weeklies *Moscow News* and *Obshchaya gazeta* and Politkovskaya's newspaper, the bi-weekly *Novaya gazeta*. How dangerous it now is to be a free-thinking Russian journalist was illustrated by the death in July 2000 of *Novaya gazeta*'s Igor Domnikov. Two months before, he had been attacked by an unknown assailant with a hammer in the entrance to his apartment block. He never recovered consciousness.

All this puts Politkovskaya's achievement into context. She is in a very select band. It is an interesting phenomenon that many of the best journalists in Chechnya have been women. One could also mention Anne Nivat, as well as Carlotta Gall, Petra Prochazkova, Yelena Masyuk, Maria Eismont – as well as the late Nadezhda Chaikova of *Obshchaya gazeta*, who was murdered in eastern Chechnya in the spring of 1996. This may be because to report well on Chechnya has required not only physical bravery but also the kind of long-term commitment that women reporters are often better at: the ability to work for the long term and negotiate with difficult and delicate situations over many months.

As I write, the war is still going on. Russian public support has begun to ebb, but is still broadly behind President Putin. Although the operation has been declared over, the Russian army continues to lose around 30 men a week. On 22 January 2001, President Putin handed overall control of the campaign over to the counter-intelligence service, the FSB. The official spin put on this in Moscow was that the army was no longer needed. It could also be seen as a recognition that the army had failed. With more than 3,000 soldiers and a far greater number of Chechens killed, the main culprits Shamil Basayev and Khattab are still at large. It seems unlikely that the FSB, who lack experience for this kind of operation, will succeed where the army has failed.

Russia has resisted all attempts to bring in international medi-ators to end the fighting – a role the Organization for Security and Cooperation in Europe played during the first war. Pointing to NATO's bombing of Serbia six months earlier, Moscow called Western criticism of its own operation "double standards". For its part, the international community has chosen mainly to ignore Chechnya – with the honourable exception of a few human rights groups. Many of the outsiders who have condemned Russia most vocally have often done so with dubious motives; some Islamic countries have perceived the war, mistakenly, as a war against Islam, while several Cold Warriors, mainly in Washington, sympathise with the Chechens in so far as they are continuing the liberation struggle against the evil empire in Moscow.

A more engaged and serious response has been entirely absent. The Council of Europe suspended the voting rights of the Russian parliamentary delegation, but has since restored them. The British Prime Minister, Tony Blair, who had promised to introduce an "ethical aspect" to his foreign policy, invited Vladimir Putin to London during the height of the fighting and even before he was elected president. Blair's spokesman said that Russia was facing a "terrorist insurrec-tion" in Chechnya.

And yet the war in Chechnya is above all Russia's agony. Leaving aside any moral considerations, it is simply not practical to wish the Russians success in "winning" this war. Moscow cannot succeed in making Chechnya a normal part of Russia again because the weapon it is using – the Russian armed forces – treats Chechnya as a foreign country, open for marauding and random violence. While the Russian security system is too corrupt and vicious to deal with Chechnya fairly – and that probably means over the next generation – ordinary Chechens will feel a deep allergy to Russian military occupation and young Chechen males will be pushed into joining the rebels. The cycle of violence looks to be self-fulfilling.

In February 2001 a Chechen friend wrote to me, after visiting her family in Grozny:

> Everything is relatively OK at home, but in the republic as a whole the drama carries on. People are dying every day, young lads vanish – they are arrested openly at checkpoints . . . When someone is arrested like this the poor boys ask people nearby to send a message to their relatives just saying where they are from. And the next day the mullah at the mosque makes an announcement to all the villagers through a loud-speaker: "Two boys were arrested at the checkpoint in Grozny, they sent a message, etc. . . . go and search for them . . . etc." My cousin heard an announcement like this in the village of Berdekel . . . I was in Grozny six days and all that time it snowed and the temperature was below freezing . . . But, strange as it sounds, I returned to Moscow full of optimism. People at home are so strong and have still not lost their sense of humour, despite all their calamities and suffering.

A *Dirty War* offers no solutions to this continuing suffering. It is the nearest thing yet written to a correct diagnosis.

THOMAS DE WAAL

The last battle of the first war. The bodies of federal soldiers killed in action in Grozny (August 1996).
© Stanley Greene/VU/Evidence X

The "Caucasus" checkpoint on the Ingushetia-Chechnya border. Chechens waiting to be allowed to go home (November 1999).
© Heidi Bradner

These Chechen refugees have travelled a long way to the border at Shatily in the hope of crossing into Georgia. But in a deal with the federal authorities Georgia has just closed its borders (December 1999).
© Eddy van Wessel

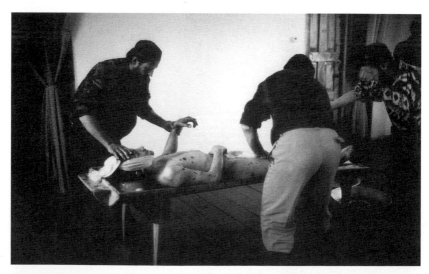

Twenty-three-year-old Mashoud was killed when Makhkety was bombed. His friends wash his body for the family (December 1999).
© Eddy van Wessel

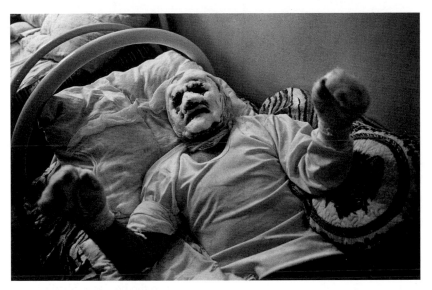

The Polipsovsk Hospital, Ingushetia. An elder from the village of Sernovodsk who stayed to watch over the family home during a bombardment. He was badly burned when gas pipes exploded after the attack (December 1999).
© Heidi Bradner

A federal soldier guards the entrance to the Grozny oil refinery (March 2000).
© Stanley Greene/VU/Evidence X

This resident of Grozny surveys the damage after a bombardment from federal forces. Written on the wall behind her are the words "People are living here" (June 2000).
© Jenny Matthews

Women rebuilding their houses in Grozny (June 2000).
© Jenny Matthews

The "Sputnik" refugee camp in Ingushetia (August 2000).
© Stanley Greene/VU/Evidence X

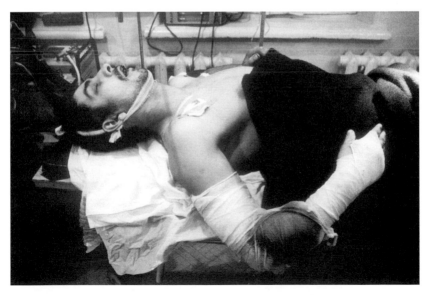

Hospital No 9, Grozny. A young man caught in the crossfire between Chechen fighters and federal forces. He died from his wounds (October 2000).
© Stanley Greene/VU/Evidence X

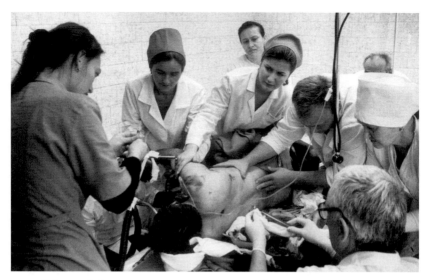

A small hospital for war veterans in Staraya Sunzha, near Grozny. The patient, Lom-Ali Timchayez, was left for dead in the market square. Diesel fuel is brought in from Hospital No 9 to make the generator work (October 2000).

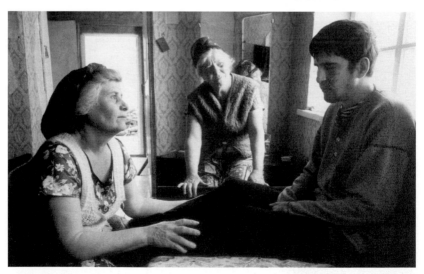

A victim of a booby-trap in Grozny is comforted by his mother and aunt. When he went to pick up a tape-recorder he saw on the pavement it exploded in his face (October 2000).

A checkpoint under Chechen opposition control in Staraya Sunzha, near Grozny. This fighter told the photographer: "Grozny needs order and it needs police. In the daytime we are the police and at night we shoot the Russians" (October 2000).

© Stanley Greene/VU/Evidence X

A federal soldier on the outskirts of Grozny. In a few days his unit will be sent into the heart of the city (December 2000).

© Heidi Bradner

The end of a superpower? Grozny, Chechnya.
© Stanley Greene/VU/Evidence X

A DIRTY WAR

PART ONE

THE BUILD-UP

July–October 1999

"You're no Muslim," I told Basayev . . . He answered me in Russian: "We're driving out the Russians, Mother, because they don't want Islam." I spat at him and said: "Yours is a dirty war, it's not a Muslim war! There aren't any Russians here."

KALIMAT IBRAGIMOVA

ANSALTA, DAGHESTAN

The regime couldn't resolve the conflict itself so it decided to go to war. Now we must hand over our children to correct other people's mistakes . . . my eldest boy was bullied quite unmercifully in the army and returned home not entirely in his right mind . . . So now they want my next son? Not for anything in this world.

LYDIA BURMISTROVA

MOSCOW

"What do you think?" I ask them. "What are the police up to?"

   "They told me themselves," replies Arslan, "the Chechens are being labelled a nation of criminals."

MOSCOW

7 OCTOBER 1999

I

GRAVE-ROBBERS

The War Dead of 1994–6

In early August few knew that only two months hence the Russian government would again send the army into Chechnya. It was clear, however, that relations with that republic and, more importantly, within Russian society itself could hardly be described as normal.

25 July 1999

Yury Plotnikov has just returned from his latest expedition to Chechnya and, alas, he has come back empty-handed. He was shown four corpses, dug out of the scorching hot Chechen soil near Grozny but not one was handed over. Instead the local committee for locating those missing in action (a body set up by the Chechen government) added these wretched bodies to eleven other captive corpses dug up some time earlier, and then, before Yury's eyes, locked them all away. We forbid you to take these exhumed corpses out of Chechnya, they told him: if you meet some of our conditions, then maybe we'll think again.

Plotnikov is a member of the working group set up by President Yeltsin for the exhumation and identification of soldiers killed during the Chechen war (1994–6). All he brought back to Moscow this time was the news that 15 bodies, identified as Russian soldiers, are being deliberately held hostage in Chechnya. Again we are forced to bargain, and this time it is the most outrageous of all the trades known to mankind, when the goods up for sale are a pile of decomposing human remains. What is going on here? Why do the Chechens behave with such insolence? Are they doing so of their own accord . . . or perhaps there are other reasons?

"To whom does a dead body belong?" Ask any normal person and they will answer without a moment's thought: "To the relatives, of course, and no one else."

Try as he might, Colonel Slipchenko could not clearly formulate an answer to this question. He is the general director of Military Commemoration Ltd; not long ago he was a colonel serving on the General Staff. Today the remains of more than 400 soldiers and officers are still lying in unmarked graves somewhere in Chechnya, and several hundred other corpses are awaiting identification at Forensic Laboratory No 124 in Rostov-on-Don, but Slipchenko, a military man himself, finds nothing particularly shocking about this.

"So they're lying there! We must work effectively, and not rush things. It'll take many years yet to finish the job," Slipchenko assured us.

He quickly changed the subject and began to talk about the American experience. Even today, he believed, not all the US participants in the Vietnam War had been found and identified. As a businessman, though, Slipchenko's odd attitude is entirely understandable. The longer the process of exhumation continues, the more profit there is for him. He earns his money from the exhumation and identification of those officers and soldiers of the Russian armed forces who died in Chechnya; his firm, Military Commemoration Ltd, where this interview took place, is located in the same Moscow building as the Chief Military Prosecutor's office. It is, to be sure, a very curious kind of commercial enterprise. And there is, of course, nothing accidental about their proximity. The Military Prosecutor's

Office, as we all know, bears part of the responsibility for locating the unmarked graves. It should be doing this job during working hours and is paid to do so. But it cannot always find the time.

Military Commemoration Ltd

Military Commemoration Ltd was formed in 1997 by the Ministry of Defence to organise the burial of servicemen and women killed in action. Formerly the Armed Forces Statute laid this responsibility on the military unit in which the individual had served. Now the task has been entrusted to these new businessmen and they make money from the location, transfer and burial of such remains.

Naturally, profit is the purpose of all business. In this case, however, it has come into blatant conflict with common sense and the Armed Forces Statute. The money for each buried serviceman comes from the budget, and the total sum allocated to the nation's defence is, in turn, confirmed each year in closed session by the Duma. Who are the deputies trying so hard to help with these funds? A private company, it would seem.

The state allocates funds for exhumation and identification and these are then transferred to the accounts of Slipchenko, among others. That was the decision of the Ministry of Defence. These sums, if you remember, were provided only after extraordinary efforts on the part of various non-governmental organisations, above all the Committees of Soldiers' Mothers. Thanks to them this item of expenditure was specified in the 1999 Budget.

The exhumation work is based on Government decree No 1052, dated 20 August 1998, and should follow an action plan approved by Deputy Prime Minister, Gennady Kulik. The plan obliges the Ministry of Defence to identify, receive, conserve and treat the remains, to ensure their despatch and burial and, finally, to erect memorials. Article 103 of the 1999 Budget, Appendix 23, details the financing of this work. The full title of the article reads: "The Search for those

Missing and Killed in Action, the Exhumation and Identification of the Deceased, the Official Publication of Lists and Informing of Parents, and the Burial of those Identified." The total sum available is 109,654,600 roubles [almost $4 million, Tr.]. This was intended for the excavation of approximately 500 burial sites and the identification of more than a thousand bodies.

In a poor country where pensioners go hungry and thousands of children are under-fed, 109 million roubles is no mean sum, and it demands the most careful and scrupulous accounting. We asked Slipchenko about this:

Q. **Sergei Iosifovich, during the period that you have been receiving budget funds has your company buried a single one of the soldiers whose remains were exhumed in Chechnya?**

A. No.

Q. **So what have you been doing with those funds?**

A. We are in possession of the entire database for soldiers missing in action [soldiers lying in unmarked graves are officially considered "missing in action", AP]. We drew up the lists ourselves, after securing the agreement of executive agencies: in 1998 this was the presidential staff and in 1999, the Ministry of Defence.

Q. **Could we take a look at your database?**

A. No, it's a commercial secret.

Q. **And how much money have you and your company already received from the budget without even beginning to do your job?**

A. That's also a commercial secret.

As well as creating this database, Military Commemoration Ltd is helping to construct an enormous cold storage facility, capable of holding up to 500 bodies, at Laboratory No 124 in Rostov-on-Don. This work is also financed from budget funds. We ask Slipchenko: Whatever was the need for such an enormous cold store? Wouldn't it be better to speed up the identification and burial of those being found? His answer is firm and categorical: "The more morgues we have, the better." In other words, the dead soldiers of the future guarantee that his company will never go out of business.

The number of war casualties used to be a military secret, now it's a commercial secret. The strictly confidential information about those missing, presumed dead, is today an entirely tradeable commodity: it can be sold, when and to whom you wish. One of the Chechen conditions for the release of the exhumed bodies, according to information obtained by the Committees of Soldiers' Mothers, is that Moscow gives them a copy of the database. Why, you wonder? In order to get the addresses and telephone numbers of those families who are still waiting, perhaps, and who would gladly give any amount of money in return for supposed sightings of their captive son?

"And just what business is it of yours, how we're spending this money?" The man at the Ministry of Defence, Sergei Aksyonov, is furious. He heads the special department for exhumation and identification work.

It proves quite pointless to ask him for detailed information. How is an exhumation actually carried out? As of today how many bodies have been found? In what Chechen village is a grave being opened at the moment? Although his department only came into being (and is now successfully expanding) thanks to those same 109 million budgeted roubles, and despite the fact that exhumation is his direct responsibility, he has no idea.

So what is his department actually doing? It's engaged in the usual pen-pushing and intrigues, allocating resources and creating new jobs – acquiring fax machines, telephones, photocopiers and so on. Aksyonov's staff cannot offer society any direct evidence of their activities. But we know what their department's only job should be: the dignified burial, with military honours, of the identified bodies of officers and soldiers.

In fact, the figures are as follows.

Since the beginning of the year, only 21 bodies of the estimated 500 servicemen and 1,500 civilians buried in Chechnya have been exhumed (figures as of 1 July 1999). Of those 21, not one has been buried. For 1998 and 1999 a total of 108 bodies have been exhumed, but only nine have been transferred from Grozny to the Central Laboratory for Identification Studies (Laboratory No 124) in Rostov-on-Don.

One telling detail: engrossed in its own reorganisation and expansion, the Ministry of Defence has not met its minimal obligation. In the budget allocation it was clearly specified that funds should be set aside for the publication of official lists, confirmed and authorised by the State, of those conscript soldiers who died in Chechnya. This is of the utmost importance. Yet Aksyonov did not even manage to make public these lists. "The Ministry has got its hands on most of this money and is simply spending it on itself," concludes Valentina Melnikova, a leading member of the Committees of Soldiers' Mothers who also sits on the presidential human rights commission. In a joint letter to the President, the Prime Minister and the country's Security Council, the Soldiers' Mothers appealed for help: "The Ministry of Defence is continuing to spend budget funds for purposes other than those intended."

"Cynical Time-Wasting"

In Colonel Konstantin Golumbovsky's opinion all unidentified soldiers could be buried within a year. He is Yury Plotnikov's superior and heads the presidential working group on the exhumation and identification of soldiers killed in action. Much must be changed and very rapidly, however, if this aim is to be achieved, he says. A major reason for the present cynical time-wasting and misuse of funds, Golumbovsky believes, is the attitude of Vladimir Shcherbakov, the head of Laboratory 124:

"Shcherbakov should spend day and night doing nothing but identification work. I am deeply convinced that now is not the time to write dissertations, conduct scientific research, engage in administrative reorganisation or pursue personal ambition. That can all come later. Now we should only be identifying bodies and burying them! And if there is a chance to identify *every single one* within a year, then you must postpone these other activities. Yet what is happening is quite different.

"The system of identification proceeds as follows. First, they identify those who can be recognised from their external appearance; then dental records, bones and fingerprints are used; the next category require more specialised methods. Finally there are remains that can be identified only by using a sequencer, a special piece of equipment for delicate genetic investigations. While Shcherbakov was lobbying in Moscow to reorganise the laboratory and purchase a sequencer, 25 of the bodies in Laboratory 124 degraded from the category of those suitable for identification to those that are unsuitable. Twenty-five bodies!

"That means that 25 families and 25 mothers cannot bury their sons. Now they have been told they must wait, indefinitely, until a decision has been taken about the sequencer. I have the unpleasant feeling that this may have been deliberate. When the other bodies can no longer be identified by methods now available in our country then Shcherbakov will get his sequencer. There's a word for this kind of behaviour: blackmail.

"Until recently no one gave Shcherbakov more consistent support than the members of our group. But then we found out that even the most basic physical measurements and features were not being recorded. And at the same time Shcherbakov was busy trying to get Laboratory 124 transferred from the North Caucasus Military District to the direct control of the Ministry of Defence in Moscow. I simply cannot understand it. Shcherbakov now has almost 70 permanent members of staff, but only seven of them are engaged in identification. What can be the justification? If you have 70 people under your command and your main task is to identify bodies then, in my view, *all* of them should be involved. If you can't manage in the course of a year to alleviate the suffering of those mothers then you should report to your superiors and say: 'I can only identify 25 bodies with my present laboratory, please help me.' The State could give you the two sequencers it already possesses, and then you'll get on with the job.

"That's what someone who is really concerned about his work should do. If Shcherbakov is now merely career-building then this is amoral behaviour. Our hospitals are starved of funds, and children in children's homes don't have enough to eat, so if the country has provided money for identification then you must get on with it and do the job! Take the lead – don't use the publicity to create a laboratory for yourself that will be the best-equipped in the world."

Unfortunately, Colonel Golumbovsky's view is supported by certain documents that have come into our possession. For example, a "Note on the Receipt and Use of Budget Funds Assigned for Specific Purposes" provided by Military Commemoration Ltd. The financial details here are quite involved: the Ministry receives the funds for a defined purpose, hands them on to Military Commemoration Ltd which, in turn, transfers them to Laboratory 124. Every conceivable item has been bought for the laboratory, as the note confirms: the usual chairs, stools and lamps, a binding machine, and computers have been purchased; a construction contract has been paid, and a security system, safes, and a digital camera, have all been acquired. Only one of the 13 listed items of expenditure is something of direct use: the chemical reagents necessary for identification tests.

The other document is even more revealing. This is the laboratory's plan of immediate expenditure, as approved by Shcherbakov. Of the budget funds at his disposal, the head of the laboratory intends to spend 10 million roubles on scientific research, 11 million on new buildings and only 1 million on identification. Yet the entire sum was allocated for this last activity. At this rate the laboratory and its staff will be fulfilling their obligations to the families of the bereaved for many years to come.

The Kosovo Contingency

The fate of those abandoned soldiers' graves in Chechnya remains unclear, but three years after the war ended this situation continues to pay dividends for the generals. The more unidentified corpses, the better. The war itself was a disgrace. How much more disgraceful it is to halt the exhumations for commercial reasons.

And that is one reason why the Chechen side behaves so insolently. You only respect those who respect themselves. The Chechens look at us, and they see a demonstration of the most fantastic cynicism at the highest level. We were the first to trade and barter human remains. We are no worse and no better than they are: the Chechens are merely playing along with the Ministry of Defence.

Ultimately everything we see today goes back to our total failure to regulate and define relations between the armed forces and civilians. We still do not have basic medical cards for all of our citizens. We don't even possess a database of identification samples for people in high-risk occupations. Nowhere do those sent on dangerous missions (to Chechnya, for instance) leave biological samples, physical measurements, fingerprints or a single drop of blood before they go. Had that elementary work been undertaken at the outset, our present financial schizophrenia would have been impossible. Only once was there a display of enlightenment. In the very last days before our forces were sent to Kosovo the main military-medical directorate and Konstantin Golumbovsky's group made enormous efforts to ensure that a doctor accompanied the troops. There, in Kosovo, and for the sake of experiment, he would begin to collect those crucial samples (albeit on a semi-legal and voluntary basis). Not one NATO officer or soldier crosses into that unsettled region without giving such samples.

Perhaps things will be better in the future. But that doesn't help Yury Plotnikov who, once again, must find something to say to families who have now been waiting for several years for their sons' remains to return home. Again he must disappoint them, and bear responsibility for the entire State. I have a suggestion. All involved in the division of budget funds should, for the good of their souls, meet one of these mothers at least once a week. If they were obliged to look them in the eye, answer their questions, and say something in their own justification, that would be a great help. They would stop imagining that they could avoid having to answer for themselves.

MOSCOW

*

That was how things were presented in Moscow. A month later, when the fighting in Daghestan was just beginning, Anna Politkovskaya went to Rostov-on-Don to see Laboratory 124 with her own eyes. The situation she found there was rather different.

2

LAND OF THE UNKNOWN SOLDIERS

A New Delivery of "Cargo 200"

23 August 1999

Senior Lieutenant (Medical Corps) Sergei Moiseyenko holds a glass laboratory dish between the palms of his hands and carefully raises it to his eyes. With a nod towards the corner of the office he indicates several bones lying on the floor, but keeps his eyes on the dish. Seven human teeth, discoloured as if they have not been brushed for a long time lie scattered there, together with small pieces of someone's lower jaw.

"Do you see?" says 25-year-old Moiseyenko, who, despite his youth, is considered one of the most gifted specialists at the renowned Rostov laboratory of forensic medicine. "That's not a filling in this tooth here, but part of a bullet . . . Together the teeth and those bones are body No 1007 according to our classification. An unknown soldier. He died in August 1996 in Grozny. My job is to establish who he was. There are already some indications. I think we'll get a result."

"Lord only knows how! You've got nothing but scraps of bone and some teeth. And that bullet, of course . . ."

The conversation moves on. We talk about the frustration felt by all at the laboratory, and the reason why they are still swamped with work though the war ended three years ago. Soldiers in Chechnya carried no metal identity discs or documents. Their superior officers cared little what became of them once they were dead. As a result, body No 1007 today fits into a small plastic bag.

"If they send back bodies from a new war without ID disks . . ."
It was the evening of 17 August. Moiseyenko did not yet know that
two days earlier, on a Sunday morning, the laboratory head Vladimir
Shcherbakov had already received a disturbing call from the Ministry
of Defence in Moscow.

"How many 'credo' bags do you have there?" someone shouted
down the line.

"I'll find out immediately," replied Colonel Shcherbakov.

"Send them all to Makhachkala.[1] Quickly! Can you get a hundred?"

Shcherbakov put down the receiver. His shoulders gave an invol-
untary shudder, as if from a chill, although it was 32°C in Rostov that
day. For those who don't know, the "credo" bag is one of those large
black plastic envelopes, closed with a zipper (you've all seen US police
films) in which they pack up dead bodies. The sort of container the
army always needs when its men start getting killed.

Neither did Lieutenant Moiseyenko know that on 18 August, the
very next morning after we talked, the bodies of soldiers killed in
Daghestan would begin to arrive. They arrived in "credo" bags, under
the code name "cargo 200", at the main reception and treatment
centre in Rostov (which serves the entire North Caucasus Military
District). And once again, they were without ID discs or documents.[2]
Body 1007 would have to squeeze up and make space on the senior
lieutenant's table for bodies 1015, 1020 and 1030. It looked as if
the entire laboratory was fated to start from scratch all over again,

1 Capital of Daghestan, one of 21 ethnic republics (including Chechnya) that with
  Moscow, Petersburg and the 66 predominantly Russian Regions make up the 89
  "subjects" of the Russian Federation.
2 In the 1990s Russia's armed forces adopted the Anglo-American ID disk or "dog-
  tag". Previously Soviet servicemen carried a capsule, resembling a spent rifle
  shell, in which personal details were sealed. For decades volunteers have searched
  for these on the battlefields of the 1941–5 war, providing confirmation of death and
  adding names to monuments.

although it still had 277 bodies to identify from the previous war.

Morgues are never cosy places, but wars are bound to happen and you need dissection rooms. There aren't any decent wars either. But they all leave us with a choice: we can either draw lessons from a war or ignore what it teaches us.

What lessons have been learned over the last three years, from August 1996 when General Lebed helped to negotiate an end to the war in Chechnya, to the present fighting in Daghestan? Why have ordinary soldiers again not left behind even a single drop of their blood to aid their rapid identification? What was Colonel Shcherbakov up to all that time? Why didn't he persuade the generals that they should never wage another war like that in Chechnya?

Body 549

"What was *I* doing?!" The colonel is indignant. "I was telling them just that. It's the reason I was in such disfavour." He explains:

"The more I pushed, the greater the pressure on me. I was accused of every failing in order to shut me up. Finally, when I could see no other way out, I drafted a law: "On Forensic Registration and Identification in the Armed Forces and Other Paramilitary Formations." And what do you think? It's been lying unheeded at the Duma for almost a year. Where was public opinion? And the human rights activists who are today shouting that the Daghestan campaign is a repeat of the Chechen war? They said nothing.

"The Ministry of Defence, on the other hand, and the presidential staff, accused me of playing 'political games' to the detriment of the job in hand. But I started to push things further, and demonstrate it was essential to have a database for the identification of all who are in the armed forces. Then they began a campaign to discredit me. Supposedly I was not fighting for identification, but only to create a nice cosy job for myself; I was exploiting these remains to push ahead scientific research. I was personally blamed because the laboratory was identifying no more than four or five bodies a month. But that was simply the reality!"

Body 549 reached Laboratory 124 from Grozny on 20 August 1996 with the label "unknown" attached to the stretcher. It had also been set on fire after death (someone had burnt the soldier after he was shot). The tissue was already in a state of total disintegration. The corpse was therefore impossible to identify visually; it had evidently lain under the southern sun for several weeks. There was no ID disc or any information about his unit. Two distinctive features: the top joint of the left thumb was missing and, by some miracle, a tin cross of the Old Believers still hung around his neck.[3]

In September 1996 when the lab's officers could see that no one was coming to claim Body 549 – neither those who had served with him nor his relatives – they sent out thousands of letters, requiring military registration offices throughout Russia to track down any of 549's surviving fellow soldiers. (It was known which units had taken part in the August battles in Grozny, and so they had a good idea which military registration offices had provided their conscripts.) It was 18 months before they received any replies. That's how things work in our country. Only many months later did the following letter reach the laboratory:

"From 24 June 1996 I served in Chechnya with unit 21617. On 9 August we were ordered to advance. We went about a kilometre and, after the company in front of us had gone ahead, we came under fire from both sides. I was hit by shrapnel, first in the foot and then in the arm. I fell down and they fired at me again. When the shooting ended I got back to the armoured vehicle. Private Ozhigov was sitting there. Perhaps they would not have noticed him, but he began to make a tourniquet above my elbow to stop the blood. Suddenly

3 The Old Believers, the "Dissenters" of Russian Orthodoxy, broke from the church in the mid-seventeenth century over its reform of texts and rituals.

he fell across my knees. A sniper had got him. Then our side gathered all the wounded and loaded them on to the armoured vehicle.

"Again the Chechens started firing at us, this time with mortars. I fell down and passed out. When I came to, the platoon leader and our driver-mechanic Khazanov were lying next to me. They said I should keep down because a sniper was watching us. We lay for four hours, pretending to be dead, until the helicopters started bombing the nine-storey building where the sniper was. Then we crawled into some cellar where our commander found us with one of the scouts. We were put in an armoured vehicle . . ."

Private Artur Kamaleyev, from the Volga republic of Bashkortostan, then spent many months in military hospitals: Vladikavkaz, then Rostov and Ufa. Only in spring 1998 did the district military registration office find him, at the laboratory's request, when he was discharged as unfit for further service. It was then that they discovered he had been saved by Private Ozhigov, who did not have the upper joint of his left thumb.

The laboratory sent a formal request to the military office in the Altai Region, for blood samples, plus thumb and palm prints from the parents of Ivan Ozhigov. His mother and father also sent a photograph of Ivan which Major Boris Shkolnikov, a forensic craniologist, compared to the skull of Body 549 – the same test carried out on the remains of the Romanovs. After five more major scientific investigations the experts could say without doubt: "This is no longer an unknown soldier."

On 3 August 1999, three years after he died, Ivan's family received his remains, and a short while ago the body of this 19-year-old private, who had died trying to save his wounded comrade, was buried in a village in Siberia.

A shocking story? Yes, but all the more so because it is no exception, but a typical and everyday example. The majority of cases at Shcherbakov's laboratory are of this type. He cannot help "spinning out" the identification procedure.

Perhaps you imagine that Moscow – i.e. the Ministry of Defence and the presidential staff – drew the same conclusion from the history of Private Ozhigov? Nothing of the kind. "For three years you've been messing around with one body!" That was the accusation thrown at Shcherbakov. The colonel's retort was just as sharp: "Don't blame me for your mistakes; all those who could have been recognised by simpler methods have long ago been identified. From now on we can only work in this way. We shall be forced to continue doing so, more-over, until you take urgent measures to finally create a database of identification samples for all soldiers and officers who are sent to areas of conflict." Keep your voice down, they told Shcherbakov: You're the one making a good living out of these corpses, it's your people who are writing dissertations and won't listen to anyone else. So now we are declaring war on you.

Slander

The campaign against Shcherbakov was headed by Victor Kolkutin, the chief forensic expert at the Ministry of Defence, and Konstantin Golumbovsky, head of the president's working group on the exhumation and identification of soldiers killed in action. They are highly respected and well-known people. However, it is difficult to describe the weapon they unleashed against Shcherbakov as anything other than public defamation. In Moscow, journalists, Duma deputies, and the Ministries of Heath and Defence were supplied with deliberately distorted information about the colonel. It was claimed, for instance, that Shcherbakov was openly disrespectful towards the remains he worked with, separating skulls from bodies simply because that was easier for his research purposes.

How can you check? The only way is to sit there, among the skulls at the laboratory, in the section headed by Major Boris Shkolnikov and read through dozens of files on unidentified soldiers. Here are the bullet wounds in the skull and here is the file. As you read, it turns out that each of these skulls represents a body: at best a few, individual bones are added to the skull and even then it's not clear to whom they belong. Lengthy molecular-genetic investigation is needed before they can be proved to come from the same person. Something else of major importance became clear to me then – the soldiers were already in this state when their remains, delivered by Golumbovsky's team, reached the laboratory.

The other accusation was that, for the convenience of research and the writing of dissertations, the army privates who serve as lab assistants are forced to boil up the bones of the deceased soldiers in the laboratory courtyard in full view of the unfortunate parents. Mothers supposedly had to pass by bubbling cauldrons full of skulls before they could view the remains of their children. It's a blood-chilling scene and makes one want to demand the immediate arrest of Shcherbakov.

How do you check this story? You must venture yourself into that devil's kitchen. There it is, exactly as described. Surrounded by filth and an unbelievable stench, soldiers are boiling the bones until the rotting flesh falls off them. It is also quite true that they do this in large vessels more usually employed for boiling clothes. But you must ask why. The reason is that money to purchase autoclaves was not allowed for in the budget estimates. Even the laundry pans were bought only recently. Before that the bones were boiled up in large tins that previously contained jam or herrings. They have no choice. Genetic investigations with contaminated remains are strictly forbidden since they will give no results and damage the equipment. What were they to do? Warn Moscow that all identification work is henceforth halted until autoclaves are provided? They might wait for years. And how then could they look mothers in the eye when they came demanding, if not their sons then at least a coffin?

As a result, the six months before the present fighting began in Daghestan have been spent squabbling, not working. The laboratory got on with its job, but in Moscow they intrigued and spread rumours and Shcherbakov had to fight back. The idea of creating a database for identification of all soldiers sent to areas of conflict has not advanced one iota. The army entered the present war in the same barbaric state as the Chechen war of 1994–6, while Colonel Shcherbakov, a unique specialist whose knowledge is now desperately needed, is a thoroughly harassed and exhausted individual. He is bound, hand and foot, by numerous investigations that do not cease from one week to the next. He is a workhorse, he says, that Moscow has driven to its limit and will soon finish off.

Graves or Monuments?

Who benefits from this outrageous squabble over bones? The immediate and obvious causes are entirely traditional. People, as always, are fighting for wealth and fame. The Moscow authorities are determined that Shcherbakov must be neutralised so that they can decide who is in charge, throughout the country, of identification research and procedures.

    Novaya gazeta has learned that very recently – just as they were preparing for the war in Daghestan, in fact – a decision was taken at the highest level by the government and the presidential staff: the unidentified "Chechen" bodies still in Laboratory 124's refrigerators must be rapidly laid to rest. The reason? The soldiers' mothers were making too much of a fuss, and it was proving too expensive for the State to pay its respects by identifying and burying everyone. A site had already been chosen in the Rostov City northern cemetery and the builders were given until 25 August to prepare the monument. When, in future, the mothers complain that they wanted to bury their children themselves the blame will be shifted entirely to Shcherbakov. It was he, they will be told, who dragged out the identification process. Any future court cases should be brought against him.

    This conveniently kills two birds with one stone. Our authorities hate to be held responsible by the living, whether they are the families of missing soldiers or that tiresomely demanding Shcherbakov. But they adore all kinds of ceremonies in commemoration of the dead – don't worry about feeding people, but be sure to place a wreath on their graves. Having proved unworthy of their soldiers and officers, politicians and military officials love annual visits to the Grave of the Unknown Soldier where they can shed a few restrained masculine tears for the benefit of the television cameras. As the Duma elections approach, the need is urgently growing for some kind of memorial to the unknown dead of the Chechen war. Politicians and the military need somewhere they can demonstrate their penitence in public. Today this is the most important and fundamental point of disagreement between Shcherbakov and the authorities. He will not hear any talk of such a monument and whenever he meets people in authority he does not fail to warn them that the State could not bring greater shame on itself than by this hurried burying of the problem. Each time he repeats the same quotation. It comes from the rules of the US Military Pathology Institute's medical examination directorate (the American equivalent of Laboratory 124):

> The goal that all of our employees strive to attain is simple. We must not permit any American serviceman or woman to be buried beneath the inscription: "Here lies an American soldier who covered himself with glory and whose name is known to God alone."

Shcherbakov follows these words with a demand for money in order to continue the expensive identification research. The more he insists, the more our authorities dream of the peace and quiet of the Grave of the Unknown Soldier.

20 August. Deliveries of "cargo 200" from Daghestan are never-ending. Shcherbakov is worn out. The laboratory has no more resources than before. As we leave, Lieutenant Moiseyenko tells us: "If they drive such people as Shcherbakov out of the army, I shall also resign."

ROSTOV-ON-DON

*

On 7 August 1999 a convoy of vehicles and armed men crossed into Daghestan. It was led by the Chechen commander Shamil Basayev and a veteran opponent of the Soviet forces in Afghanistan, the Saudi-born Khattab. They had come supposedly in support of local Wahhabites. Army and police units were sent to repel them.

3

"A DIRTY WAR"

Basayev and the Daghestan Refugees

In January 1996 we were told that the Chechens would never take Pervomayskoe in neighbouring Daghestan.[4] When they captured the town, we were told they would never get out alive. When they left, the then Head of the FSB, Barsukov, convincingly explained how they got away: early one frosty morning they crossed the ploughed fields very quietly in bare feet.

This time no one has offered any explanations. We were simply and triumphantly told that "the territory is being cleansed". Our information is that the Chechen guerrillas were not barefoot as they left Daghestan, but drove out, unimpeded, in a motorised column led by Shamil Basayev's jeep. Furthermore, we have good reason to suppose that someone paid a very large sum of money to ensure that things ended this way.

Novaya gazeta, 6 September 1999

---

4 Retreating from his raid on Kizlyar, Salman Raduyev and the fighters with him were caught by Russian forces near Pervomayskoe village just before reaching Chechnya.

6 September 1999

On the evening of 28 August, Akhmet Omarov suddenly arrived at the Pearl Hotel, formerly a holiday resort for the rail-workers' union. Twenty-two women from his village, with their 30 children, were waiting for the news he brought and, at the same time, afraid to hear what he had to say. In August everything they had thought eternal, unchanging and resistant to any natural catastrophe – their large families in their sturdy massive-walled houses – were not simply shaken, but rapidly ceased to exist.

Now one of 30 newly created refugee centres is located in this beautiful hotel in the foothills, away from the mountains, and away from the refugees' village of Ansalta, just across the border with Chechnya. Akhmet's own family took refuge in the hotel: his wife, little daughter, six-year-old twin girls and his 14-year-old son. After embracing them all, Akhmet finally went to director Mahomed-Ali Abdurakhmanov's office to talk to all the other women. There was a fierce downpour on the street but Akhmet did not shake the rain from his jacket or even notice the water streaming down his chest and back.

"It's no good," the farmer told his fellow villagers. "Our homes are gone. They've been destroyed or burnt, or only the cracked walls are left standing. It will be impossible to rebuild. My home is also gone. The homes of my brothers and parents no longer exist. There are piles of rubble on all sides. There is no electricity or gas in Ansalta, and our cattle and orchards have been destroyed. We couldn't survive there this winter. Yesterday there was a meeting of the villagers. The men decided that we would move to another place and build there. We can't remain where we are any longer. We must wait for the prefabricated houses that Putin promised. The old Ansalta is gone for ever."

This was the worst news anyone could have expected. In the southern mountainous area of Daghestan a family home is a potent symbol and someone without their own house is the most wretched of all human beings. A man who cannot put a roof over the heads of his wife and children is no longer a man. Until the last minute the women of Ansalta just like their sisters from the other villages obliterated in the August fighting (Rakhata, Tando and Shadroda) – could not believe their men would take this decision. Too many generations had toiled to build the massive houses now bombed out of existence. Too many tears and too much sweat had been mixed with the foundations of these fortified buildings that, it seemed, would last for ever. And now they had just got up and left, carrying only their children.

None of the women shed a tear on hearing Akhmet's harsh verdict. They are strong-spirited women who are used to surviving in the most severe climatic conditions. They merely shook their heads, "Even this rain is not doing any good." After the stifling heat that accompanied all the fighting for these mountain villages, Daghestan was subjected to thunderstorms interrupted by a low-lying fog. News that arrives with the rain is by local tradition always considered good and a herald of hope. Alas, the torrential rain that met Akhmet on his return to the camp was contemptuous of such ancient beliefs.

Wisdom beyond Moscow's Capacity

The refugees have spent days now discussing why this all happened, and who is to blame for their misery. The question they most often ask a visiting stranger is: "But why did you Russians forgive Basayev for what he did in Budyonnovsk[5] and everything else he's done?"

It was something that people in the camps now scattered in the Buinaksk, Sergokalinsk and Karabudakhkent districts could not understand. In the answer to this question they see the cause of their own present misfortunes. The problem is not some "wretched" (as they themselves describe it) Wahhabite doctrine, but the customs

---

5 In June 1995 Shamil Basayev and 148 Chechen fighters invaded the southern Russian town of Budyonnovsk and for a week held up to 1,000 hostages in the hospital. He negotiated their release with the then Prime Minister Victor Chernomyrdin in exchange for safe passage back to Chechnya.

and ethics of those ruling the State within which they want to live. Hundreds of perplexed women asked: "Why didn't your Russian men avenge themselves on Basayev for the blood he shed in Budyonnovsk? What words did they use to justify themselves in the eyes of their womenfolk? And what will your mothers in Siberia say now, when their sons are dying in our mountains and all for that same Basayev?"

That was what I heard from Rakhimat Yusupova, a mother of five from the no longer extant village of Rakhata, as she wrapped a borrowed dressing gown about her; an Ansalta mother of four, Sukainat Abdulmultalipova, supported her words. They were both now temporarily housed at the "Oil-worker" holiday camp. I was told the same by Asma Umakhanova, a widow with ten children at the Cosmos camp, and by Patimat Khan-Magomedova, a pensioner in the Danko camp. They are very simple and naive women. The majority of them had never left their mountain villages before the August fighting. Hundreds of them had never seen the sea and, incidentally, did not enjoy their first sight of the Caspian. At the "Oil-worker" camp, for instance, 70 kilometres from the capital, Makhachkala, Zalina Iduyeva told me, in all seriousness, that she did not want to send her child to boarding-school No 2 in the town of Kaspiisk because it was next to the sea, and that was dangerous.

"Why is it dangerous?"

"Because the sea is there."

But it's best to let them describe in their own words their recent encounters with the Chechen fighters.

"I went out to do the morning's milking. An enormous monster, covered in weapons, was walking past the house. I took fright, ran away and began to hide the children. Then they told me this was a Negro woman who was fighting with the Wahhabites."

Zarina Tadueva from Rakhata had seen her first ever black person.

Many of the refugees do not speak Russian. With the help of a translator they tell me:

"When Basayev arrived he told us that this was a commercial war."

"And did you believe him?"

"To begin with, no. Now I do. Because the Russian soldiers let Basayev leave Ansalta and only then bombed our houses. But we'd told them: You can knock down the houses, but make sure you kill them all [i.e. the Wahhabites]."

Finally, the mountain women speak words of condemnation and judgement:

"Our menfolk will never forgive Basayev for what he did to us."

"Did he threaten you?"

"No. He insulted us."

"In what way?"

"He wanted to make us do his bidding."

"But some of the villagers were on his side. He didn't force everyone, some went of their own accord . . ."

The women fall silent. It is left to Akhmet Omarov to tell us the first thing the Ansalta villagers did when, after the fighting was over, they were allowed back to their village. They found and dug up the graves of two villagers who had helped Basayev, but had been killed in the fighting and buried by Basayev's men. The returning villagers carried the two corpses out into the mountains so that they did not lie near their ancestors, who had never brought such dishonour in their lifetime.

"But Akhmet, we know that some of your fellow villagers left with the Chechen fighters."

"One man. But that won't help him. He'll run around for a while, then we'll track him down and that'll be the end of him. That's our custom. His time will certainly come." As Akhmet answers, he gazes at the women and it is as if he is taking a vow before them. A look of pride in their men appears on the women's faces.

"You did well," says Kalimat Ibragimova, an elderly woman from Ansalta, to the approving tongue-clicking of her companions. "If you hadn't dug them up, I would have done so myself. They cannot lie there next to my mother. On 7 August when those bandits came it was exactly 52 days since her death. I had made all the preparations to perform the prayer for her, and then they drove me out. 'You're no Muslim,' I told Basayev, 'if you don't let me commemorate the 52nd day.' He answered me in Russian: 'We're driving out the Russians, Mother, because they don't want Islam.' I spat at him and said: 'Yours is a dirty war, it's not a Muslim war! There aren't any Russians here, but you'll drive us out all the same.' I'll never forgive him."

They are, as you see, very simple people. Some might even call them primitive. However, they can see to the very heart of the matter, while we remain blinkered and confused by our complexes and sophistication. These women speak with a decisiveness and clarity that we have long forgotten: "Basayev is a bloodthirsty bandit and traitor and he has no place among normal people." Their questions and answers expose Russia's ill-defined policies in the North Caucasus. Our own answers hint at some involved game we are playing, and it is never clear to whose advantage: "Things aren't that simple," we say. "It makes sense to negotiate with Basayev . . ."

Meanwhile in Moscow various media commentators again hold forth about all these savages from the hills, and how we should be much tougher on them. With increasing frequency it is suggested that the Daghestanis be kept out of the struggle with the Chechens: let them stand by while we defend their freedom. Unbelievable stupidity, and yet just another of the thousand foolish judgements uttered over the last few years. Such arrogance on the part of the Moscow elite in its dealings with Daghestan is both unacceptable and dangerous. That becomes quite clear if you travel to the remote mountain areas of the republic, talk face to face with the people, listen to what they say and see with your own eyes the results of their struggle in August to defend their freedom. These direct and unsophisticated villagers are infinitely wiser and more principled than all of our Moscow politicians put together, no matter how many advisers crowd round them. Listen to the Daghestani hillsmen, and open your eyes.

"Your Russian men must be braver and take a hard decision," says Zeinab Baisarova, a music teacher from Rakhata village, now in the Swallow camp. "Let your men decide what Chechnya means for Russia. And when they've decided, let them act. As long as they do nothing we shall be forced to fight and flee. Our men will die because yours weren't worthy of the name."

Did You, By Any Chance, See Some Aid?

Several years ago Termenlik was a flourishing tourist centre, one of the most popular not just in Daghestan, but in the whole country. Now it houses a refugee camp. The director, Kerim Murtazaliev, is bitter: "Do you remember how, not long ago, we used to joke about the old Soviet toast? 'Peace to the World'? Well, it's been given new meaning now, hasn't it?"

For the first time in his long life Kerim is taking in refugees and he does not hide his deep sorrow at the fact:

"I have 237 people here. They came with only the clothes they stood up in. The children were in pants and barefoot. The women wore slippers. No money or belongings. Nursing mothers' milk dried up . . . You don't know where the aid has got to, do you? The television said it was on its way."

Every time we finish discussing the main subject with the refugees – Who is to blame for the present war? – they ask about humanitarian aid. Regrettably, we were unable to detect the faintest trace of any such help in a single one of the camps. Someone was certainly unloading boxes at Makhachkala airport in front of the TV cameras. Everyone saw that. But not one of the mountain women has yet been able to feed her child with the baby food from those boxes.

The only Russian woman living in Rakhata village is Irina Gasanova. From Tyumen in West Siberia, she married a local man 16 years ago and now she and her three sons are in the Pearl Hotel camp. She tells the following story:

"After watching that programme several of us women asked the director to lend us a car. We drove down to Makhachkala ourselves to the command centre for allocating refugees on Chernyshevsky Street. 'Where's our share of the aid?' we firmly demanded. 'There's nothing for you lot,' they said."

The director of the Pearl Hotel, Mahomed-Ali, comforted Irina. "We'll survive without them. I'll do everything to make sure you don't starve or freeze. And we'll organise classes for the children – I used to be a schoolteacher myself."

Which sums up how the refugees are coping in Daghestan today. Once again the State is nowhere to be seen. That the refugees are fed and have somewhere to sleep is only thanks to the kindness of others. While Moscow is hyping up reports of "humanitarian aid" it is others who bring food and clothes to the camps because they consider it a matter of honour. On 20 August, Dalgat Mirzabekov, general director of the "Electrosignal" factory in Derbent, transferred half the month's salary for the entire workforce to the refugees. He did not wait to be asked and, naturally, he had the full agreement of his employees. They spent 150,000 roubles buying bowls and powder for washing clothes, and baby food for the young. Mirzabekov's business, incidentally, is not very wealthy, although well known in Daghestan. When asked why he helped the refugees, however, he replied: "We had to help. That was how our forbears behaved."

On 28 August the head of the local administration in Ametirk (they are Lakks there, a different ethnic group) brought 5,000 roubles to the "Oil-worker" camp from his fellow villagers. By local standards that is a considerable sum for a poor place like Ametirk. He told the women: "Take it and spend it as you wish. You must be able to dress your children for school." To the same camp came the most fearsome Daghestani of the present day, the head of the Avar community, Hadji Makhachev, who is, at one and the same time, a deputy premier in the republic's government and general director of Daghestan Oil. As everyone knows he is a wealthy man and he gave every refugee, man, woman and child, 250 roubles. He gave a further thousand roubles to each family.

There are hundreds of similar stories. Fresh milk is brought each day for the children at the Swallow camp from the village of Ullubui-aul. Why? "After I saw a woman with a small baby get out of the bus, scared, weeping, and without even the simplest knapsack, I went and organised our lads the very next morning so they should have milk," Mejid Mejidov, who is farm manager here, tells me. When I ask if he expects anyone to pay him someday for all this milk, he does not reply. He is offended.

The present catastrophe in Daghestan has once again shown that ordinary people are a hundred times better and purer than our authorities. At best our clumsy and unresponsive regime thinks only of itself and does nothing. One other sad observation. Unlike the Chechen war in 1994–6 not a single Moscow human rights organisation has done anything to aid these hapless people – and yet several of those organisations are specifically for refugees and not lacking in resources. Only the Daghestanis today are helping the people of their republic and this does not bode well. Moscow is thereby sowing the seeds of separatism. When they take root and begin to grow, the federal authorities will complain that you can do nothing with these people.

And it's high time to return to the questions the mountain women asked most often. Of course, they're naive people. They simply cannot understand that Russian men are going to say nothing to Siberian mothers to explain how they are dealing with Shamil Basayev. They'll keep quiet as usual. Yet again they'll do nothing about Basayev and swallow this disgrace. Then they'll shield themselves behind clever words: discussion of the status of Chechnya has been "postponed", we must not increase tension by arresting Basayev. Madness. The women are right. As long as our men behave in this way, their war will never end.

MAKHACHKALA–BUINAKSK–KARABUDAKHKENT

4

TAINTED TINS

How the Soldiers are Fed

30 September 1999

If it had not been for the fighting in Daghestan the two of us might never have met: the tinned meat of the Semikarakorsk meat-processing plant and my digestive system.

It was getting near suppertime and the men of the Lipetsk Region OMON [riot police] who were off-duty invited me into their improvised kitchen. They are currently based in the Kazbekovsk district next to the Chechen border, and are guarding the approaches to Dylym, the main town in the area. I should have been warned by the mysterious winks and smiles they exchanged.

The kitchen turned out to be in a cellar, down two dark flights of stairs. The lower we descended, the greater my reluctance: the foul stench rising to meet us suggested that chemical weapons had been used not far away.

"May I offer you a gas mask?" a pleasant young man asked.

"You're most kind, but if you can take it, so can I."

"Oh, you mustn't compare yourself with us, we're already used to it."

At that moment we reached our destination and the dishevelled character in charge of the kitchen came into view. With a knife he was opening one after another of the latest rations from the Semikarakorsk plant. They had received them the day before from the OMON quartermaster at the food depot in Kizlyar. Plunging his blade through the pliable aluminium he counted aloud:

" . . . Tin 23, rotten. Tin 39, likewise. Tin 41, the same . . . That's enough! Tin 42 is for you. Take it back to Moscow and show them what they feed us. Perhaps you'd like me to disembowel it here and now, so there's no mistake?"

"Better not," jokes Alexander Pavlovich Ponomaryov, the lieutenant colonel in charge of these Interior Ministry forces (to them he is simply Pal'ich), "everyone on the plane might die before the tin reaches the capital of our great country. Try a sample of what they regularly serve us."

I sniffed and licked. What else could I do? My organism reacted instantly.

"We have stomach infections all the time," concluded Pal'ich. "And that's the condition we fight in."

"But do you have enough to treat it? Did they give you anything?"

"Medicine, you mean? Not really. We're chronically short of everything here."

I pulled out all of the anti-diarrhoea tablets I'd taken with me on the trip and handed them over to Colonel Ponomaryov. Then I decided to investigate local life and its chronic shortages.

Food Fit for Heroes

This unit of the Lipetsk OMON is already famous throughout Daghestan. They are in charge of the Kazbekovsk section of the *cordon sanitaire* that runs along the Chechen-Daghestani border and they recently performed a feat of heroism. In early September they were guarding the small town of Novolakskoe. With them were the town's fearless policemen and an army unit under the command of Infantry Major Zhenya (in Daghestan officers do not introduce themselves, even to fellow officers). At one point it became clear that things were going badly and the bandits would soon have the area completely surrounded. No one wanted to die. So while there was still a way out of the town, Major Zhenya grabbed an armoured personnel carrier and drove away from the fighting, leaving his own soldiers and the policemen to their fate, and to almost certain death.

"Why didn't you save yourselves and run?"

"We had wounded men with us."

When resistance became almost futile and they faced capture or death, the Lipetsk OMON decided to break through enemy lines. Of course, they had almost no chance of getting through alive. It was simply a case of despair, resentment, and a desire to live. Guided by their senses, they crawled out at night, stealthily and silently, tracing a great arc across Chechen territory, beyond the surrounding fighters, where death waited behind each hill.

Discussing their feat of bravery in that stench-ridden kitchen only sharpened everyone's perceptions. How could people who have shown such bravery in impossible circumstances and, weeks later, continue to face mortal danger every day, now be living like stray dogs that no one cares for? Is this how the Motherland repays their valour?

The next subject proved highly sensitive for these resentful people whose nerves have been stretched to the limit. The Lipetsk OMON escaped from encirclement in worn and tattered clothes. What was left when they reached freedom could have gone straight on the fire. But did anyone hurry to issue them with new uniforms? The military quartermasters now running Daghestan did not even blink. Instead they had to rely on their well-disposed comrades to cover their nakedness.

Their heroism was not reflected in their pay, either. Prime Minister Putin may frequently offer the nation therapeutic TV sessions, but the OMON are still getting a mere 22 roubles a day [about $0.70, Tr.], and there's no hope of any more. Not for them the $1,000 the Chechen fighters are supposed to get each month! It makes no difference whether you're a hero, or a Major Zhenya. Pal'ich supposes that some-where, perhaps in Makhachkala, at staff headquarters, some of the generals may already be doing quite nicely. On the front line, here in Dylym, where they expect the Chechen fighters to break through again at any minute, no one has seen any extra money.

Hence their hungry existence. They live little better than savages and our beloved country blows the smell of tainted meat in their faces. The Lipetsk OMON men are greeted by this stench in place of supper and can expect nothing else. There are no street-side kiosks here, only ravines and mountains, and even if they could buy something to eat they have no money. If it were not for the tins from Semikarakorsk then the Motherland would be offering its heroes nothing more than gruel. When the local women notice how thin the soldiers defending them are, they bring them food out of the kindness of their hearts.

Alexander Ponomaryov, their commanding officer, is 42 and 27 of those years he has devoted to the army. His shoulders constantly twitch and jerk, from the cold and from a nervous tic. He huddles up in his shapeless old sweater and is sunk in melancholy. His life, for the most part, has been wasted, he believes, fighting difficult military campaigns for which the country has never even offered a grudging "Thank you."

"Do you know why you're fighting here?"

"Because of someone's political ambitions. And for 22 roubles a day. Otherwise everything would be different. You can see for yourself. The furthest post where our men are on duty is 15 kilometres from this barrack. If anything happens there we don't even have a car or the money to buy petrol – they don't supply one, it's not standard issue. So we run out into the road, flag someone down and ask for a lift. And what if it's night-time? Who can you ask here in the village? It's a joke. But when something happens you feel nothing but hatred for the powers that sent us here. As you can see, they have created all the necessary conditions for feats of heroism . . ."

Pal'ich laughs. Our dear Pal'ich who knows from bitter experience that the brisk reports delivered by the generals from morning to night on all the TV channels are very far from the truth here on the front line.

At this point someone will certainly say to himself: What a green creature this Politkovskaya is! Just imagine, the tinned meat was off, and the colonel got emotional like some delicate college girl. Well, if you're sitting comfortably and safely in Moscow, then indeed there is little need to become overexcited. But if someone is aiming at you, every hour of every day down the barrel of a gun, and if you take your life in your hands simply by glancing out the window, then your nerves will be in quite a different state. The complaints about living conditions are entirely justified. If the country wants acts of bravery then it should give more practical expression to its rapture at such heroism. As long as the authorities think they can buy off their heroes with awards and decorations – and dozens are being proposed for decorations in Daghestan today – then the heroes will desert them.

Semikarakorsk

My two last phone calls were to Rostov-on-Don and Semikarakorsk. At supply headquarters for the North Caucasus Military District the answer was simple:

"The meat-processing plant in Semikarakorsk won the public tender. You can't hold us responsible. It's impossible to open every tin. When we made spot checks the results were good. All complaints to the producer."

In Semikarakorsk someone who describes himself as the plant director answers the phone. He is very evasive and lengthily assures me that these rumours are lies, nothing more than the newspapers trying to concoct a sensational story.

"But how much were you paid for these consignments to Daghestan?"

The moment money is mentioned the director turns nasty:

"Get lost. I'm not telling you," he snaps, "it's a commercial secret. We're a private company."

Then our Semikarakorsk butcher gets carried away. Like a real old-style Communist he tells me that the soldiers have become too demanding, they are asking for the impossible and should be more modest. The Motherland "is in no fit condition . . . Do you understand?" And a lot of other nonsense.

Finally I reach the end of my patience:

"You're a real bastard, aren't you? Are you really too thick to understand that your rotten meat may be the last thing one of those young soldiers ever eats?"

There is an unpleasant, disparaging laugh:

"Fax us your questions and if we see the necessity, we'll provide answers." Without a word of farewell he slams down the receiver.

You want to know his name, of course. The businessman I was talking to is called Igor G. Lisakonov. And if you wish to personally express your revulsion at a scoundrel who has been turning a pretty penny from these tainted supplies then you may ring him on the following telephone numbers: Rostov (886356-2) 13-94 or 14-94. Perhaps then he'll finally get the message.

At all times and under all regimes wars have been profitable business. While others carried the dead off the battlefield, the quartermasters and their kind in supplies were lining their pockets. The longer the war, the fatter their wallets. The more soldiers despatched to the front, the finer the *Mercedes* some ministry official can obtain.[6] You tell me that the Chechens are to blame for our troubles. Don't worry, we're doing quite well on our own.

A Minefield

Today more than a dozen unexploded bombs, dropped from the air, lie about the churned-up mess that is Novolakskoe. They didn't go off, unfortunately, because they were rather old; someone says they

6 Pavel Grachev, Minister of Defence during the first Chechen war, was famous for his acquisition of several *Mercedes* for himself and his leading officials.

were made in the 1950s. Naturally people returning to their homes asked the military to remove these dangerous and unpredictable lumps of metal as quickly as possible. The soldiers replied that the bombs could not be safely moved and must be detonated where they are. The explosive force of each bomb, they added, lowering their gaze, is equivalent to that which demolished the high-rise block in Buinaksk.[7] Did no one think of that before? Now Novolakskoe will acquire a dozen large craters and suffer extensive new destruction. People are horrified.

That's how our soldiers are living at the front. No one cares for their safety and they are forced to stroll past unexploded bombs all of the time. One bomb waiting to explode is their semi-starved existence; another is the lack of normal warm clothing; a third is their miserable wages; a fourth . . . Do the authorities really not foresee the consequences? Do they expect people who have served in these conditions to return home, calm and confident, convinced they are real heroes?

An armoured personnel carrier races through the maize-fields along the road that borders the *cordon sanitaire*. It is full of soldiers. An officer leaps out and introduces himself: "Colonel N." All of them here say that: Colonel N., Major N. and so on. Among themselves the officers say that if they give their surnames the Chechens will find their families "in Russia" and wreak vengeance on them. The colonel is in a highly nervous state. Restlessly he struts back and forth, twitching and sometimes breaking into a run; he gives an odd and unbalanced impression. At his command the soldiers point their weapons at everyone who isn't in uniform or riding in an army vehicle. No one trusts anyone else here and they're all afraid of each other.

7 On 4 September 1999, 62 soldiers and members of their families were killed when a residential building in their compound in Buinaksk was demolished by an explosion. Over the next ten days there were two bombings of residential blocks in Moscow (see Chronology).

That's how we now behave, yet the land around is part of our country, it's not a fascist, gangster-run republic. We created this situation. Only officers who are daily shown how little they count could behave in this way.

MAKHACHKALA-DYLYM

5

CRIMINAL MOTHERS

Hundreds Break the Law

On 30 September ground operations effectively began in Chechnya. On 1 October Putin declared that the only legal authority in the republic is the 1996 parliament "elected according to the laws of the Russian Federation. All other bodies formed in the Chechen Republic can be termed legitimate only with serious reservations." Such a statement by the Prime Minister amounts to no less than the renunciation of the Peace Treaty signed by Yeltsin and Chechen President Maskhadov on 12 May 1997. The authorities have taken yet another major step towards making this war irreversible.

VICTOR POPKOV[8]
Novaya gazeta, 4 October 1999

4 October 1999

Kidnappers

The story Sergei has to tell might astonish even those who have served in our army and know what it is like (we know Sergei's surname but cannot make it public as yet). It is the story of how the Daghestan

---

8 Popkov was among the human rights activists who acted as neutral intermediaries during the first Chechen war, providing news for the civilian population and helping to organise exchanges of bodies and hostages.

events began for Sergei, a private in the self-propelled-artillery regiment (Unit 52157B), and for his fellow soldiers who were based in Mulino village, Nizhny Novgorod Region.

For a long while rumours that the regiment might be sent to the fighting were no more than idle talk when the soldiers were allowed to break for a cigarette. Their officers stubbornly denied the suggestion and yelled down the phone at parents who were panicking and calling from every end of the country in search of reassurance.

"The regiment won't be sent there, will it?" mothers and fathers sobbed, and shouted to make themselves heard across the defective telephone lines. What naiveté, to suppose that military secrets would be revealed to them so simply.

The reply was firm and authoritative: "Under no circumstances."

There is no more dangerous path to travel than that which is firmly paved with lies. To this day the untruths those officers were telling in August have created so many tragedies that we shall not soon see the end of them.

Finally the decisive moment arrived. That evening nothing was as usual in Unit 52157B. The officers were uncharacteristically kind. Numerous crates of vodka were carried through the guardhouse quite openly, even escorted by a corporal. The experienced soldiers, seeing this, hid themselves away as best they could and did not appear again. When the green young conscripts staggered out for a breath of fresh air they were not met by the usual obscenities. On the contrary, they were given cigarettes and hints were dropped that soon some of the regiment might be sent to Daghestan. Sergei and the hundred or so 18-year-olds like him decided that they would not be affected, since they had been called up late in June and had only once since then been shown how to use an automatic rifle.

After the evening meal the officers invited the soldiers to join their table, something that had never happened before. There was a great deal of delicious homemade food there and an impressive number of bottles.

By 10 p.m. all had drunk their fill. The next day 50 men were missing from the barracks. Half of those who disappeared were among the new recruits who had fired a gun only once in their lives. At 2 a.m. the officers had woken them up when they were still completely drunk and, ticking names off a list, loaded them on to trucks; at 3.30 a.m. they despatched them to Daghestan.

These ominous drunken parties would happen again at the unit. But now none would drink themselves senseless, since they all feared being sent off to fight. The scenario remained the same, however. Each time at the dead of night, more groups were woken, rapidly assembled and despatched . . . The officers provided no explanations where they were going or why; there were no special briefings or preparation, let alone, of course, an official request from any of these unfortunates "to continue their service in an area of conflict". Many soldiers described the whole business in letters home. As later became clear not one of these envelopes ever reached its addressee. Staff at the Mulino village post office were ordered to sort them into separate bags and then they were all burned.

I repeat: the soldiers were encouraged to drink and then, before they came to their senses, were sent off to the war. At the very same time, in late August and early September, speeches by the highest government and army officials were shown on all TV channels in which they lulled the soldiers' mothers into complacency with the lie that the "voluntary principle" of service in the new war was being most rigorously respected. Next our TV news, copying the crafty Movladi Udugov,[9] confidently announced, on the authority of the Security Service and the Ministries of the Interior and of Defence, that only well-trained and prepared fighters were being sent to Daghestan.

How did our military leaders and the officers in Mulino expect people to react? How should the families of these young conscripts

9 Spokesman for the Chechen side during the first war, Udugov displayed an effective grasp of PR techniques and constantly wrong-footed the Ministry of Defence in Moscow.

have responded to these secret, dishonest and illegal intrigues? Their reaction was entirely natural. Having tried one army hotline after another, the mothers of soldiers with the Mulino regiment were briefly told: "Your sons are at the unit." Why then had none of them received a single letter? The mothers went to Mulino themselves. Those who were in time found their sons still there and each decided to take their own measures against the State that had so insolently deceived them. Driving their cars up to the compound fence, they asked the officers on duty to let their sons out "for an hour or so, so we can feed them and have a chat". Then they drove off with their children, transforming them into deserters and themselves into accessories to the crime.

To be honest you don't envy Sergei now. He regards all around him with a heavy and fixed gaze. And with good reason. He's sorry for his mother and for himself, but many of his friends have been sent to the Caucasus. What will he do when he meets them again? How will he look them in the eye? "I know, I know. But I couldn't risk leaving it any longer," says Sergei's mother Nadezhda Ivanovna:

"It's true, I tricked him into coming with me. I took away all his documents. I locked him in the apartment. I argued and insisted. And I'm sure I was right. We mothers, whose children are now serving in the army, have no choice. There's no 'voluntary principle'. Young lads who have come as mere conscripts are being forced to go and fight, without any explanation or preparation. I consider the State has put us in an impossible position."

Hundreds of mothers today, kidnappers against their will, would repeat her words. On 16 September Lydia Burmistrova, a Muscovite, took away her 19-year-old son Ivan, a private with the Taman division (Unit 73881), just before the next contingent was setting out and after more than 2,000 of the division's soldiers had already been sent to the Caucasus. This is her disturbing and moving tale:

"Ivan was very reluctant, but I broke his resistance. I brought my sons up by myself. The State gave me nothing, not a kopeck. But when they needed someone to die for them, then they were there at the door, in a flash. The regime couldn't resolve the conflict itself so it decided to go to war. Now we must hand over our children to correct other people's mistakes. Never! No one cares that my eldest boy was bullied quite unmercifully in the army and returned home not entirely in his right mind. I'm the one that's bringing him round, and healing his nerves and his mind, which have been unbalanced by that army for many years to come. The State has done nothing to treat him. So now they want my next son? Not for anything in this world."

Mothers who were too late to stop their children have now rushed to Daghestan and Ingushetia where, risking danger and even death, they wander the roads and villages in search of their sons. Their aim remains the same. To find their child and not let him go again. Before they set out for the Caucasus the majority come to the Committees of Soldiers' Mothers for advice. There they hear only one thing: steal them back and take them away, and the sooner the better. It's easier to help you now than when you have a disabled son to look after.

"They Owe Us Nothing"

What is the "impossible position" the State offers its citizens? What should parents know whose children find themselves in the middle of a new war in the Caucasus? "'You must think very clearly and soberly about the situation,' that is what I tell mothers who come to me," says Maria Fedulova, joint chairwoman of the co-ordinating council for the Committees of Soldiers' Mothers. "'Will you be able to look after your children all your life? They will get only 280 roubles a month from the State.' I have not yet met one mother, and you can see how many there are here now, who has replied: 'I can. Let him do his military service as required.'"

Don't imagine that Maria Fedulova thinks only about money. Nothing of the kind. It's just that she knows better than most how

OCTOBER 1999   47

things really are. She knows all the laws, the edicts and instructions of the government, and the internal orders issued by the Ministries of Internal Affairs and Defence, and by the FSB. She knows that there are no allowances or benefits for invalids, either for those who survived the slaughter of 1994–6 or who are now in Daghestan. This is the first thing parents must know: those who return from the fighting will enjoy no allowances or privileges; not for re-training, artificial limbs, medicine, jobs, or, least likely of all, accommodation. Everything will depend on whether they can find some kindly helper where they live: if the head of the local administration feels so inclined, he will pay for an artificial leg, but nothing can force him to do so. If the lad can find a sponsor to support his job training then all is well; if he can't, there's no hope. The regime stresses that it has taken a decision to begin the war, but accepts no responsibility for the consequences. They owe us nothing, we owe them everything!

These are the rules by which the State plays with its people today. Nothing changes, moreover, for those who perform feats of valour and demonstrate unexampled bravery to the glory of the Fatherland. The only reliable support for those lads who return from the war will be their families and relatives. It is as if their fathers and mothers had sent them to fight in the first place.

The tragedies swell and multiply before our eyes. Alexander and Marina Klochkov's son had served with the Interior Ministry's forces (Unit 3642N) for only nine months before he was sent to Daghestan. On 6 September he received severe leg wounds and one leg was torn away. On 30 September they amputated part of the other leg. This boy from Krasnogorsk, a few miles outside Moscow, was not 19 before he became a lifelong invalid. On his birthday, 8 September, he was already lying unconscious in the Khasavyurt military hospital. His father, Alexander, is beginning to understand what this means:

"I've realised that soldiers and invalids get no benefits or allowances. When I read that about the veterans of the Chechen war I thought journalists were exaggerating. Now I go round all these offices and can see for myself. I can't even get them to pay out the insurance for my son's injuries. At the military registration office in Krasnogorsk they say they might pay out some of it if any money is transferred to them. When that will be no one knows. I ask them: 'What will Alyosha do now? Work or study? Where? Can you help?' And they reply: 'The law makes no provision for that.' What does that mean? They found the laws for fighting, but none to help those crippled by that war? Then I ask: 'What am I to do about my younger son, who's 16? Probably he won't have to do military service now?' It turns out that he would be exempted only if Alyosha had died."

On 22 September Tamara Panina, a pensioner from Votkinsk (the town where Tchaikovsky was born), saw her son Alexei on television. A military doctor was describing how a soldier had been brought back from Daghestan with a bullet wound through the skull and brain: he did not know his own name, could not speak, and remembered and understood nothing – amnesia and paralysis. In addition, the ID disc hanging round his neck, thanks to the disgraceful slovenliness of his commanding officers (Unit 3537), carried not a single letter or number. Tamara immediately recognised her son and flew straight away to Moscow. Now she sits beside Alexei's bed in the brain surgery department of the Interior Ministry's central hospital. She finds herself in exactly the same position as Alexander Klochkov. She has no idea whether the boy's superior officers will help pull him through and how long that support will continue after he is released from hospital. Tamara is only sure of one thing: she and her husband will not be able to cope on their own.

Now she greatly regrets that she didn't use every legal – and illegal – means to keep him at home after his summer leave, but let him return to his unit two months before the war began.

But perhaps there are signs that the regime, which started this whole escapade, will not limit itself to words of admiration for the wounded and invalids? Perhaps this time it will not abandon those crippled exclusively through the fault of the State and reduced to a miserable existence for the rest of their lives?

More Wheelchairs?

It's shameful, but I have not detected the slightest sign that the authorities are coming to their senses. Not a single State body has yet made the least move to help the invalids of the new war. When we talked to people in the government they replied: As you know, those who fought in Chechnya have no benefits or allowances. Do you want those fighting in Daghestan to jump the queue?

And the Duma? They haven't woken up yet. Perhaps the upper house of parliament, the Federation Council, is stirring? No, the same somnolent condition. I got the impression they simply didn't understand what we were talking about. They are only too ready to express support for military operations, but fall silent at the suggestion that more wheelchairs are likely to be needed as a result.

The Ministry of Social Security? Invalids come directly within their remit. They confessed that so far they had sent no documents to the government on the subject. They have not begun to draft them, and did not intend to anyway.

As for the Ministry of Defence, the Interior Ministry, the Federal Security Service and the Federal Communications Service – i.e. all those government departments whose officers and soldiers are now fighting, and being wounded and maimed – alas, they are too enthusiastically involved in war-planning. What will happen afterwards does not interest them.

It's quite evident that the new war in the Caucasus also caught Russian society off-guard. Where are the human rights activists? The intelligentsia, the conscience of the nation? Where has all that army of socially active people gone? Why do we not hear their voices raised in defence of the victims of the war? Or at least in support of the truth. There is a war going on, but those taking part continue to be officially described as no more than "participants of an anti-terrorist operation". As long as there is no legal qualification of these events we shall pretend there is no war. What war invalids in 1999? There is no war, how can there be invalids?

Again our country has no time for the truth. It is being run by the military and they feel no pity for ordinary soldiers. The minds of the majority are becoming rapidly and totally militarised: they talk of "wiping out", "crushing", and "smashing" the enemy, while the minority, faced by this rising tide of military euphoria, lapse into a state of apathy. In such circumstances it should come as no surprise that the most effective antidote to war as in any primitive society is the maternal instinct.

Tamara Panina recently tried talking to her severely wounded son Alexei. Just a little, and in words he might now be able to follow. She put a felt-tip pen in his hand, guided it to a sheet of paper and Alyosha drew two letters. However, he was too exhausted to complete the word, and the senior sergeant's weakened hand fell back on the bed. Overjoyed at even this much success, Tamara decided to guess what her son was thinking and added two more letters. Now it spelled "papa". She thought he wanted to know about his father who had remained behind in Votkinsk.

But Alyosha burst into tears. His mother thought it was hurt and frustration that she had not understood him. So Tamara added different letters. This time it spelled *patsany*: the boys, the lads. When Alyosha saw this he went into hysterics. She had guessed rightly. He wanted to tell her what had happened to his fellow soldiers. Some had died in the fierce fighting in early September. Others survived and, after leaving hospital, would face our dishonest life. We would very soon try to forget that these lads were heroes, but they would never forget.

Who understood Alyosha? Only his mother. Even the doctor did not understand. And that is the answer to the question: Did these women do the right thing when they committed their crime?

MOSCOW

CONSCRIPTS TO THE FRONT

Several weeks later, Roman Shleinov published the following comment in
Novaya gazeta (*15 November 1999*):

On 16 May 1996 President Yeltsin signed edict No 722: by
spring 2000 the army would be entirely professional in its
composition. The military were particularly amused by this
assertion.

This year Yeltsin ordered (edict 1347, 16 September 1999)
that only volunteers who have served no less than a year be
sent into battle. On 15 October he issued edict 1366, whereby
any soldier who has served six months could be sent to fight,
no matter whether he wanted to go or not. The edict was
retrospective, moreover, coming into force as of 6 October.

We have analysed more than 200 appeals to the Committees of Soldiers' Mothers. They show that the majority
sent on these operations come from distant and remote parts
of the country.

6

A TALE OF LOVE
AND FASCISM

7 October 1999

They are a charming, ordinary couple, who should be enjoying the best years of their life. A fiancé and his betrothed. He gently brushes something from her hair, she softly strokes his hand. They're no different from a thousand others: Romeo and Juliet, Natasha and Seryozha, Arslan and . . .

"No, please don't put her name in your paper. They might arrest her as well, because she's connected with me."

Arslan is a Chechen who found love in the Moscow of 1999. Today this is much the same as being a Jew in Germany sometime after 1933 or in German-occupied Minsk or Kiev after 1941. His Muscovite fiancée in Yeltsin's declining year in power has to hide Arslan from the Moscow police, just as simple Russian women once concealed their Jewish neighbours from the Gestapo. Encouraged from above, a pogrom against anyone from the Caucasus is under way in Moscow. But sooner or later you have to leave the apartment, even when they are hunting down people. For instance, to renew your residence permit.

Arslan Gatiev, 28, was born in the Daghestan village of Osman-Yurt. Nothing helped in this case. Not the fact that he had come to Moscow long ago and, as a teenager, was given a quite official passport[10] at police station No 111; nor that he answered his call-up papers and, after serving two years in the army, has been working in Moscow for the last eight years.[11]

On 16 September Arslan and his fiancée collected together all the papers required for the re-registration imposed by Mayor Luzhkov three days earlier on those without permanent right of residence, and went to the police station at 10 Samarkand Street. There they reported to the local policeman, a certain Nechaev. They spent the entire working day standing in the queue, because there were hundreds of others who wanted to keep on the right side of the law enforcement agencies.

17 September, the same story. On 18 September it was finally their turn and Nechaev met the young lovers. After looking at their papers he said: "You're a Chechen, you must go to Room 4. I'll take you there myself . . ." His fiancée asked if she could accompany them. "There's no place for you there," joked the policeman.

Another policeman was also in the room, inspecting documents at the same time. "You can expect to see him again in two or three months," he added. She was panic-stricken.

Meanwhile Arslan was already on his way to "the centre", the Vykhino police station on Sormovskaya Street. "I've brought in a Chechen," said Nechaev, following Arslan into the room where the plain-clothes men were sitting.

They came to life. Arslan was made to sit on a chair that was evidently waiting for people like him. The scenario was carefully thought out. The entire room remains behind the person on the chair. Some time passes, and the sounds of preparation are heard – one of them plays with a pair of handcuffs, the policemen laugh a

10 The basic Russian (and Soviet) identity document that includes a stamp indicating place of permanent residence and an entry for nationality (ethnic identity).

11 Outside Grozny, the largest urban concentration of Chechens is the community of over 50,000 in Moscow.

little – then, suddenly, someone jerks the end of Arslan's coat: "Why are you slumping like that? Sit up! Hands on your knees!"

At that moment two witnesses are brought into the room. Alcoholics, detained for some formal infringement of the laws. The policemen make Arslan stand and they turn out his pockets. Heroin: 0.03 grams. Article 228:1. Case No 0504. Temporary detention centre.

"But why heroin?" Arslan demanded, "I won't sign a thing!"

"All right, don't sign," came the reply. "We have a slogan now: 'Chechnya for the Chechens.' Go back to your own country."

"But I was born in Daghestan!"

"So?"

There were only Chechens and Ingush in the cell at the detention centre. They had each been picked up in the same way. All were charged under Article 228 after coming of their own free will to re-register. Then they were escorted here, to be fixed up with a dose of heroin. Those in the cell felt genuinely sorry for one lad: there was not enough heroin left to plant on him, so they put an explosive charge in his pocket and now he stood accused of terrorism.

What next?

A constant turnover. More were brought in, others were taken away. They all remained in prison, none were granted bail. First, the plain-clothes men beat people until they offered a "sincere confession" and "declined the services of a lawyer". Then those same policemen and interrogators reassured them: "Don't worry, it'll only be for six months; while we're at war with Chechnya, we must put you all in prison."

It was Arslan's misfortune to rebel against this smoothly run system for reclassifying all Chechens as criminals. He would not sign anything. He demanded to see a lawyer.

Meanwhile his fiancée was doing exactly the same. She demanded to see both the Head of Investigations at the Vykhino police department and the district prosecutor and she asked for an explanation. As she discovered, no one even pretended to look through the case file of these "Chechen heroin addicts". If someone was Chechen his place was in prison. But she would not accept the system and day after day waited outside their offices. In the end they saw her.

The defenders of law and order became very indignant when they found out that Arslan's fiancée had agreed bail for her future husband. At midday on 23 September Arslan was pushed out of his cell without a single document and ordered to walk straight ahead: "Your lawyer is waiting round the corner and he has all your papers." A baffled Arslan tried to understand what was going on and stopped in front of the entrance to the police station. The next thing he knew, a six-foot bystander had grabbed him and tied his hands. A minute later he was back in the cell. After some time he was given a deposition to sign. It said that he had "attacked" someone and "used obscene language". In other words, that six-foot giant was his victim.

"Tomorrow you'll be in court on a charge of delinquency."

Arslan spent the night of 23 September in the same cell, but now the charge was different. His cellmates explained that this was "politeness training". The prisoner is worn down by repeated accusations of "crimes" fabricated by the police and is never released in between.

The next morning the case was heard. After Judge Vladimir Shumskoi of the Kuzminki district court had read through the formal complaint compiled by Arslan with the help of his lawyer, he said: "This is much too serious a matter. I'll fine you 20 roubles and I don't want to hear anything more about your affairs . . ." Arslan was released in the court-room after he formally agreed not to leave Moscow and was ordered to wait for a summons to appear in court again.

Today Arslan and his fiancée sit before me at our newspaper offices and ask: "What can we do now?"

His fiancée keeps running her hands over his pockets. She sewed them up so that no one can slip anything into them when they have to go out on the street again, for instance after leaving our offices.

"What do you think?" I ask them. "What are the police up to?"

"They told me themselves," replies Arslan, "the Chechens are being labelled a nation of criminals."[12]

What is the thinking behind this? Putin can now tell the country that the proportion of Chechens involved in crime has been rising sharply, but their activities are being just as rapidly exposed and frustrated by the police and security services. We'll expose and imprison them and everyone will start living much better. Then we'll elect those who promised that this would happen.

It is the madness of racial discrimination.

The theory of the criminal nation was particularly fashionable in Nazi Germany. Then they targeted the Jews and Gypsies. Filtration and concentration camps were opened for them everywhere, and they were also confined to ghettos. There seems little to choose between that and what is now going on in Moscow with our mute (or in some cases vociferous) participation. Shall we be forced to admit to our children and grandchildren that we aided this fascism, and did nothing to prevent it happening?

One other parallel. The tragic terrorist bombings in Moscow, Volgodonsk, and Buinaksk, are far too rapidly coming to resemble another distant event: the burning of the Reichstag.

"When we're together it's not so frightening," say Arslan and his fiancée, and they go back out into the city that they once had thought their own.

MOSCOW

---

12 See Amnesty International's December 1999 report, "For the Motherland" (www.amnesty.org).

PART TWO

WAR

November 1999–March 2000

In unity and concord, our society is moving towards the abyss, led by the blind and those who deliberately stir up a "patriotic" and "anti-Caucasian" hysteria. A new puppet ruler has been appointed for Chechnya; the army is on the move. The land operation will begin successfully and then encounter serious problems. Even in the small victorious war[13] in Daghestan our losses were officially 250 dead and 750 wounded out of the 5,000 taking part. By December we shall face the choice: either we conclude a new agreement with Chechnya or, knee-deep in blood, we shall wade towards a "final solution" of the Chechen problem, "using every type of contemporary weapon to physically destroy Chechnya", as some of our passionate commentators now demand.

ANDREI PIONTKOWSKY

The other day our Prime Minister [Vladimir Putin], who has a university education, amazed the entire country when he promised he would "corner the bandits in the shithouse and wipe them out". The Bolsheviks evidently had good reason for considering that ordinary criminals were "a socially close element". Freed of any ideological restraints, our leaders now speak the language of thugs and gangsters from our TV screens.

ANDREI CHERNOV

Novaya gazeta, 7 October 1999[14]

13 "To hold back the revolution", asserted the Tsar's Minister for the Interior, von Plehve, in the early twentieth century, "we need a small victorious war." When war with Japan loomed he advocated caution. The first defeat of that conflict was soon followed by the minister's own assassination and the 1905 Revolution.

14 Andrei Piontkowsky is a political consultant in Moscow; Andrei Chernov writes on cultural issues for *Novaya gazeta*.

7

INGUSHLAG

A New Concentration Camp

4 November 1999

A tragedy is today unfolding in Ingushetia. It has grown to such catastrophic proportions that, believe me, it is now hardly less terrible than the war in Chechnya. What difference does it make, in the end, if you die from hunger or from bombing? During the month that they have spent in the refugee camps – in these poultry and old stock-raising farms, in cellars, tents and out in the open beside campfires – thousands of people have become deeply embittered, with no regular food or place to wash, and without any occupation or work.

Hopes of returning home have finally melted away. Now people in the camps are desperately struggling just to survive. They await the first snows in November almost as though they were death itself. Each night their fear of bombardment is magnified a hundred-fold by the roar of weapons being fired nearby. All the food they brought with them has now been eaten and there is a chronic shortage of humanitarian aid: the little there is, is totally inadequate for the number of refugees. Cold, hunger, sickness and everywhere pale children with blue lips. Adults squabble over each crust of bread. People ask only two questions: "Why?" and "How many more victims do you need?"

Death from the Skies

We are standing in the middle of the camp and even laughing, although it's no laughing matter. We're looking up at the sky where rockets fly over our heads. Insolently they rip through the air above us as though we are not standing below and, instead, this were some weapons-testing site. Why the laughter? It helps us save face in front of each other and conceals the nervous trembling that has seized hold of us all.

27 October 1999. It's sunny and there is no wind. Soon it will be midday. We are on the outskirts of Karabulak, a town in Ingushetia. The camp – more than 3,000 refugees squeezed into 98 army tents – is in a shallow gully beside the River Sunzha. Most people are now gathered in the centre of the camp. Behind the hills to the right stands the town of Mozdok. To the left are more hills, and beyond them the capital of Ossetia, Vladikavkaz.

At last it's midday. We feel a shock wave of uncertain origin pass through our bodies, and pick up an inner rumbling of the earth through the soles of our feet. A 25-year-old from Grozny with a degree in Russian Language and Literature and the wonderful name of Mir[15] explains: "They've just launched a rocket. Now we shall be able to follow its tail. We saw them yesterday as well."

He's quite right. In a second two white trails stretch across the sky from the direction of Mozdok. At 12.10 there is a repeat performance. Only this time the missile has been fired from near Vladikavkaz and again there are two trails.

Mir Khadjimuratov thinks aloud: "Doesn't all this remind you of the famous password: 'The Spanish sky is cloudless'?[16] Are they deliberately provoking us? What feelings can you have, other than a desire for revenge, when you sit watching death fly towards your home town?"

15 It means "Peace" in Russian.
16 The signal for Franco's forces to begin their rebellion in 1936 was broadcast as part of the weather forecast on the radio.

Half an hour later it is as if those vile traces of the rockets had never been there. People are no longer laughing, nor are they trembling. Now their eyes are hard and dull, clenched teeth show through their jaws and their hands in their pockets are bunched into fists. No one even smokes. The men leave the square with the comment: "27 October, between 12.00 and 12.10 another 100 people died. None of them fighters."

Mir Khadjimuratov asks: "Why do they continue firing missiles into Grozny after the tragedy in the Central Market?[17] Each missile immediately hits a great number of people. That many fighters never gather in a single place, even our children know that. So it's genocide. And those who didn't want to fight are now ready to."

Vakha Nurmagomedov is 40 years old and comes from Moscow. He had permanent domicile registration in the capital's Mitino district, but police harassment forced him to move. He returned first to his native Urus-Martan in Chechnya and then, with his family, left the republic. Vakha is very keen for his point of view to be heard – not by Putin (that would be a waste of breath, he thinks), but by the millions who today are ready to vote for a continuation of this cruel war in the North Caucasus. "You don't win people over to your side by firing rockets. Missiles spell the end of a friendly attitude towards Russia, even among those who used to feel that way. You must understand, we can never allow ourselves to forget all this. Otherwise we are not the fathers of our children or the children of our fathers."

"We could not forget and forgive deportation,"[18] I constantly hear this refrain from the crowd of refugees. "We simply had no right to do

17 On the afternoon of 21 October 1999 the Central Market in Grozny was struck by a rocket attack, leaving many dead and wounded. Despite denials it seems clear that this was authorised by the Russian government.

18 In February 1944 the Chechens and Ingush, accused of intending to aid the invading German forces, were deported en masse to Kazakhstan. Many died on the journey. The survivors could not return home until 1957. (The Germans captured Mozdok in August 1942, but could never get close enough to take Grozny and Baku, then the Soviet Union's greatest centres of the oil industry.)

so. The first Chechen war joined those memories and so will the present war."

The main focus of their life in Ingushetia in the refugee camps is the accumulation of hatred as they daily study the missiles flying overhead and observe the fighting which can easily be followed from here. By heading for Ingushetia in late September and early October the refugees were leaving the war behind them. Now it has caught up with them again, in their temporary refuge.

Children Fated Not to Survive

Above the Sputnik camp, not far from the village of Ordjoniki-dzevskaya, it is the Grad [Hail] missiles that swagger across the skies.

Here at Sputnik anyone who wants to can easily guess what the military are planning. The camp is roughly seven kilometres from the small town of Sernovodsk in Chechnya. In late September tents were erected here for the convenience of the refugees. Taken in by the Kremlin spokesmen, local officials believed that the "anti-terrorist operation" would not last long nor affect Ingushetia. It would there-fore be easier and quicker, the republic's Ministry for Emergency Situations decided, for the refugees to return home from here.

These good intentions have backfired on everyone. Today the tents sit directly in the zone of bombardment. If the officer aiming the weapon has had a little too much to drink (and the military do take to drink here – it's also bad for them to go on fighting this long) then a tragedy is inevitable. The refugees are in a shallow gully between mountains. On one hillside are the Russian forces, on the other, the town of Sernovodsk. From one hilltop they are firing at Sernovodsk and a stream of murderous metal flies over the heads of almost 5,000 people living in the camp, half of them children. The volleys produce an unpleasant hissing sound, like snakes, and they make the already hard life of the refugees unbearable.

Take, for instance, one half-hour around midday on 28 October:

12.45, volley; 12.47, another; 12.51 yet another . . . Then, there is a brief respite until 13.11, when the firing again resumes every two minutes.

"They're trying to catch Basayev," decide the women in the weeping, worn-out crowd. "Those officers up on the hill probably don't know that Grad missiles can't pinpoint a target, they're a weapon of mass destruction. But we know that all too well."

Meanwhile some boys between five and seven years old are digging a trench beyond the furthest tents. Gradually they disappear below the ground, and pay no attention to what the adults are saying.

"What are you doing?" I finally ask them.

But the children look at me as though I'm from another planet. They don't speak Russian because they were born after the first war in 1994–6. It is their mother Toita Elimkhanova, from the Pervomayskaya village where 157 of their clan are living, who explains:

"The boys themselves took the decision. No one asked them. They say it's just in case: we left home under a terrible bombardment."

It's interesting that the children a little older than two or three do not react at all to the Grad missiles. They are a very strange sight. "Hunger makes them apathetic and lethargic," says Hasan Tempieva from Gudermes. She is without her husband and has eight children. "There is starvation here. Bread is handed out free, but there isn't enough for everyone. In my family, for instance, it is three days since any of us ate. We just drink hot water."

Small children, still entirely dependent on their mothers, react quite differently. Their short lives are threatened by each volley. On the night of 25–26 October, when there was a particularly severe and unrelenting stream of Grad missiles and sparks from the sky burned holes in the tents, many refugees lost control of themselves. The screams of women rose over the Sputnik camp and drowned out the howl of the rockets. Seven months pregnant, Malizha Derbieva from the Ishchorskaya village in Naurskaya district (now she is in Tent 8, Block 6) was so frightened that by morning she gave birth prematurely. Her little baby girl died immediately. Malizha is still being treated in the Sunzhensk district hospital. The doctors cannot guarantee she will ever have children now, the shock was too great.

Aina Terekmurzaeva, from the small village of Betimokhk in the Nozhai-Yurt district, is 17 years old. Only a short while ago she married someone from Gudermes where she herself was born. When Aina arrived at the camp she already had Ibrahim her newborn son with her. He's now four months old. The skin on his face is transparent and his bluish but still smiling lips try to find something to eat. Aina herself has wasted away and is barely alive.

Aina's milk failed as soon as the Grad missile volleys began. A four-month-old cannot eat bread, so for a week now they have been giving him nothing but weak tea. If you've ever had children then you'll know that an infant cannot survive long like that. Aina went to the camp administration and asked if they could get hold of some baby food. So far they have found nothing. The warehouses of the republic's Ministry for Emergency Situations are empty.

You probably think I'm writing all this to stir your pity. My fellow citizens have indeed proved a hard-hearted lot. You sit enjoying your breakfast, listening to stirring reports about the war in the North Caucasus, in which the most terrible and disturbing facts are sanitised so that the voters don't choke on their food.

But my notes have a quite different purpose, they are written for the future. They are the testimony of the innocent victims of the new Chechen war, which is why I record all the detail I can.

The Warehouse

The measure of our present kindness is the warehouse for humanitarian aid on the outskirts of Ordjonikidzevskaya village. Officially it's a local depot of the reserve supplies of the Ministry for Emergency Situations. We arrive unexpectedly and accompanied by Major Tugan Chapanov. He heads one of the Ministry's departments, and on

23 October a decree issued by President Aushev made him commandant of the Sputnik camp (replacing the refugee leaders who
had held the post).

Being a refugee is demeaning, not only because you are without a
home and of no concern to anyone else. But for days on end there is
nothing to do in the camps, apart from go out in the morning to collect
sticks and twigs for the fire and chat with your fellows in misfortune.
In these endless conversations a great many myths are born. For
example, people said that the relatives of Shamil Basayev and Alla
Dudayev[19] are living peacefully in the Ingush capital Nazran. The
government pays all of their bills, no one is in pursuit of them and
they have the best cottages the rich could buy. The conclusion? The
war is not against the "bandits", but against "us" and they aim to
exterminate "us" completely.

Another persistent myth concerns the aid warehouse. The refugees are certain that it is overflowing with supplies and that those
distributing the aid are to blame when it does not reach the right
people. They are selling most of it at the market, goes the myth, and
pocketing the money.

Alas, on inspection the "supply depot" is almost empty. The
local deputy director, Hasan Bogatyrev, shows us several metal beds
that could not be issued because there were no mattresses, let alone
pillows and sheets (they're waiting for a delivery). There were also
some black olives that were well past their sell-by date, so they did
not risk sending them to the camps. (They would certainly be eaten
there, no one has any doubt about that, but who can tell with what
consequences?)

Also standing idle in the warehouse were the military kitchens
and mobile bath units. People are starving in the camps and they are
lousy because they cannot wash. Why then are such valuable items

19 The Russian widow of Chechnya's first president, Jokhar Dudayev (see
   Biographies).

left here? The answer is very simple. Ingushetia already has serious problems with its water supply and now is quite incapable of providing for the refugee camps as well. The camp commandants are afraid to take the bath units since they have no fuel to run them and their many urgent requests to the Moscow authorities to increase the water allowance in the republic's supply network have gone unanswered.

"But what about the kitchen?" demands Major Chapanov.

"What will they cook?" His question is met with a question. "And who will take responsibility?" continues Bogatyrev. "To begin with the federal Ministry of Labour was, apparently, ready to pay the services of cooks from among the refugee women as persons engaged in socially useful work. Now they're keeping quiet. It has all remained at the level of good intentions and the Ministry officials, after tossing out these promises, have gone back to Moscow. We have to sort things out for them."

This is the honest truth. The refugees are extremely bitter. It must be said that they do not accept everything that happens with calm and understanding. There are constant quarrels and fights. Harsh measures are directed against every "newcomer" to the camp. The Chechens are now almost certain that their brother Ingush[20] are brazenly cheating them. A dangerous feud between the two nations threatens, though when the refugee exodus began nothing of the kind was in the air. It must also be admitted that we came across people in the camps who were stirring up anti-Ingush feelings.

What will be the outcome? Only one conclusion is possible, that some dishonourable person of dubious sanity passionately desires to extend the war to Ingushetia.

---

20 Until 1991 the ethnically close Chechens and Ingush were united in the autonomous republic of Checheno-Ingushetia. When Chechnya declared independence, the less numerous Ingush (135,000 in 1989) decided to remain within the Russian Federation.

What Can We Do?

All these passions will abate to reasonable levels if the refugees are clothed and fed. Warm clothes are urgently and desperately needed, for children and adults. The majority of women are still wearing only socks and need warm tights. Medicine is also in urgent demand. So are shoes, toothbrushes and toothpaste (families of ten or twelve members have been issued with two or three brushes). Most urgent of all is the need for baby food and milk.

The best thing would be not only to collect the above-mentioned items, but also to hire and equip a convoy of trucks to drive to Ingushetia and hand out these goods ourselves. Where is our fellow feeling? If you want to know what is needed today in which camp, and its exact location, ring the author on her pager (232-0000, #49883). We must get the better of this appalling misfortune. And we must do so together. The last consideration is the most important of all, because we will only remain united in future if we act together now. Otherwise we shall become so many wild and hunted wolves each retreating to hide in its lair.

The refugees in Ingushetia are suffering inhuman deprivation. Despite everything, though, they dream of remaining human beings. They need not only our practical help but also our moral support. Where are all the actors of our great country? Where are its singers, musicians, performers and satirists? Don't tell me they're all too busy with the Ukrainian elections. Where are our own de Niros (remember how he flew to the refugees in the Balkans?) who are trying to reach out to these unfortunate people?

No one is visiting the camps in Ingushetia today, apart from the republic's equally exhausted officials from the Ministry for Emergency Situations who are responsible for their administration. No one is talking to the people or explaining what's going on. The information war has been won, but for the time being the battle for human souls has been completely lost.   INGUSHETIA

8

CAMP GUARDS

Using the Jailers' Long Experience

11 November 1999

In Ingushetia and Chechnya they call them "criminals", plain and simple. The refugees say they are the most brutal during various "cleansing operations" – it is no good pleading with them, they don't know the meaning of mercy. The story now circulating widely among refugees is that the most vicious offenders were selected and then released from prison or the camps under an amnesty if they agreed to fight in Chechnya in these "criminal units". It's one thing to hear such talk, quite another to witness it with your own eyes. Now here they stand before me.

The men in camouflage fatigues, which bear no indications of service, rank or unit, make up the very first line, holding back the refugees at the famous "Caucasus" checkpoint. They create a contradictory and strange impression. Men and women alike are greeted with foul-mouthed obscenities and a machine-gun poked in their ribs. The insolence is reinforced by pockets visibly bulging with grenades. And it proves pointless to ask the most innocent questions. The armed men in this cordon simply spit insultingly at your feet. I had to return to Moscow to find out any more.

"Remember, you are a soldier not a bandit." This is an intriguing exhortation, you must agree. Without this reminder, would the people addressed really be so uncertain of their social status? Perhaps amnestied criminals had been let loose, after all, in Chechnya. One clue provides the answer. These parting words are nothing less than motto No 1 of the special memorandum signed by Yury Kalinin, Russia's deputy minister of justice. It was intended not for gangsters seeking personal redemption but for officers in the service of the State.

Our quest for the "criminals" led us to the Ministry of Justice in Moscow. A profoundly civilian establishment, its purpose is to help maintain the rule of law throughout the country. In September 1998 the Ministry was expanded to include the State Directorate for the Penitentiary System, i.e. it acquired a million prisoners and the 300,000 staff in charge of them. Before that they came under the control of the Ministry of Internal Affairs, but at the firm insistence of the Council of Europe[21] the penitentiary system was finally transferred to the civilian staff of the Justice Ministry.

The effect seems not to have been as expected. The Ministry gradually succumbed to a powerful infrastructure that had been built up over decades. The Justice Ministry did not impose its rules on the modern Gulag but, instead, was being swallowed up by it. As usual, this only became apparent by chance. At the "Caucasus" checkpoint the leader of the "criminals" had introduced himself as the head of a special detachment from the Justice Ministry.

At first I could not believe my ears. Two Ministry officials in Moscow agreed to answer our questions. Mikhail Nazarkin heads the penitentiary service's Security Department while Sergei Cherkai is the immediate Moscow superior of the "soldiers not bandits" – to be exact, he is Deputy Head of the Special Services Section (a mouthful but that is his official title).

NAZARKIN: Our special detachments are indeed serving in Chechnya,

---

21 An association of European States, founded in 1949, committed to defending parliamentary democracy and to encouraging the economic and social progress of its members. Russia was admitted in 1996.

on the orders of the Justice Minister, Yury Chaika. There they are at the disposal of General Kazantsev, the commanding officer of the combined forces. We have been seconded to the combined forces group and must carry out all the orders and instructions of General Kazantsev. The experience of the last Chechnya war made this a necessity: then there was no co-ordination among the different federal forces and this led to enormous losses. As regards the "Caucasus" checkpoint: if General Kazantsev decided that our lads should stand between the army and the refugees then he must have had a good reason.

Q. **But you are, at least formally, a civilian organisation. How can your subordinates come under the command of an army general? What written authorisation is there?**

NAZARKIN: We're not a civilian department, that's a fundamental error on your part. For more than a year we have been one of the power ministries.[22] The basis for that is a presidential decree. And the decision was entirely correct and proper.

Q. **What is the main purpose of your special detachments in peacetime?**

CHERKAI: We are there to ensure that the penitentiary system keeps functioning in the event of various excesses and conflicts.

"Excesses" and "conflicts" are terms the prison authorities use for riots and the taking of hostages in prisons and detention centres. Cherkai's men have been specially trained to disarm and kill desperate convicts with nothing more to lose and nowhere else to go. Such detachments, according to Cherkai, have been set up in every region throughout the country. They shun any publicity: Cherkai has served in the prison camps for 13 years as a special service man, but our interview is his first for ten years.

---

22 A term applied to the Ministries of Defence and of Internal Affairs, and to the Federal Security Service (FSB).

Q. **What's happening in Chechnya is also an "excess", in your view?**
CHERKAI: Yes, in Daghestan and Chechnya we are facing unusual situations. When necessary the Government and the President have every right to call on our forces to carry out duties that, perhaps, are not entirely familiar to our men. We cleansed Karamakhi and several other villages in Daghestan. I myself took part in the summer events. And we more than earned the thanks of the soldiers there. Today our men are stationed at five checkpoints [refugees are being "greeted" at the "Caucasus" checkpoint by a detachment from the Kalmyk republic's prison camps, AP]. We are also cleansing Chechen villages, in particular, Goragorsk and Naurskaya. It's hard to understand you journalists! You wrote that inexperienced soldiers should not be used in Chechnya. Now they send experienced men down there, and again it's all wrong.

Q. **How many of your men are stationed in Chechnya today?**
NAZARKIN: Nine hundred. They'll be replaced in December and we must provide the new replacements from our own "fresh" forces. Incidentally, several of our people have already been put in charge of liberated population centres, in particular, in the Naurskaya district.

Q. **How do you mean? A specialist in the suppression of prison-camp disturbances is suddenly responsible for organising the work of schools, hospitals, farms – something quite alien to him! Your special services men are trained for destruction not construction. How will they organise civilian activities? They know nothing about it. They've spent years being trained for quite another job. Evidently someone needs them urgently to do his dirty work. And how could your people be put directly in contact with the refugees? With our vast military presence in the North Caucasus was there really no one but prison-camp riot police to stem the flood of civilians fleeing the bombing in Chechnya?**
CHERKAI: The reason is simple. There is a catastrophic shortage of manpower here! [He admits his men "are hired out by the Ministry of Justice" and are doing jobs they have no training for, AP.] But

there's nothing you can do about it – there's a war on. It's hard to foresee everything and keep things neat and tidy.

Q. **Aren't you uneasy that the "Caucasus" checkpoint and the events we've been describing are all on Ingushetia's territory? Your people were in charge there, though there is no fighting in the area. Does that mean you consider Ingushetia to be the arena for a new war?**

NAZARKIN: From a legal point of view everything is quite in order here. I'd advise you to carefully read through the presidential decree authorising the present anti-terrorist operation. There it clearly specifies "the territory of the North Caucasus". Not Chechen territory, note. That's of fundamental importance. Acting on that decree, the military can today carry out their activities where they're needed. Ingushetia is also a part of the North Caucasus. Therefore, there has been no bending of the rules, all these actions are well within the framework of the official documents. Now as concerns instances of tactless behaviour towards the refugees, I can well believe it – under extreme conditions anything may happen. Some of the soldiers simply lost control of their emotions.

Q. **And the refugees are at some holiday camp, are they? Isn't that an extreme condition for them as well? Just imagine if the roles were reversed. If it wasn't your men who were cursing the refugees, but they who were insulting you, and if they then came nearer and poked their machine-guns at "your boys", what would your men have done? Of course, they'd have killed them and said they were terrorists. Your people represent a civilian ministry and they are behaving disrespectfully towards the civilian population only because they have machine-guns in their hands. Isn't that right?**

NAZARKIN: The answer to all your questions is as follows. Our men have to carry out their assignment using *any means.* That was the order they were given.

Q. **Even those methods they use on rioting prisoners?**

NAZARKIN: Any means.

The entire conversation, I should add, was frequently interrupted by long digressions about recent history and the first Chechen war. In each case these leading officials of the prison-camp special services argued that no matter how badly their men behaved they would be forgiven and their actions justified. There was only one argument: what was happening now paid back the Chechens for the losses of the first war and the chief purpose of the present fighting was revenge for those who had died then.

CHERKAI: Among those supposed refugees, you didn't see any teenage suicide-bombers there, at the "Caucasus" checkpoint, did you? They've been trained in Basayev's camps to carry out terrorist acts in Russia. None were detained when you were there? Not one? Well, we've been told it's going on.

Q. **I saw nothing of the kind. Are you sure it's true?**

NAZARKIN: Not entirely, of course. Basayev also likes to push a good story. Nevertheless the way I see things, one Chechen is a Chechen, two Chechens are two Chechens, but three Chechens – and it's already a gang. And there are no exceptions to the rule.

Cherkai then, without any inhibitions, began to expound his ideology. Our fighters, he is convinced, must learn from the Chechens. Brother must answer for brother and if someone in the family has been fighting for Basayev, then all of his relatives are accomplices and deserve extermination. Incidentally, Cherkai also wants the blood feud to regain its place in the Russian mentality.

Q. **So we should reply to their mediaeval ways with something similar?**

CHERKAI: I don't see why not.

Q. **But, tell me, why are your men really there?**

CHERKAI: For kicks, and the rest can't wait to get there either.

There is a Plan

It's hard to find any major difference between the attitudes and behaviour of Minister Chaika's fighters and those supported by their "colleagues" who fight for Basayev and Khattab. A code of military honour? As a rule, neither displays anything of the kind. An idea of how to deal with the civilian population – with children, pregnant women and old men? Very vague. Blood lust? Now that's ineradicable.

At the end of our conversation Sergei Cherkai recognised that the only proper use for the cruel and merciless Justice Ministry fighters in this war would be if they captured and liquidated Basayev and his gang of cutthroats. That is a job they could do. The rest is not really their scene.

At which point the most important questions arise. Was it, then, mere accident that they were sent to the war? Why was it Chaika's prison guards who were chosen to deal with the refugees? What will we consider victory – the head of Basayev? Who exactly are they pacifying in the present operation?

The latest information from Chechnya confirms that the incidents at the "Caucasus" checkpoint were not the result of the chaos of war but part of a deliberate plan. It has now been announced that the special detachments of the Ministry of Justice will guard the new refugee camps – those that are now being set up in Chechnya itself under the control of the military (as Sergei Shoigu, Minister for Emergency Situations, recently declared). Neither Russia's journalists nor Western observers will be able to move freely there. Moreover, these Gulag guards are now forming the backbone of the "territorial self-defence groups" for towns and villages in the liberated areas. A special guard for these special settlements. Again a "wicked" nation is being held in a ghetto?

All that remains for me is to recount one conversation I had in Ingushetia. Those I spoke to are major actors in the present "anti-terrorist operation in the North Caucasus". I said to them that there was no sense, from a military point of view, in treating the refugees so harshly. The officers replied: No, it makes a great deal of sense and is done to "soften up the Chechen fighters". Once they learn that their families are in the hands of prison camp guards they'll most certainly become more amenable.

The name for it is a concentration camp. All they need now is to start designing gas chambers. And for as long as one set of gangsters faces another we can feel nothing but doomed.

INGUSHETIA-MOSCOW

9

BOMB, DON'T SAVE

The Old People's Home in Grozny

15 November 1999

The refugees in the camps in Ingushetia fall into one of two groups. Some hate the Russians and anyone from Moscow. Others cannot and don't want to imagine a future outside Russia. However, when they begin to describe the pitiful state of those left at the old people's home in Grozny they are all in full agreement. Almost 100 old men and women, 30 of them bedridden, remain in the Chechen capital with bombs falling indiscriminately all around. "What can you [i.e. Russians, AP] do right, if you can't even save your own old folk from being bombed?"

It was painful and shaming to hear. Left without relatives, these elderly men and women were reduced to desperate begging, wandering the city in search of food. Those still able to walk brought food for the bedridden. The staff had abandoned them. There was no water, electricity or gas. And behind all these tales, alas, lies the issue of nationality: for the most part those spending their last years at the home are Russians and other Russian speakers,[23] "your people". Chechens do not usually send their old people to such homes.

And that was how the idea first arose. We had to get these

---

23 Those assimilated to the dominant Russophone culture but not themselves ethnically Russian. The last Soviet population census in 1989 found 15 million people across the USSR who defined themselves as such "Russian speakers".

unfortunate old men and women out of Grozny at any cost and find them somewhere decent to live. But how?

"What Can You Do Right?"

We made a start. All of Moscow officialdom, probably, received the same question. Who should help the Grozny old people's home? Whose responsibility is it? Tell us his name, patronymic and surname.

The answer, it turned out, was no one. During both wars, it is true, representatives of the Russian Ministry of Labour and Social Development came to inspect the home, supposedly to provide aid. But now? When bombs were falling? Political considerations and the "struggle against terrorism" had made them forget all about their charges. Then the military added their contribution: all who had remained in Grozny, they declared, were accomplices of the bandits. That was an end of it. There was now no way of calling the Ministry of Labour to account: it was easier to bomb them than save them.

We could only conclude that the way our State is run today there is not one official who accepts responsibility for the fate of 100 old and lonely people, stranded on the front line of the great military and political venture in the North Caucasus.

At this point emotion took over. At first sight the rescue of these helpless old men and women was an almost impossible task. It only began to appear a reality once we started appealing directly to people's emotions. The first to take our idea to heart and bring his considerable personal connections into play was Yevgeny Gontmakher, who heads the Department for Social Development on the government staff. He did everything he could, acting as an individual, to ensure that the Minister of Labour and Social Development, Sergei Kalashnikov – who until then refused even to talk about the Grozny home (while fully aware of its terrible plight) – received the necessary order from Valentina Matvienko, the Deputy Prime Minister. Very soon Kalashnikov's deputy, Sergei Kiselyov, had found places for the old people in homes located in nine other regions of the country.

Here we committed a fundamental and fateful error. In order not to dampen their stirring enthusiasm we ignored too much of what these federal bureaucrats were saying. We pretended not to hear, for instance, when those involved in the operation loftily declared that it was "politically unwise" to evacuate the old people from Grozny. We even agreed to a compromise, promising not to publish a word until the happy end had been reached. When that moment came, we assured them, we would give a lyrical description of all the participants and forget every unpleasant moment there had been.

And there were more than enough of those. Kalashnikov, for instance, demanded our guarantee that there were "only Russians" in the Grozny old people's home; a little later, when he found out there were "also Chechens there", he accused us of deceit. We pleaded with certain politicians, battling to enter the new Duma, for money to buy warm clothes for the old people, and to pay for the bus to get them out of Grozny. Those aspiring tribunes of the people also insisted on guarantees: yes, they would do something but only if they were shown on all the main TV channels, greeting the helpless old people from Chechnya. Without a shade of embarrassment, these future parliamentarians mused aloud to themselves: "Only 100? That's not going to bring in many votes . . ."

Our compromise with this cynical company served no purpose. We kept quiet about the story while the government officials and Duma candidates were just looking for a chance to avoid doing anything. Their main concern was to ensure that no one later learnt how indecently they'd behaved.

"Who's She? Matvienko?"

While we continued trying to win over the political elite in Moscow the military completely encircled Chechnya. It was now 100 times more difficult to move the old people's home out to the frontier with

Ingushetia. For hours I stood at the Caucasus checkpoint. I looked the commandant, Colonel Khrulyov, in the eye and I begged, pleaded and explained to him that the Deputy Prime Minister, Valentina Matvienko, had already issued the relevant order. His answer was simple: "Who's she? Matvienko?" Or: "What are they to you, these old people?" He hinted persistently that the enemy was vigilant and that "terrorists could enter Russian territory" disguised as busloads of pensioners.

I asked colleagues who were working nearby, some of them very well known TV journalists, to help. They listened attentively, but did not show the slightest inclination to get involved.

According to Sergei Kalashnikov's instructions Ruslan Tsetsoyev, the Minister of Labour for Ingushetia, was to help in transporting the elderly. However, Tsetsoyev was so engrossed in the preparations for his own birthday party that he shamelessly pushed me out of his office when I began speaking about the old people's home. Most important of all, he let us down whenever we needed his help. If we reached agreement that a bus should be at the checkpoint by 9 a.m. then it was not there at 9, or 10, or 11 . . . It took a while before we understood: he had been told by Moscow to do nothing.

We got in touch with the Chechen side. Perhaps the people struggling to hold on to power in Grozny would like to demonstrate their own magnanimity and themselves deliver the old people to the frontier with Ingushetia?

Alas, the Chechen reaction was indistinguishable from that of the federal authorities. There were a great many promises.

First from the lips of Mate Tsikhesashvili, Aslan Maskhadov's personal representative, who heads the department for inter-governmental relations of the Chechnya cabinet of ministers.

Second from Vakha Dudayev, a deputy of the existing parliament of Chechnya. He was especially insistent that his was the only legitimate representative assembly in the republic and so it was a matter of honour for the deputies to see that the old people were evacuated.

Third from the Red Cross representative in Grozny and from dozens of private individuals. They swore oaths and gave us heartfelt looks.

These words all proved so much hot air. Gradually it became clear that those in charge of Chechnya today, or their close allies, wanted exactly the same as their opposite numbers on the federal side: as much blood and horror, as many deaths and bombs, as possible. The two were in direct and uncompromising confrontation and knew that neither could back down. We were repeatedly told by the Chechen side that the old people's home had been bombed out of existence and its inhabitants were now all dead. Not once did they offer the slightest proof. The federal side played the same game, assuring us that Chechen fighters had destroyed the home. And not once did they offer us a shred of evidence.

The well-informed in Nazran told us there was only one remaining chance: we should throw ourselves on the mercy of Valery Kuksa, who was Ingushetia's Minister for Emergency Situations, the all-powerful local equivalent of Sergei Shoigu. He was the only one who could help. Kuksa was closely linked to the generals leading the combined forces group and he had connections with the equivalent ministry in Chechnya. He had fought alongside Ruslan Aushev, President of Ingushetia, during the Afghan war – and he was not just a friend, but had been Aushev's commander. Kuksa would find out if the old people were still alive, he would get them out.

So we appealed to him. And Kuksa promised. He was surprised, though, at my persistence. I appealed to him a second time. Kuksa again gave his word. But asked me not to pressure him too much. I appealed to him a third time, and Kuksa promised yet again.

And that's as far as we have got.

Strong, brave, active and ambitious individuals have now gone into hiding to avoid facing the plight of the weakest, loneliest and most abandoned people. It does indeed disgrace the nation.

What now? They say you should live quietly and not go poking your nose into other people's business. They say that Putin's rating is growing because he has shown how tough he is. They say that Valentina Matvienko is his right hand and can do anything she wants.

Let me tell you, it's all lies. These heartless tough hands are signing death sentences.

INGUSHETIA–MOSCOW

10

THE BASIC INSTINCT OF EMPIRE

Two Faces of the Russian Army

28 November 1999

We already had enough problems with the weather – it was cold, damp and windy – when the helicopter appeared, flying low over the ground, intimidating us and stirring up a veritable hurricane. It's chilly in Russia and frightening.

With a crazy determination, worthy of better application, the helicopter circles towards us a fifth time. It rumbled, descending still lower towards the field, letting the gunner examine us at point-blank range and again flew away.

Finally Bagaudin Batygov, administrator of the "Southern" refugee settlement in Ingushetia (nine kilometres from the Nesterovskaya village) could stand it no longer. He grabbed a piece of paper from his briefcase and quickly began to write something on it. And at the same time he muttered:

"I always do that when the helicopters start buzzing us. Then 'they' think that I'm here on official business and don't start shooting. I'd much prefer to stay alive! Don't look up, they might misinterpret that. The gunner . . ."

He's right. It really did help.

Now I can get on my way. My mission could not be less warlike. The Southern refugee settlement is an open field on the border between Chechnya and Ingushetia where they erected 95 of the

"Luzhkov" caravans a month ago – humanitarian aid sent by the city administration in Moscow. But no one has moved in there and today they present a pitiful spectacle. The military were roving all around the area. To begin with they used the caravans as winter quarters, but then they went to live in dugouts and now they come here on raids every evening. The doors have been broken, the roofs stolen, windows smashed, and all the valuable fixtures and fittings – heaters, sinks, cupboards and tables – have been carted off to some unknown destination. Of the hundred or so panels brought here to construct outdoor toilets only four remain.

As the helicopter flew away, we called out: "Hey, soldier! We know you're there. What's the problem?" We could even see these filthy hunted soldiers. But they kept silent. Then there was a burst of machine-gun fire. Their ill will expressed in lead. Thankfully it was not directly aimed at us.

This was the road to Nesterovskaya village and by the roadside, two kilometres from the Southern settlement, the officers of these pillaging soldiers stood in a group. It was 10.16 a.m. and they were knocking back vodka as fast as they could. This is what people in Chechnya and Ingushetia fear most of all today: the lawless behaviour of the army. If you're unlucky enough to fall into the hasty hands of a drunken or hashish-crazed "man with a gun" then you've had it.

It is quite clear even now how the war is changing as the cold weather sets in and the operation drags on. The lives of thousands of civilians become dependent not on the will of those who write the orders in Moscow and Mozdok[24] but of the man who actually carries out the order. Everything depends on his intellectual level and moral qualities. Anyone can shoot where they like in this war. Survival now depends on a whim.

24 The main military base for federal forces in the North Caucasus.

Monsters and Human Beings

We know of instances when air-force pilots jettisoned their bombs into the river on the outskirts of villages so as not to commit the sin of bombing their peaceful inhabitants.

We know cases of quite the opposite kind. The pilots deliberately fired on the Rostov-Baku Highway when refugees were fleeing along it from the war zone, and then flew past a second, third and even a fourth time when they saw that someone below was still moving. The war is rapidly acquiring two faces and each potential victim hopes and prays that they will be lucky and meet the "kind" face of this war.

Asya Astamirova, a young 28-year-old inhabitant of the Katyr-Yurt village in the Achkhoi-Martan district, has looked at both the one and the other. She survived physically because some soldiers saved her. But she is now dead to the world because other soldiers carried out a dreadful and cynical atrocity before her very eyes.

On 16 November Asya was bringing the body of her husband Aslan back to be buried in Katyr-Yurt. He had died in the Sunzhensk district hospital from the wounds he received when he came under fire. With her in the car were her children, six-year-old Aslanbek and two-year-old Salambek. In another car were Aslan's older sister Oeva, a mother of two, and their two uncles who were no longer young men. At the checkpoint between Achkhoi-Martan and Katyr-Yurt they were stopped and, without a word, the soldiers opened fire on both vehicles. When the first burst into flames Asya and the little boys leapt out. "For Allah's sake, save us!" they cried. The contract soldiers in their bandannas, who were not raw youths, continued shooting and told her: "There's no Allah, you Chechen bitch! You're dead."

They fired directly at her and the children. Aslanbek fell unconscious, Salambek screamed and Asya saw the car and her husband's body burn. Young conscripts observed the whole scene from a distance. When the contract soldiers had finished and went off to rest, the conscripts loaded the wounded Asya into an armoured vehicle and took her away. After several hours driving across the fields, avoiding the military posts, the soldiers unloaded the wounded family outside Sunzhensk hospital and without a word to anyone they left.

Asya is still in a state of shock. She gazes blankly round ward No 1 where she and the children were placed. Her mother Esita Islamova asks each new visitor: "How can I tell anyone after this that we belong together, that we're citizens of Russia? I can't!"

I try to stroke tiny Salambek's hair – his right leg is encased in plaster where fragments hit him – but the boy begins to scream and cry. He turns away and hides in the pillow.

"He's afraid," Esita explains. "You're a Slav, like the contract soldiers."

"But what about the conscripts, they're also Slavs?"

"He's only a child . . . It's what he remembers and that's what he's reacting to."

Our losses are immeasurable as we let the army get out of hand and degenerate into anarchy. By allowing such a war to be fought in our own country, without any rules, not against terrorists but against those who hate their own bandits perhaps even more strongly than we do, we are the losers and the loss is irreversible.

INGUSHETIA

II

KALASHNIKOV AND THE OLD PEOPLE'S HOME

29 November 1999

This should have been a profoundly optimistic report describing the successful evacuation, under bombardment, of the inhabitants of the old people's home in Grozny. For the last month and a half, our newspaper has spent every day preparing this complex operation. A permanent team was formed and it worked to gain the goodwill and assurances of the General Staff and the Ministry of Defence. Meanwhile readers helped us to collect enough money for guides and coaches. (No one would do a thing without payment – it proved quite unrealistic to expect that – and we discovered that government departments had no funds to spend on such activities.)

At long last, a date and time were agreed.

What then happened was shameful, and we can offer readers no words of consolation. The fighters defending the Chechen capital suddenly realised that the federal authorities placed a certain value on these old people. So they simply turned them into hostages. How and why will become clear from what follows.

Here and Now

The last week we had been full of hope. Leaving home and family, all our energy and determination went on ensuring that no later than 10 a.m. on 25 November, our long-awaited red *Icarus* coach would return from Grozny to the Chechen-Ingush border. There, at the "Caucasus" checkpoint on the Rostov-Baku Highway, we would meet "our old people". Then we would escort these sick and lonely old men and women, whose lives began with a war and were closing with two more, back to a peaceful and quiet existence.

25 November arrived. At 10 a.m. so did our *Icarus*. But instead of the old people, the guides brought us a written note. It said, in effect, that the local authorities had forbidden the evacuation. The Chechen guides, who only a few days before had been so courageous and admirable, sat uneasily before us. They fidgeted. They gave muddled explanations about the people who had been there to meet them when they reached the old people's home. Finally they passed on the following verbal message: the journalists were expected at the home tomorrow morning and then, perhaps, they might let the elderly go.

"Who's expecting us there?"

"The people who didn't let the old ones leave today."

Ruslan Koloyev's drawn face darkened. He had welcomed, and then nursed through, the entire operation, and in its final stages, as Ingushetia's Deputy Minister for Emergency Situations, he had shouldered the main burden. Powerless, he stood and silently left us. He was gone for a long time, at least half an hour. We were stunned. As we waited our guides told us more of the fantastic tales they had been spun by those thugs. Finally Ruslan's absence became a reproach. I went to find him.

"Where's Ruslan?"

"He's praying," his colleagues quietly replied.

Ruslan is a devout Muslim. But you'd never know it. Not a single word, look or movement betrays his inner faith, let alone

demonstrative green bandannas or cries of "Allahu Akbar!" Ruslan
returned from his prayers to our room, sent out the talkative guides
and said: "Last night I already knew this was going to happen. Only
a miracle could have changed things."

And this, day by day, is how it came about.

On 23 November, following a carefully agreed route, the *Icarus*
coach left for Grozny. It was to go to 194 Borodin Street in the city's
Staropromyslovsky district, where the old people's home was located.
We had already sent volunteers there several times before to investigate and test the ground. Each time the story was the same. The old
people were exhausted and starving, all the staff had long ago run
away, no one had any money and those who could still move went out
in the streets begging. We must hurry. Since the end of September,
while the Moscow bureaucrats idled their time away, twelve of the
old people had died. There were now only 85 left.

Finally the evening of 24 November arrived. Anticipating a
happy end, I could hardly wait. Then, like a bucket of cold water, at
9.30 p.m., following the main evening news, came the Channel One
TV programme *Here and Now*. The presenter, Alexander Lyubimov,
was talking to Sergei Kalashnikov, the Minister of Labour and Social
Development.[25] Kalashnikov is in charge of homes for the elderly
throughout Russia, and whenever we needed his support he had
unfailingly obstructed us, doing everything to ensure that the old
people in Grozny never crossed the border into Ingushetia. His
greatest concern was about the issue's "political aspects" and he was
determined to ensure that no solitary *Chechen* pensioners would
somehow be included in the mission.

The interview went roughly as follows (I'm reporting not the
exact words, but the fatal message they sent). One, the elderly had

25 Kalashnikov is a leading member of Zhirinovsky's nationalistic Liberal Democrat
Party.

been evacuated from Grozny. Two, the Ministry of Labour had been working long and stubbornly to achieve this goal. Three, the successful outcome was the result of an undercover operation by the Russian government on the territory of the Chechen Republic.

More of a public slap in the face for our operation would be hard to imagine. You already know the rest. The guides then came back and told us they had been forbidden to evacuate the elderly from Chechnya.

26 November. From early morning the following day, as informed army officers had repeatedly warned us, Grozny was subjected to the most powerful artillery and aerial bombardment of the present war. Moreover, the shells were falling precisely on the Staropromyslovsky district where the old people's home was. We had been in such a hurry because the military had told us: "After the 26th it will be too complicated. Get a move on."

But surely, you are saying to yourself, a government minister like Kalashnikov must have known as much as journalists and senior officers? Of course, he knew. That's exactly why, perhaps, he took the risk and, from midday on 25 November, began to issue quite false claims over the wires of the Itar-TASS news agency that the elderly had been successfully evacuated. As he knew only too well, it would be very dangerous to go and check whether these announcements were true or not. Later that day he repeated his cheap lies live on Channel One TV. Guided by the overriding principle that "War justifies everything", Kalashnikov was evidently quite happy to abandon the old people's home to bombardment from the ground and skies. He also had reasons of his own.

The minister was covering his tracks using every means at his disposal. And, considering his status within the government, he had access to some significant means. Throughout 1997 and 1998 Kalashnikov's ministry had poured money from the federal budget into that same old people's home. Funds were transferred from Moscow, and no account of their expenditure was demanded. At the ministry they were well aware that not a rouble was being spent for the purpose intended. The money went on presents – not to the elderly, but to members of Maskhadov's government. As a result, the home was ruined and abandoned by its staff, with no one left to feed the elderly or give them essential medicine.

The money was siphoned off and Labour Ministry officials knew exactly where it was going, because they had punctiliously ensured it reached its destination. If the elderly left Chechnya, however, there would now be living testimony of this embezzlement of state funds. For Kalashnikov and those who actually made the transfers this spelled ruin. That's why he took the risk.

The following scenario is, in my view, highly probable. On the day the guides and our coach appeared in Grozny, Kalashnikov was alerted from Chechnya (despite all that people say, lines of communication remain open). He was warned that the evacuation was about to begin and asked to take measures. And he acted. On the very evening the guides were in Grozny this fact was publicly announced on television. It was the equivalent of saying: "At this very moment American intelligence agents have entered the Kremlin and are trying to steal top secret documents . . ."

The lives of these lonely and helpless old people finally lost any value of their own. They had become no more than a means to an end.

A Powerless State

The moral of this story is that the State does not exist in Russia. We have been hearing a great deal of talk from Prime Minister Putin, in the run-up to the forthcoming Duma elections. They are building a powerful State, he tells us, to take the place of the once great superpower. But the State led by this premier does not exist. The Russian Federation is a case-study in total and irreversible impotence.

That vacated arena is now filled with the ambitions of some, and the laziness and indifference of others; some publicise their ludicrous stupidity, others tell barefaced lies, while idiocy is raised to the level of government policy, and all are guilty of a slovenly inefficiency.

The evidence is here, before your eyes. This was a tiny and quite specific case that demanded specific and exclusively humanitarian action – it did not require the authorities to mobilise the army and send in tanks and armoured personnel carriers. But the State sets no value on such people. The situation has become quite intolerable. What earthly use to me is the Putin we see, prancing about on TV and telling us that he's going to "wipe out" the bandits after they're cornered "in the shithouse"?

I want a Putin who will defend the weak – according to the Constitution our State exists, first and foremost, for the good of the people. Give me a Putin who at least can control his ministries. Let's have a Putin who does not kow-tow to the army, police and security service, but instead appeals to ordinary citizens: to the people who are suffering and dying under bombardment, as though they are at the mercy of blood-crazed terrorists! I want a different Putin. Not the man who, in front of the TV cameras, climbed into the cockpit of a bomber wearing a pilot's helmet that was evidently the wrong size, but someone who will go to the Staropromyslovsky district and visit the Grozny old people's home.

Isn't it strange, though, that a newspaper whose job it is to provide information, should so persistently shoulder the functions of the government? Why should journalists do the job we pay ministers to do? Obviously because the authorities with the same stubborn persistence refuse to carry out their duties. As soon as ministers are appointed they are cosseted and protected from popular pressure. Their power and privilege is all that interests them.

The only reason we started this operation was because not one official could be found in the entire State who would do the job for us or without our help. We acted because there was no alternative and because the State was immobile and indifferent. And, at the same time, we were perfectly aware that we could not take the place of those authorities and that this situation was public proof of the State's absence.

The end result was that, while we were doing Kalashnikov's job, he started doing ours. He suddenly became hyperactive and began posing as a journalist. He was convinced that anyone could do the job. He was mistaken. A journalist is above all someone who does not lie and will check facts many times before risking an error.

Our Colleagues

I also observed the behaviour of our colleagues in the media during this crisis. Their only interest in our operation was to capture some dramatic events. "You create some news for us, and then we'll react," was their principle. From morning onwards they came up to us in Nazran and asked: "Are the buses going to come? You couldn't be more precise about the time so that we can be sure to broadcast live?" Not once did we hear an offer of help. The only news team that became truly involved and lived through the entire tragedy of the last few days with us as if it concerned them personally were the camera crew from Channel One TV, led by correspondent Olga Mezhennaya.

All attempts to interest Western (or our own) human rights organisations in the fate of these helpless old people from Grozny were also futile. Today such organisations are based in Ingushetia and mainly engaged in the theoretical defence of human rights. The practical side of things does not greatly worry them. The majority are enthusiastically collecting information about mass infringements of Chechen human rights. They can be seen every day in contact almost exclusively with representatives of the Chechen parliament and other similar organisations.

When it became clear that the elderly were being held in Grozny by Chechen fighters, people representing a powerful and influential organisation such as Human Rights Watch did not show the faintest desire to help. Every day they issued press releases about the Russian army's acts of genocide (also undeniable) against the Chechen people. There is a thorough filtering of information to serve a single point of view. If it's a question of a press release, based on Chechen accounts, about the shelling of the Samashki psychiatric hospital, then they are only too happy to oblige and very quick about it. They have no intention, though, of writing and despatching to New York a press release about the inhuman ban on the evacuation of elderly people from Grozny, a ban imposed by Maskhadov's followers who have long since sent their own families to Ingushetia. Sad as it is, that is the fact of the matter.

What Next?

Clever people, including some in the government, have told us that following Kalashnikov's public statements there is now almost no chance of evacuating the elderly from Grozny. The only hope of saving anyone is to make a personal appeal to Basayev.

And that says it all. Basayev has more influence over the fate of our fellow citizens than Putin. It's a vicious circle. The old people must forgive us, but we cannot bring ourselves to appeal to the Conqueror of Budyonnovsk, a man who held the mothers of the maternity hospital there hostage, and ask him to take pity on these lonely old men and women. In my mind the images of Kalashnikov and Basayev are now totally blurred and confused. (The latter's beard makes no difference.)

You can see where all this is leading. By tolerating such things on our own doorstep and allowing the State's officials to perform these acts of violence against us we shall very soon have our own Pinochet. We shall be so relieved, in fact, when he comes that we'll throw ourselves at his feet, and beg him to save us.

INGUSHETIA

POSTSCRIPT

The editors would like to thank all who tried to help us perform this mission of conscience and duty. Their names are listed in order of the magnitude of their personal contribution, starting with those who did most: Ruslan Koloyev, Deputy Minister, Ingushetia Ministry for Emergency Situations (MES); Yury Shum, Head of the North Caucasus Regional Centre, Federal MES; Valery Kuksa, Minister, Ingushetia MES; Tugan Chapanov, Section Head, Ingushetia MES; Marina Kurkieva, Deputy Minister of Labour and Social Development, Ingushetia; Anatoly Khrulyov, CO of the "Caucasus" checkpoint; Ruslan Aushev, President of Ingushetia; Yevgeny Gontmakher, Department Head for Social Development, Russian government; Valery Vostrotin, Deputy Minister, Federal MES; and Valentina Matvienko, Deputy Prime Minister, Russian government.

12

WELCOME TO HELL

The Parasites of War

2 December 1999

Lyuba Zubareva, a nurse from Grozny Hospital No 9, has two rouble coins in the pocket of her light jacket and four children, each smaller than the next, standing behind her. Elina is two and a half years old, Andrei is six, Olya is eleven and the oldest boy, Ruslan, is twelve. None of them has anything to eat. At Lyuba's insistence Ruslan goes each day when bread is handed out free of charge, but he is not given so much as a crust. Lyuba admits that she doesn't know how they will survive. Her earth-coloured face is emaciated, her hands are covered with a bloody eczema and she clutches Elina, who has a high temperature and is constantly losing consciousness.

"But why don't you call the ambulance?"

"I've no money."

"But for free?"

"No one would take me."

Lyuba does not want to expose or offend anyone. She's just seen how, not long ago, a young man, Ruslan Khasayev, was taken to hospital from the neighbouring carriage, dying from an acute suppurative infection. Another quite penniless refugee. For two weeks Ruslan's relatives tried to get a doctor to see him, with no success. When he got to the state where he did not recognise his wife they organised something like a protest meeting and a passer-by took pity and drove Ruslan to the doctors, who said that another half day and he would have died. What condition will tiny Elina have to reach before a protest is organised for her? Lyuba does not even want to think about it and, in spite of everything, hopes that she will get better, that the little girl's organism will itself overcome the illness.

A Freezing Railway Carriage

"How can she recover? They have nothing to eat! Nothing at all, just like me," shouts Lena Shilova, a railway conductress from St Petersburg, her voice roughened by years of shouting matches with her bosses – the same railway bosses who sent her and her train carriage to Ingushetia and abandoned them both in that refugee-stricken land.

"Oh yes, they gave me my expenses when they sent me here. All of a thousand roubles. And as many promises! Who knew that we'd end up in such terrible conditions? I've been travelling across the country for ten years, but I've never seen such a nightmare. Lyuba turned up here and I gave her all I had. I don't have anything to eat myself. Why? Because I'm a human being, no matter what, and I couldn't bear to see it any more!"

The conductress hoarsely ends her speech and wags her finger at a group of filthy, undernourished creatures, the little ones hiding behind their big brothers and sisters, who are looking out into the carriage corridor. She takes me to one side and quietly adds: "Our camp is one big filthy stench. Lice. Rashes. No water, toilets or baths. Hell on earth. Don't hang around here."

Who are these children? What are we doing in a railway carriage? And what on earth is a cheap sleeping carriage from St Petersburg doing on the far siding of the tiny station outside the town of Karabulak? How can Lena Shilova, while performing her duties as a conductress, now look no different – with her filthy face and dirty clothes – from refugees who have already been here two months?

The rare visitors to Carriage 21408, where Lyuba and her children have found a refuge, are struck by the icy cold. After 15 minutes sitting on the bunk you are frozen through and through, as I myself discovered. Nevertheless, the report sent promptly to Moscow says that the 64 carriages have been successfully prepared for the accommodation of refugees near Karabulak. Mission accomplished.

I can testify that this ingratiating report was sent by the local Karabulak authorities, at their head a man called Abukar Aushev. He and his subordinates were supposed to ensure that the camp, set up on territory under their control, was properly organised – something for which, incidentally, they were funded. The reality is different. The money has gone somewhere else and unless you pay they'll do nothing for the people in the carriages. The rule is harshly enforced: if you don't give them a bribe, there will be no coal for heating, and if you don't show your gratitude there will be no water for the boiler. But since it is a crowd of the most destitute and powerless women who have been sent to these carriages in Karabulak, under the care of Lena Shilova, there is neither heating nor water. People sit here for days on end, in a strange state of numbness, having lost the will to live or to organise their lives, turning their faces to the mattress.

Malika Saidova from Grozny, here with her husband and four children, is convinced that she has little chance of surviving. She is disabled, with only one kidney, and in constant pain: she will not survive this cold. Her husband, Mohammed, tried to find a warm room for his frozen family, if only for a few nights, but his attempts all came to nothing. The ones who are doing well now are those who possess something resembling four walls, a roof and a floor. They demanded 380 roubles from Mohammed for one night in a warm room! Mohammed says he's sure that the Ingush are deliberately not heating the carriages so that other Ingush in Karabulak can make some money from the coal.

Lyuba Zubareva and her family came here having finally fled Grozny a week ago. To the very last moment they crouched in a cellar, until 137 Mayakovsky Street was bombed from the air. Lyuba's tragedy today is that all of her documents, and those of her children, were burned with the house. Without documents, they cannot be registered and without registration they get no bread. Only money can break this vicious circle, but Lyuba doesn't have any.

Like Lyuba we wander through Ingushetia and demand: Who can help? Who *should* help her? It's not such an unusual situation during a war, after all, for someone to be left without documents to confirm their identity. People take me aside and say, "We'll do it, just for you." But I don't want things to be done "just for me". I demand that a proper system for the reception of refugees be organised. After two and a half months something of that kind should already be up and running! I want to know how those officials who personify authority for the refugees act in special circumstances, such as Lyuba's case. Again they whisper: "You want to know? No money, no documents. We're fed up with these refugees."

In the end people simply took Lyuba and her children into their cold carriage. For pity's sake. They squeezed up and freed the lower bunks for the children. Lena took pity on them. But what must we do now? How can we make the system work?

Through the knee-deep, unbelievably oily local mud a car slithers up to the carriage. A large fat man with a kindly face gets out: he looks like some Caucasian Father Christmas. He's wearing the dark blue jacket of the federal Ministry for Emergency Situations (MES). The women rush towards him. They're going to tear him limb from limb, I think. This is Major Alikhan Dakayev, who was appointed on behalf of the republican MES to keep an eye (no more than that!) on the Karabulak carriages.

Soon I find out that he is the only person who comes here. It is not part of his job to provide lighting, bring water or organise toilets. The existing rules make that the business of the migration authorities and the district administration in Karabulak. But they don't want to do anything and Alikhan is a kindly man. So it is he who brings things here against the rules. At the end of the day it is Alikhan who goes to the district administration yet again to demand better conditions for these people. Again Alikhan puts Lyuba and Ruslan in his warm car and takes them off to straighten out their documents. There he stands in the rubber boots he wears for days on end, listening to the nonsense talked by Temirkhan Akiev, a man who wears a French silk tie, a white shirt and perfectly polished shoes and heads the Karabulak office of the migration service. Akiev repeats that he will "raise the matter with his superiors".

"That's all? You'll just raise the matter – for the second month?"

"That's my job."

While conversing with these bureaucrats who have grown fat on other people's misery, Alikhan resembles a tank. A kindly tank, since it does not fire at anyone and is used only for intimidating shameless scoundrels. But Akiev is no simpleton. He knows it is not a real tank and is not particularly afraid. Alikhan regards him with quiet revulsion and takes Lyuba to the next office. Not to raise the matter, but to resolve it. Hurriedly Akiev tries to convince me that these difficulties in the carriages are the exception rather than the rule.

Help Me Die!

Over the last few weeks something new has happened. A great many Russian civilians have appeared in the refugee camps. If some reader is particularly worried about nationality and classifies old people and children according to the shape of their nose and the colour of their hair, then let me tell them that many Russians have been leaving Chechnya recently. As a rule, they are very poor people. When you ask why they stayed in Chechnya until mid-November they say that they truly believed that residential areas would not be bombed, that "the army knows everything" (i.e. where the fighters really are). Nevertheless the bombs began to fall and they had to leave.

I am walking through a small town of tents called Bart, which means "Friendship" in the Chechen language. It is also near

Karabulak, but quite different from the railway carriages. I already know many of the people well. They exchange the latest news and reports from Chechnya. Suddenly there's a penetrating scream. No one has any doubts: it's a cry of pain. "Let me die! I can't stand it any more!" It comes from tent No 40.

There on the bed, an elderly man with a blank expression is sitting bolt upright and constantly rocking from side to side. Nikolai Zubkov is 85 and for half a century, as a professor of the Grozny oil institute, he has taught his subject to half the republic: "the exploitation of gas and oil reserves". The professor did not want to leave his old home and go anywhere else, the Zubkov family have lived in Grozny for more than a century now. But on 14 November his wife, 82-year-old Zoya Georgievna, a mathematics and physics teacher, was knocked down by the shock wave from an explosion and something happened to her hip joint. Those were her screams that everyone could hear.

But why doesn't anyone nearby do something? Their son, Lyova, a backward 60-year-old alcoholic, is with them. But he has just finished a drinking bout with his mother's last 200 roubles, money set aside for her funeral.

"Why don't you call an ambulance for Zoya Georgievna?"

"It's pointless. No one will come."

"But have you told the commandant?"

"He never comes here."

When the Zubkovs appeared at the camp on 18 November there was not a single free tent. Out of compassion, Zalikhat Khildikhoreva gave them hers: she is a medical assistant and also from Grozny. Zalikhat is indignant at Lyova's behaviour but says that the ambulance really won't come here. Meanwhile Zoya Georgievna begs them: "Help me! I want to die. I need nothing else!"

Through the pleas of his mother, Lyova continues to talk about the library of more than 10,000 books which they left behind in Grozny. He is filthy drunk. Yesterday a foreign TV crew came and, mistaking what they saw and heard, gave Lyova some money.

*

Chechen women from neighbouring tents stand around and quietly discuss Lyova and relations within Russian families where the old man is not in charge. I run over to the first-aid station which, it turns out, is only two tents away. Here in the refugee camp you must constantly set aside your work as a journalist and do other jobs. In this case, it is the job of those officials who receive money to organise medical treatment and supply the camps with medicines.

There is an attractive eye-catching sign above the first-aid station. It is a branch of some Geneva-based organisation called Médecins du Monde. Among themselves the inhabitants of the Bart camp refer to these doctors as CIA operatives.

"Why do you call them CIA?"

"Because all they do is to constantly collect information, about us and about what is happening in Chechnya," say the refugees. "They couldn't care less about our illnesses."

I yell at the prim figure in a white cap and coat who looks out of the tent: "Surely you can hear someone screaming in pain next door?"

"I hear her," she answers calmly.

"Then why don't you help her?"

"Because I don't have anything."

"Not even painkillers?"

"No."

"But yesterday evening I saw you give an interview on TV and you told the whole country that you were fully supplied. Why did you deceive people?"

"I was afraid they would sack me," concludes Asya Yasayeva.

Wonderful! She is unafraid to break the Hippocratic oath and not go to the aid of a sick person, but she fears to speak the truth, and do her duty as a doctor. Where is the logic in that? It is to be found in the official documents concerning the camp. For those who are interested, I can say that the Karabulak administration has documents showing that there are two fully staffed and equipped first-aid stations in the Bart camp.

What can you do? The investigation and allocation of blame will come later. For now I pull out my remaining travel expense money and give it to Zalikhat. It's enough for her to run and immediately get some painkiller for Zoya Georgievna, and later buy the old woman a ticket to Yalta where we managed to find some of her relatives. Then their other son, Vladimir, who has come to take his mother and father back to Yalta weeps and says he never imagined that such horrors could happen. A little time passes and Zalikhat's husband leaves her in protest: she spent the money some journalist gave her on these old people and not on him. Zalikhat's husband, it turns out, used to drink with Lyova and neither of them forgave Zalikhat for sending the old people to Yalta.

If people survive in the Karabulak camps it is down to chance and miracles. It only happens *in spite of* the now-established system where everyone expects payment for helping the refugees. The only thing that's clear is that, as winter begins, the life of the refugees from Chechnya has become even harder than before. Some aid is getting through to Ingushetia, but the convoys are chaotic and irregular and do not always bring what is needed: why send hundreds of thousands of bottles of shampoo when no one has water to wash with? State support has now reached the level where, occasionally and in certain areas, the refugees are given half a bowl of hot soup once a day. But we know perfectly well from our own experience that we need and want to eat more often than that.

There is little to console us. The refugees' most dangerous enemies, the cold, hunger and sickness, remain unvanquished. By the beginning of December the system set up by the State for the reception of refugees in Ingushetia was disintegrating. The federal ministries and departments drawn into this system have shown their incompetence and are now washing their hands of it all. But the job still needs to be done. All of these unfortunate people are now the responsibility of the Ministry for Emergency Situations (MES). You need medicine? Go to the MES! You want a toothbrush? Ask the MES. School textbooks? Or baby food? Turn to the MES. But the ministry is not Christ Himself and cannot make five hundred loaves out of five.

The employees of the MES in Ingushetia are working themselves into the ground each and every day, from early morning to late at night. Even so they are not coping and their activities are more and more reminiscent of the war hero Alexander Matrosov, who could only halt the fire of a German gun emplacement by blocking it with his own body.

INGUSHETIA

13

TELL THEM: THIS WAR IS SENSELESS

6 December 1999

Abandon all logic, ye who travel here. Shake off your Moscow stereotypes and conceptions. Forget all you have been told about this war. Then you will rapidly see that the army you were shown, confident in its sacred purpose and storming one enemy position after another with ease and no tangible losses, does not exist.

Instead you see exhausted men with unbalanced minds. Then there's the cold, the filth, scabies, rotting feet, drunkenness and hashish. And they all desperately want to come through this alive.

Fatal Confrontation with a Cow

"If those ***** in Moscow are not going to pay me then I'll . . ." – the General yelled with such gusto that the sound echoed around the hills and drowned the howls of the artillery salvos – ". . . go back to Moscow and demand my money! Why come here causing mischief?"

We were standing outside the village of Muzhichi, in the distant foothills of Ingushetia. For no reason whatsoever this army general had just shot dead a skinny, young brown cow that provided the milk for one Ingush family. It's not far from the border with independent Georgia and no distance at all, across the pass, to rebellious Chechnya. So the troops and howitzers have long been billeted in the village and the children sleep badly at night, disturbed by the crash of the artillery.

The cow met its end as follows. She was ambling back from the pasture through the twilight with the other cattle towards her familiar shed. She could already see the fence, where she enjoyed scratching herself, and her owner, Khadizhat, whose warm hands would gently pull at her stubborn teats each evening. Suddenly the path to her familiar and understandable world was blocked by the General. (We know his name and surname, but are not publishing them because he has children of his own, and they are not to blame.)

He was young and handsome, a striking figure. A real fighter. Bare-chested, camouflage hat at an angle, he had fury in his eyes and was as full of testosterone as any teenager after three months at the front. Leaving his men behind him he placed his (by local standards) Very Important Person in the middle of the path and faced the herd. The General was obviously selecting a target. Then, he rapidly fired his machine-gun one-handed and from the hip. Khadizhat screamed and the village shuddered. Tomorrow they would be burying someone else they thought.

First the General shot the cow with his own gun. Then he lifted the body onto the armoured vehicle and, to the wails and laments of the cow's owner, ordered his men to drag it back to the field-kitchen.

"You had nothing to eat?" I asked.

"No, I'm not hungry. It's just that those ***** aren't paying me any money!"

"Who? The Ingush from Muzhichi?"

"No, the Muscovites in Internal Affairs."

The soldiers listen very attentively to this conversation.

"What's your name?"

"It's a military secret." The cow-conqueror smelled of stale alcohol. "We are forbidden to associate with journalists. One more question and I'll arrest you for spying."

*

In the given circumstances our General has evidently lost "the ability to analyse events and understand his own thoughts and actions". It is that capacity, supposedly, which defines the professional war-worthiness of our senior officers – just as those with warm and gentle hands are chosen to milk the cows. Perhaps, though, you are consoling yourself with the thought that this was a regrettable mis-understanding. It only reflects, you say to yourself, the tolerable percentage of monsters that somehow have found their way into the disciplined ranks of those who defended the Motherland from inter-national terrorism. Before I answer, let me show you the second picture in our North Caucasian military exhibition.

A High the Size of an Ammunition Box

Yura's tongue had obviously got the better of him and Volodya also felt an excessive and strange urge to chatter. It was clear they were both mildly stoned. Their thoughts became confused and tangled, and constantly turned back on their tracks but they each have one endlessly repeated, muddled and obsessive theme. Anyone who has smoked grass can tell what the problem with Yura and Volodya is.

They are both serving with the OMON [riot police], a lieutenant and corporal respectively, and we met them at their post near the Chechen village of Assinovskaya. Both were proudly showing off their new sleeve badges: the OMON are no longer snow leopards or lions they're TEAM SPECIAL (the words are written in English). Our special-ist, Lieutenant Yura, could not stop talking about the blood and dismembered flesh of "persons of Caucasian nationality"[26] and several times repeated his fantasies of how "yesterday they slashed a *dukh*[27]

26 A euphemism, widely used by the police and other Russian officials, to legitimate a
   common racial stereotype applied to anyone from the post-Soviet states of Armenia,
   Georgia and Azerbaijan or the seven North Caucasian republics within Russia.
27 "Dukh" (lit. "spirit"), Soviet army slang for their opponents in Afghanistan
   (1979–89).

to pieces in the drainage channel, just over there". Volodya was just
as obsessed with his wages, which were too low in his view.

Volodya felt deeply offended; Yura saw himself as a hero in some
American action film. He described more revolting scenes, watching
to see how his listeners reacted. The FSB distributed videos among
the soldiers in the North Caucasus, he said, and they watched them
every evening to "get in the mood".

"What do they show?"

"How they kill and rape. Don't you know how they raped Shamil
Basayev's brother, Shirvani, in Nazran? A whole gang of them. Well,
I saw it." Yura is very pleased with the nauseating effect this has.

"Did you enjoy that?"

"Not bad." Yura is satisfied. It doesn't take long to realise he is
mentally unbalanced. All that's lacking is a formal confirmation.

People are now so used to seeing mentally ill men clutching
Kalashnikovs at the front line in the North Caucasus that they might
not notice it any more. It would be foolhardy of them, however, to
ignore it. One curious detail. Standing next to Yura is his unit's staff
psychologist. He's also a little strange, if only because Yura's behaviour
seems to have no effect on him.

By December these men are worn out by the war. Around Yura and
Volodya we see the faces of their fellow-OMON men tormented by
gunfire in the night. Further off are the army soldiers who are hungry
and dirty, and all with athlete's foot because they never take off their
rubber boots, even at night. Before their eyes flows a constant stream
of misery and grief, as the refugees shuffle across Assinovskaya
through all the shortening hours of daylight: weeping women and
children, scowling old men. The wounded fighters are carried through
from Chechnya, men with amputated limbs and oozing wounds.

"I wouldn't wound them," comments Yura. "I'd just finish them
off." Think for a moment, and you're likely to go mad at the thought:
they are taking men for treatment in Russian hospitals who were
crippled by Russia's own soldiers, and the same budget is today

financing the murderous bombing attacks and the treatment of their victims.

The landscape before the man with a gun is too doleful for him not to brighten it up somehow. By the end of the autumn, thoroughly commercial relations had been established on the border between Chechnya and Ingushetia, not far from the "Caucasus" check-point. The soldiers drive up in armoured vehicles from the nearby "liberated" villages. They are met by the black marketeers from the Ingush side.

Policemen from the Ingush OMON man the first post on the road to the "Caucasus" check point. They tell us the going rate for "intensive care". For two zinc cases (i.e. boxes of ammunition) you get either 20 bottles of locally produced vodka (at 10 roubles each) or one glassful of hashish. Usually the deal works as follows. The soldiers bring the cases in the evening or at night, whenever it's dark (and always accompanied by an officer), and by that time their partners with the vodka or hashish are already waiting at the Ingush post. The police are convinced that all the participants in these exchanges have earlier reached agreement on the time and place and that the whole system runs very smoothly.

Why then do these well-informed Ingush policemen simply sit and watch? Where are the seizures of contraband, the arrests and widely publicised investigations into these cases of corruption?

"We've received no order to act," say the valiant OMON, averting their gaze.

If you believe them, I don't. But it's impossible not to think about the other side of this coin. The military have become so mercantile that they are selling the very bullets that, sometime later, will almost certainly fly in their direction.

100-Rouble Gateway

Picture No 3 from our exhibition. There is one more very curious checkpoint in this war. The "October" checkpoint allows you to travel from Chechnya to Mozdok (where the headquarters of the combined forces in the North Caucasus are to be found). Refugees at the Sputnik camp near the Ingush village of Sleptsovskaya (Ordjonikidzevskaya) have extraordinary tales to tell. The soldiers at the checkpoint supposedly tell women from north Chechen villages who are taking food to sell at the market in Mozdok: "You're not allowed there! Mozdok is a prohibited city for you."

But as with all else in Russia, never be in a hurry to go away. After a little while the town becomes quite open and the soldiers tell the most persistent women how much they must pay. One person on foot must pay 100 roubles; a light vehicle costs about 500–600 roubles, depending on the mood of the bribe-taker. To cross with a body (forgive this cynicism!) costs 1,000 roubles. "If you pay the soldiers they don't even look at your passport," the refugees assure me.

Can you believe such assurances? Of course not. Or not until you've tried it yourself. I travelled there, driving about two hours by car from the Sputnik camp. The refugee women were quite right. I paid 100 roubles and got past without showing my passport, with its "permanent resident" stamp from the Moscow authorities, or any other details of my life and work.

At which point a treacherous suspicion entered my head. What if you offer them 200, 300 or 500 roubles? Could you then carry back arms and ammunition into Chechnya without any hindrance? And then leave the republic again without showing up on their computer? All this talk as though it is the frontier with Georgia that matters!

Cleaning Up

And what are we to make of the military trucks that drive back and forth across Ingushetia? Suddenly their interiors are hung with carpets to make them warmer. It's unheard of. I hope no one imagines that our generals, like modern-day Suvorovs,[28] have indeed taken the comfort of their men so much to heart that they added carpets to warm the interior of the trucks.

There is as much plundering in this war as there was last time. Stories about "cleansing of property", at the same time as "liberated population centres" are "cleansed" of real and suspected fighters, are some of the commonest tales among the refugees in the tent camps. Of all that I have heard I have chosen the monologue of Yazirat Dovletmurzaeva, an 85-year-old grandmother from the village of Samashki. Today she lives in Tent 3, Block 13 of the Sputnik camp. She is illiterate, and all of her life she has worked on the land, tending her cows, never getting involved in any political events. She finds it hard to understand the motives behind the wars that have raged around her for the last five years. She's quite clear about one thing, though. She has never acquired any wealth during her life and has no possessions in her home.

"Yesterday [21 November, AP] I walked over to Samashki to see if I could return home at last. I want to go back very much. When I got there some soldiers were climbing out of the windows. The house had been plundered. They had taken away everything they could find, all my pickles and conserves. They took the cow. They even took the door. I'll never save enough to buy a mattress as good as the one I had."

If the military can listen calmly to this tale, then I think they'll agree with me: when such things happen the war could go on forever

---

28 Russian Generalissimo Alexander Suvorov (1729–1800) insisted that his soldiers have cool heads and warm feet.

and each new trainload of troops for Chechnya will be very happy to be transferred to the North Caucasus.

And how can we leave out the vile story about the Interior Ministry soldiers in Sernovodsk? Berlant Magomedova describes what she saw:

"The soldiers walk around the market demanding vodka. Sometimes they bring sacks full of tinned meat and exchange it for vodka. Once they're drunk they begin shooting. On 15 November they shot our neighbour Mohammed Esnukayev. He was a very good man, an orphan who had been looked after and brought up by the entire street, but when he told the soldiers 'I don't have any vodka' they shot him dead."

It was from Sernovodsk, remember, that a platoon of soldiers came in their armoured vehicle to the village of Sleptsovskaya (Ordjonikidzevskaya) on 25 November. Led by their commander, they demanded that same accursed vodka and, in similar circumstances, shot dead a young female shop assistant. All Ingushetia was stunned by this event. But it is a natural consequence of everything that has happened to the army in the North Caucasus. Something of this kind was bound to happen sooner or later.

The Costs of War

Inevitably someone will say: "That is the cost of war. It always carries with it a certain element of evil and unpredictability." And he or she will take comfort in the thought. Those who have actually been there know that things are much worse than anyone could imagine.

As winter progresses the mood in the army is changing rapidly. Too many feel themselves caught in a dead end. They're confused and uncertain. After the soldiers have sat for weeks in a dugout that is more like a swamp, wearing rubber boots day in, day out, and their commanding officer is forced to wander around collecting enough money to go to the baths in the next village, then the war ceases to appear a sacred feat of liberation – even supposing they arrived in the Caucasus with such feelings.

The men in uniform are today physically exhausted and psychologically worn out. They can no longer tolerate these inhuman conditions and begin, as a consequence, to behave inhumanly themselves. They're not supermen, but ordinary people like you and me. So we must stop lying to ourselves: what is going on in Chechnya is not at all what many in Moscow dreamt of!

I'm not reporting these particular offences to encourage the staff officers in Moscow and Mozdok to immediately track down those who committed them. That would be stupid and inefficient. They must act quite differently, either focusing the war within clear limits or a local arena, or else halting it altogether. The present "struggle with the terrorists" is spreading across the entire country and is becoming a deadly danger to many who have not the slightest connection with the terrorists.

Dusk began to fall rapidly at the checkpoint near the Chechen village of Assinovskaya. We could stay no longer. Night-time was when the trade in bullets and vodka began. Lieutenant-Colonel Gubich, head of the Kursk OMON stationed here, despairingly drove away all non-military personnel, in accordance with his orders. As we were leaving, however, he told us: "Pass this message on to Moscow: 'This war is quite senseless.' And that," he added, "is the most important truth of all."

INGUSHETIA

14

STRANGE BATTLES

Fighting for Grozny

16 December 1999

She was lying on her back, arms by her side, shoulders square, like a soldier on parade, unaware of anything in the world around her apart from her pain. Some people came up, threw back the sheet, and looked at the eleven bullet holes scattered across her slight, girlish body and sewn together by the doctors. But even then Mubarik Avkhadova did not react. Her enormous dry eyes were fixed on the ceiling. Her arms lay helplessly by her side. Her only link with the world was the drip running into her vein.

For the third week 22-year-old Mubarik has hovered between life and death. No one will give any guarantees. No one who visits her in Ward 8 of the Nazran republican hospital talks about the future. And everyone looks away when, worn by her struggle to keep alive, this once cheerful and carefree fourth-year student at the languages faculty in Grozny university suddenly shifts her gaze from the ceiling and stares at them as they repeat their meaningless phrases.

"A Car Full of Bandits"

What happened? By current standards it was a very ordinary case. The Russian army were advancing on the village of Alkhan-Yurt, only a kilometre from Grozny. Mubarik, the younger daughter, had stayed there on Suvorov Street with her elderly parents, her mother Tumish and father Ali, convinced until the last that the soldiers would not open fire on peaceful civilians and residential areas. On 1 December Ali decided that they could wait no longer and, stopping a passing *Zhiguli*, which already contained six people, he persuaded them to also take his wife and daughter. He stayed behind.

Round midday the vehicle with a white flag tied to its radio aerial was moving towards Goity. The village is now overflowing with refugees and it was there, a few days earlier, that Mubarik's elder sister, Aiza, had gone with her four small children. Two kilometres down the Goity road, off the main Rostov-Baku Highway, a plane began to pursue the unfortunate *Zhiguli* and finally opened fire.

An old woman and her grown-up daughter died immediately. To this day their names are not known. Mubarik and a 13-year-old girl, the old woman's granddaughter, were wounded. While the plane prepared for a second swoop, Tumish dragged the girl and her own daughter out of the car and shielded their bodies with her own, already bleeding from a number of wounds. She feverishly tucked their arms and legs under her and when the plane returned and again fired it only killed Tumish. On the evening of 1 December it was announced on TV that the air force had destroyed a *Zhiguli* full of Chechen fighters who were trying to flee. Only on 11 December, on a Saturday, was Aiza able to get her wounded sister to hospital in Ingushetia, after bribing each and every post now set up on the Rostov-Baku Highway. (At Goity the village elders had collected 3,000 roubles to help her.)

And what about Mubarik's village? On 9 December the federal forces arrived at Alkhan-Yurt. What did they gain there at the cost of such torment to this pretty young woman?

The same day that Mubarik was brought to Ingushetia, 11 December, the area around the village was swarming with soldiers and their officers, tanks and armoured vehicles. At first sight it looked exactly the way the books describe the front line in a war or the fictional versions of the present Chechen campaign that they show, hour after hour, on every TV channel. Machine-guns, bullet-proof jackets, mud, and helicopters boastfully zooming overhead.

The closer you look, however, the stranger the sights you see. The officers, for instance, are standing with their backs to the front line. Whoever heard of such a thing? The soldiers follow their example. They sprawl over their armoured vehicles in such a way that they cannot possibly observe the territory of their opponent because it is located directly behind them.

"Where's the front then?"

"Over there."

All cheerfully pointed to a pile of tree trunks that have been chopped down and laid straight on the road to Grozny. This means that from where we're talking to the front line, beyond which there was fierce fighting, is at most 50 metres. You could hit the trees with a slingshot, let alone a machine-gun or a sniper's rifle.

"And the fighters are over there, in that belt of trees," the officers continue, with no concern for the absurdities they themselves are offering me.

"But we're no distance from them, and you're not even wearing bullet-proof jackets? Why aren't the fighters firing? Where are those snipers that everyone is so scared off? We're sitting ducks here."

The ordinary soldiers are even more open targets on this strange front. Contemptuous of the dangers concealed in the surrounding area (if, that is, one believes this talk of a front outside Grozny), they stand on the roofs of the ugly concrete bus-shelters and seem in no fear for their lives.

So where are the Chechen fighters? Are there any here at all, and were they ever here? It all feels like some show put on by the military and not really the front line in an uncompromising struggle with international terrorism. What physical evidence can we see here of the fierce war that Russia's forces already, in their tens of thousands, have been waging in the North Caucasus since mid-December?

Slaughter in Alkhan-Yurt

The refugees are unanimous. They talk today of a slaughter only of the civilian population, and the death of children, pregnant women and old men, instead of Basayev and Khattab. That is why I am here to record such testimony from those around Alkhan-Yurt. This is the area the military call the front. We know that here, one kilometre from Grozny, there were particularly fierce battles and pitiless operations to "cleanse" the territory. I want to understand the reason why the nameless passengers of that *Zhiguli* on the Goity road lost their lives, and Mubarik was shot.

I want to know why 23 people died here in Alkhan-Yurt between 1–8 December: farmers, their wives and children. Only three died as the result of bombing, the rest perished during a check on "ID documents and residence permits" (information from Human Rights Watch):

1   Alkhanpasha Dudayev
2   Humid Khazuyev
3   Isa Muradov
4   Musa Geikhayev
5   Arbi Karnukayev
6   Nebist Karnukayeva
7   Enist Sulimova
8   Turka Sulipova
9   Musa Yakubov
10 Sharani Arsanov
11 Marvan Karnukayev
12 Aset Karnukayeva
13 Kantash Saidullayev
14 Sovdat Saidullayeva
15 their child
16 Isa Omarkhadjiev
17 Doka Omarkhadjieva
18 Zara Omarkhadjieva
19 Matag Abdulgazhiev

20   Belkiz Madagova
21   Birlant Yakhayeva
22   Alimpasha Asuyev
23   Amat Asieva[29]

How are we to go on living after this? Who is our friend or enemy now?

On the eve of Constitution Day[30] the "liberated" Chechen settlement of Alkhan-Yurt was as empty as a film-set in the middle of the night. There was not a single human being anywhere, not a cow, a chicken or a goose. Not a single living thing, nor any sound that might distantly suggest a mooing or clucking. If someone had been weeping, shouting or lamenting it would have been less frightening.

Silence. On the hill a churned-up graveyard. The officers tell me that Chechen fighters had dug themselves in there, so they had to fire straight at the graves. But where then are the dead fighters' bodies or the prisoners?

"Where they should be," the officers reply.

Perhaps it would be better to show them to everyone. To put the survivors on trial. Then that would really be the triumph of the legitimate authorities over international terrorism.

The silence that greets these elementary proposals is the most tell-tale sign of this war. We continue gazing in silence at Alkhan-Yurt. The cupola of the mosque has been turned into a sieve. A few jagged rafters are all that remain, at best, of the roofs of hundreds of houses. The walls are like some worn and discarded garment, with gaping holes of all sizes (depending on the calibre of weapon the officer chose to shoot with). Alkhan-Yurt lies quiet and deathly still, in the tight grip of the encircling armoured vehicles. If people can be wounded, so can the villages they leave behind them.

29 See the April 2000 Human Rights Watch report "No Happiness Remains" (www.hrw.org).
30 Since 1993, 12 December is marked as the day on which independent, post-Communist Russia adopted its new Constitution.

"We're Not Shooting at People's Homes"

So this is the "fierce struggle with the Chechen fighters". The army tells us "We are not shooting at people's homes", and the result is a devastated village and not one piece of evidence that the fighters have been there. And the front? There are no fighters there either.

But where are all the people? There must be someone on the front-line in Alkhan Yurt. Where is Mubarik's father, Ali, who couldn't get into the *Zhiguli* on 1 December and stayed behind at their house on Suvorov Street?

The commanding officer issued a very straightforward order. The civilian population has the right to leave their cellars and basements only between 11 a.m. and 1 p.m., carrying a white flag. If there is no white flag, they will be shot and also if they come out after 1 p.m. But why, I ask? The village has already been "liberated". And why only at those times, why not from 9 a.m. to 9 p.m.? The military here prefer to answer every question with a brief and clear "Because". That's how General Shamanov, our newly decorated Hero of Russia, has taught his subordinates to reply when asked about his imposition of this 22-hour curfew, an unfathomable addition to the theory of military strategy at the close of the twentieth century.

That is why they do not allow journalists here who have not first been thoroughly tested and processed by the press service of the combined forces in Mozdok. Without such ideological preparation the picture is all too clear. They call it the front, but it's nothing of the kind. And there can be no justification for the sufferings of Alkhan-Yurt. Who then are they fighting against? When the remaining inhabitants are allowed back, to walk again through their village and fields as they wish, they will know the soul-wrenching answer. Well, what would you say if you found yourself in the position of these hunted and tormented villagers who have been deprived of every human right?

The answer is obvious. But let me offer one more picture, this time from the "liberated" northern areas of Chechnya, a region opposed to Maskhadov, Dudayev, Basayev and all of their kind. The snapshot comes from Goragorsk[31] on 10 December. This large and once unbelievably beautiful village, spread out like Moscow over "seven hills", lies roughly 80 kilometres northwest of Grozny. There were also fierce battles here and people died on both sides. A great deal of destruction is evident, as are the fresh graves. A rough-hewn cross commemorates Private Alexei Mitrofanov, who died fighting for Goragorsk, and stands next to the vast and gaping holes left in the oil tanks by heavy artillery shells. This speaks more eloquently than any briefing: Mitrofanov died for someone else's oil.

You can't help noticing that they took particular and malicious delight in targeting the mosque in Goragorsk. It has been reduced to its foundations. The villagers give a welcoming smile to all visiting "persons of Slav nationality", but their silent response came during the night. The statue of the Unknown Soviet Soldier, which stands as always in the central square, was neatly decapitated. No one can find the head. There are those here who fought the Germans in the Great Patriotic War,[32] but even that did not halt the villagers who have driven inwards their feelings of hate and desire for revenge.

The memorial itself suffered from the fighting nearby. The words NO ONE IS FORGOTTEN, have fallen off; the words NOT ONE DEED IS FORGOTTEN remain.

INGUSHETIA-CHECHNYA

ALKHAN-YURT, GORAGORSK, NAZRAN

*

31 See Chapter 8, "Camp Guards".

32 In 1945 at the end of the war the male Chechens who had fought the Germans did not take part in victory parades (even the 132 among them who as Heroes of the Soviet Union had won the ultimate accolade for their bravery) but were sent off to join the old men, women and children deported to Kazakhstan in their absence the year before (see fn. 18).

On 19 December elections to the Duma, the lower house of parliament, were held throughout Russia. A new bloc supporting Prime Minister Putin and calling itself Unity (or The Bear) won wide support. Headed by Minister for Emergency Situations Sergei Shoigu, Alexander Gurov, the senior police expert on organised crime, and one-time wrestling champion Victor Karelin, it offered few policies, but promised to stop talking and get things done.

A few days before, the surviving inhabitants of the Grozny old people's home were finally evacuated as the federal artillery continued to shell the Chechen capital (see Chapter 24).

15

REDUCING MORTALITY

The Hidden Losses

23 December 1999

On 12 December in Ordjonikidzevskaya village, on the administrative boundary between Chechnya and Ingushetia, two deaths were recorded: soldiers who had died from their wounds.

As dawn broke a 20-year-old conscript, Misha Moshtyrev, military card No 8709472, died without coming round, in the intensive care unit of the district hospital. He had been brought there several hours earlier on an armoured vehicle by a group of soldiers who said they were serving with him. Early that morning Aza Tseloyeva, the doctor on duty, accompanied Misha's tormented body, which bore the marks of the surgeon's battle to save his life, to the tiny local morgue. She was astonished that no one, especially an officer, came to claim the soldier's remains.

At midday an all-male funeral procession crossed through the "Caucasus" checkpoint from Chechnya into Ingushetia. On one of the streets in Ordjonikidzevskaya the old men began to gather, as is the custom, in order to accompany and bury the body of their neighbour, 40-year-old bachelor Bagautdin, with full honours. He had died that dawn defending Grozny. He was a mercenary there and he did not hide the fact. For $1,000 a month, from early September he had fought the "feds"[33] and at times had come back to visit his

---

33 A slang term (in Russian "federaly") first used for the federal forces during the 1994–6 Chechen war.

home, his mother and his sisters. On his short holidays in the village he squandered his pay on heroin and it was no secret that he hired himself out entirely because of his fatal addiction.

"But if that is the case, why are they burying Bagautdin with full honours? His name was cursed publicly in the mosque as a drug-addict. So the old men should not visit his family home to perform the rite." We were talking with a neighbour of the man they had just buried.

"But he redeemed all his errors."

"How?"

"By going to fight," said the neighbour, who admitted that when Bagautdin was alive he had very much disapproved of him. "But now that is all in the past. Now he has become a sacred figure . . ."

Just don't imagine that Bagautdin's neighbour is also a fighter. On the contrary, his views are strongly pro-Russia. He was celebrating Constitution Day and is now going to vote for the Communists in the Duma elections: "Not because I like Zyuganov, but because it was that ideology that kept us all from fighting each other."

After these conversations I returned to the morgue, to the youthful and totally abandoned body of Private Moshtyrev. Forgotten by the army he fought for, he lay there awaiting an uncertain future. Why was Doctor Aza more upset about this than anyone else? Why did not a soul utter the same words of rapture about his sacred feat as met Bagautdin, who had until then been one of life's losers? I wondered whom the army, the government and the country as a whole intended to defeat when they showed such contemptuous indifference to what happened to their soldiers after death. Did they really think they could win against people who would never forget, no matter what the circumstances, to pay their last respects to a fallen warrior? Bagautdin's fellow Chechen fighters risked their lives to accompany his body through the checkpoint.

As we leave the morgue, Aza Tseloyeva is brief and to the point, as you'd expect from a doctor working in intensive care:

"Are you flying back to Moscow? Then go straight away, today, to the Ministry of Defence and tell them it's inconceivable to behave this way! Our attitude to death is a continuation of our attitude to life. That is a universal rule, no matter what your nationality. Why are they bringing soldiers to civilian hospitals? Why don't they collect the bodies of the dead?"

Manilov at Work

Several days later I was in Moscow at the first major international conference about the present war – "Chechnya: The Unlearned Lessons" – which was extremely well organised by the Itar-TASS news agency and the weekly *Moscow News*. There I managed to put Aza Tseloyeva's questions directly to the main ideologue of the present campaign in the Caucasus, First Deputy Head of the General Staff, Colonel-General Valery Manilov. He may be the namesake of Gogol's character,[34] but his fantasies are not at all endearing or funny: he is behind the constant assurances in all the media about the unprecedented concern for our soldiers' survival, the minimal losses being suffered by the army and the clockwork efficiency of the medical system serving the combined forces operating from Mozdok.

Manilov, his face red after telling the latest lie about "only 400 dead", half-listened to my story: of Misha Moshtyrev's unclaimed body, of the wounded soldiers who were, for some reason, brought to a district hospital in Ingushetia, and of the chronic shortage there of medicines and equipment. Disgruntled with what he was hearing, Manilov turned to his aide: "Write that down. We'll investigate." His aide began slowly and unwillingly to draw his pen across the page, but quickly abandoned this unrewarding task. "It's a pack of lies," he retorted, and disappeared into the crowd behind his hefty boss's uniform.

34 The daydreaming landowner in *Dead Souls*, who is charming but ineffective.

What is going on here? We seem to be rolling towards some black tunnel and where it leads no one knows. The story of these two deaths in Ordjonikidzevskaya village leads me back to one of the main disputes of the present campaign in Chechnya, the level of army losses. How many are there, in reality? When they talk of 400 losses, do they mean those who died on the battlefield or does it include those who died later from their wounds? And where did they die? And to which department and category will the wily General Staff statisticians assign Misha Moshtyrev?

There is hardly anyone who continues to believe that the number of killed and wounded soldiers corresponds to the official figures. How, though, can we catch the military officials red-handed and prove that they're lying? In present conditions, the opportunity only surfaces by chance. Only those journalists in special favour with the high command, who have been carefully vetted for any "unnecessary talk", continue to be admitted to the field hospitals. Therefore only a strictly controlled amount of information reaches the media, and only that which shows the military in a favourable light and conforms to the principles announced by the General Staff ("a war with very low losses"). It is only the chance occurrence, such as the incident I encountered at the Sunzhensk district hospital, that enables us to prove how successful the military have become at concealing their own losses.

A Night's Work

"What did you say? He was ex-what . . . ?"

"Exat. In other words, departed from us . . ."

At the entrance to the emergency department of the Sunzhensk district hospital the gloomy local medical assistant is trying to explain what happened the previous night. Only later do I realise that he is describing Misha Moshtyrev.

"To begin with, at nine in the evening, they brought a soldier on an armoured vehicle with blood gushing from the open femoral artery. The lads with him said they had come from Bamut and had been driving for three hours. Why had they dragged him so far? Where were the army doctors? Why had no one qualified travelled with such a seriously wounded soldier? It was strange . . ."

The story is continued by Igor Listov, the anaesthetist: "The boy was in a very poor way. There was little chance of pulling him through. He was almost in his death throes when they arrived. Fifteen minutes later he was clinically dead, but we managed to get his heart going again. Then the operation began."

The surgeon on duty, realising that he would have difficulty coping on his own, got in touch with doctors from the mobile hospital of the "Medical Catastrophe" organisation. Since the arrival in Ingushetia of several hundred thousand refugees this unit has been in operation not far from the Sunzhensk hospital and aims to provide skilled first aid.

"We began to operate, although we realised that the soldier had lost five of his six litres of blood," says Victor Popov, head of a team of doctors from Yekaterinburg who is now working with the Emergency Relief hospital. It was Popov who tried to save Moshtyrev's life. "We extracted a very large calibre bullet – incidentally no one came to collect it and the military prosecutors showed no interest in it. We gave the lad a so-called artificial artery because the bullet had torn away about five centimetres of the artery. Just at that moment, as chance would have it, there was a power cut, quite a usual occurrence in Ingushetia. The artificial respirator stopped working and we had to pump air in by hand."

"Was that what finally killed him?"

"It's hard to say," the surgeon replies. "At least we did everything to ensure that he left the operating table alive. We battled as only we know how. He died just before dawn. We were then already operating on the next soldier."

"So there's a constant flow of bodies coming here, like a field hospital?"

"Judge for yourself. Over the last 48 hours we have received three soldiers," Popov continued. "The one with the torn artery died. Another wounded private was operated on by Igor Piven, our traumatologist, and survived, though only by a miracle. He has lost half his brain. Only one of them stands a good chance. I think he's called Artyom. Incidentally, we don't bother with names here, there's no time for that, we must operate. Artyom should live. We extracted bullets that had pierced his intestines in four places. He was haemorrhaging severely. Now he's in intensive care, recovering."

Doctor Popov insists on calling the soldier Artyom. Several minutes later, however, we find out that he is called Ramil Abdurakhmanov, a 19-year-old from Kazan. For the present he talks very badly. His speech becomes garbled, but his eyes are calm: he knows that he has survived. Aza Tseloyeva, who is in charge of the intensive care unit, allows me to sit and chat to him.

Ramil has extraordinary tales to tell. To begin with, he is serving with Unit 73745 of the railway's armed detachment. What are they doing here? Their unit is located on the boundary between Chechnya and Ingushetia at the Sleptsovskaya (Ordjonikidzevskaya) oil storage plant. They are serving at the "Caucasus" checkpoint, taking the place of the Migration Service men. Ramil and the others filled in special forms agreeing to their "enforced relocation". In the evenings they are brought back to the plant. That fateful evening Ramil was about to enter the compound when someone tried to push him into a white *Zhiguli* car, an attempted kidnap. He fought them off as best he could, and when he shouted was rewarded by a stream of bullets at point-blank range from the window of the retreating vehicle.

An attempt to kidnap a soldier, who was severely wounded in the process. This is a much too serious offence to be passed over without the attention of the military prosecutor. Especially since Ramil displayed considerable bravery. Well, that's the conclusion any normal person would reach. Alas, when I was back in Moscow I discovered that Abdurakhmanov, born 1980, conscripted in June 1998, was everywhere listed not as a wounded soldier, but as a deserter ("having voluntarily left his unit" is the phrase). The formal justification is that he had not entered the compound of the plant at the moment of the attempted kidnap. The officers used this to quickly disassociate themselves from yet another "loss of manpower", and to transfer the incident to quite a different category for which they would not find themselves held responsible.

Indeed, who among the high-ranking military officials will bother to get his hands dirty and discover that there was, in strict terms, no "unit" located at the oil storage plant? It worries no one that they had absolutely no right to force conscript soldiers to sleep where there were no defensive posts. Nor that it is plainly indecent to conceal the mistakes officers have made behind the supposedly improper behaviour of Ramil.

Incidentally, the other soldiers in Unit 73745 say that Ramil is one of the best, and fought the bandits to the last of his strength (he was unarmed), and did not let them capture him although he was severely wounded. That's what our ordinary soldiers are like, although they are unbearably young. And that's what their officers are like. Their main worry is submitting the kind of report their superiors expect.

Ramil looks down at his hands, which appear black against the hospital sheet, and explains why they're so dirty: "You remember there was rain and slush yesterday. I crawled through the mud to the fence to hide myself. I thought the *Zhiguli* was coming back to get me."

"When did help come from the oil plant?"

"I don't remember."

The officers made good use of this circumstance. I should add that the doctors who operated on the three soldiers – Misha Moshtyrev, Ramil and Andrei Batrakov (the lad with the head wound) – take not the slightest interest in how they were wounded. That is entirely in accordance with the Hippocratic oath. Still, they're very surprised that there are more and more soldiers in this war who are "by chance brought to the wrong place", and who are transported not to military

hospitals but to ordinary civilian medical centres. Doesn't this contradict Manilov's statements about the General Staff's efforts to keep
losses to a minimum?

Doctors are firm and decisive people only when they are operating.
The rest of the time they are gentle and thoughtful. Therefore, it is
up to me to take their thoughts to their logical conclusion: soldiers
are deliberately being denied the protection of military medical aid.

Just consider the Sunzhensk district hospital. It is certainly one
of the best in Ingushetia. However, it has very limited facilities and
resources. It was built to meet the needs of this peaceful town and
the surrounding villages, not to fulfil military purposes. It doesn't
have staff with a narrow specialisation in field surgery. Neither does
it have its own generator. The electricity is constantly going off and
an operation is often successful only because a patient was lucky not
to be treated during one of the frequent power cuts.

Myths and Reality

These "chance admissions" do not square at all with the talk about the
Ministry of Defence's smooth-running system of medical treatment.

Had the case of the wounded soldier from Bamut been included
in official reports, it would raise many other questions. Bamut is
one of those villages that has been "liberated" for a long while. There
are no more Chechen fighters there, if one believes the General Staff.
Ramil's story suggests the opposite. Perhaps we are again the victims
of shameless deception by the authorities. If we admit this is a lie,
then the whole encouraging picture of the planned and steady advance
of the Russian forces begins to fall to pieces.

The superior officers must conceal the fact that the war continues
in Bamut. That's the only reason why wounded soldiers were dragged
three (!) hours on an armoured vehicle – not by helicopter! – along
poor roads, during which the soldier with a severed artery lost his
chance to live. It also means that there are no military doctors or, at

least, medical assistants in Bamut who can assess the severity of someone's wounds. Otherwise they would certainly have warned his superior officers that Private Moshtyrev would not survive the journey. And why Ordjonikidzevskaya? There is another small hospital with an operating room at Galashki in the foothills of the mountains. Don't these people have local maps?

There are too many questions and too few answers. But we are waiting for Ivan Chizh, the head of the armed forces' chief military-medical department, to give us his answer. If he keeps silent, then we shall take it as an acknowledgement that our suppositions are correct.

To be frank, like the doctors, we don't have much chance of making ourselves heard. All we can do is wait, though these delays are shaming and offensive. We know that wounded soldiers are steadily being sent out of Chechnya and not to the hospitals that are especially equipped to treat them. They go instead to Ingushetia, because it helps the Russian authorities look better and increases their popularity rating.

The ordinary soldiers, as before, remain no better than dirt beneath the officer's boot. No one regards them as "sacred", like Bagautdin. Though the TV constantly tries to persuade us it is so: it shows us leading government officials, press spokesmen, and the army's professional political advisers – like Manilov, who will not rest until he can equal the achievements of Movladi Udugov,[35] the man who brainwashed so many during the first Chechen war.

We're fighting in Chechnya the only way we know how. And the things we're best at are lies and cynicism. It is by shortening the lists in this way that we have successfully created "a war with very low losses".

INGUSHETIA

---

35 Minister of Information in the Chechen government during the last war (see fn. 9).

16

THE CHECHNYA
RESERVATION

27 December 1999

Tragic news has reached Moscow. Refugees living in railway carriages have been attached to a locomotive and shunted, against their will, six kilometres into Chechnya. At first sight, this is nothing special. We might be inclined to agree with Vladimir Kalamanov, head of the Federal Migration Service: "What's the fuss? It's only six kilometres. And nearer home."

However, half of those in the carriages grabbed their children and belongings and leaped out as they moved off. They preferred to become illegal residents in Ingushetia, although that republic is gradually ceasing to be a welcoming host. Those living in the tent camps who do not want to go back are deprived of their daily ration on orders of the commandant: they no longer get their half-loaf of bread and plate of hot soup.

A notice hung up in Aki-Yurt village in the Malgobek district of Ingushetia reads as follows:

ALL REFUGEES FROM THE CHECHEN REPUBLIC IN AKI-YURT! WE INFORM ALL REFUGEES FROM THESE DISTRICTS IN CHECHNYA: NADTERECHNAYA, SHOLKOVSKAYA, NAURSKAYA, ACHKHOI-MARTAN AND THE TOWN OF SERNOVODSK, THAT THEY ARE TO RETURN TO POPULATION CENTRES IN THOSE AREAS. IN ACCORDANCE WITH THE DECISION OF THE

MINISTRY FOR EMERGENCY SITUATIONS AND FEDERAL
MIGRATION SERVICE OF THE REPUBLIC OF INGUSHETIA
THEY WILL NOT HENCEFORTH BE GIVEN HUMANITARIAN AID.
THE ADMINISTRATION

Why are refugees being shunted from one place to another like so much unclaimed luggage? Why so little respect for people's feelings and desires? We are continuing to create a nation of outcasts who lack all civil rights. Is it deliberate? I'm afraid so.

Why They Don't Want to Go

The refugees don't want to go home because they know very well what awaits them. "We shall go back only after the troops have completely left," says Kulady Aidayev, a 53-year-old from Grozny. He used to live at 2 Tovarny Street and run the depot for the Chechen Bus Company, but now he lives in a tent at the Bart camp near Karabulak.

Kulady is adamant and his words are supported by all around him. He found himself at the camp in early November when his 25-year-old son Adam was killed during one of the bombing raids. The body was so disfigured that they could not find the head, and buried him without it. The father says he cannot look at the soldiers strolling around Grozny. The others are all in agreement with him. The majority have similar distressing experiences to recount concerning their relatives and friends.

"But what if they send you back to Chechnya by force?"

"Force will get them nowhere," comes the immediate and uncompromising reply, fast as a sniper's bullet. The speaker is Adlan Tepsayev from Grozny.

Obstacle No 1: none of them wish to live next to the soldiers on principle. Indeed, it would be better if the majority of men here do not come across any of the federal forces: they must avenge the dead members of their family or be shamed as men without honour.

Looters

Abdurashid Aduyev is *yut-da* of the Chechen town of Assinovskaya, 45 kilometres each way from Nazran and Grozny, and 12 kilometres from the "Caucasus" checkpoint. *Yut-da* means *father of the village*. On such people depends the decision whether fighters are allowed into the village or not, which young men go away to fight and which stay at home. I should remind readers that federal forces entered Assinovskaya at the very beginning of the "anti-terrorist operation" and met almost no resistance. *Yut-da* Abdurashid is an old man, a pensioner, who has lived most of his life under the Soviet regime and carries his title with pride. He did not flee the town, and he did not want to go to Ingushetia or any other Chechen village. He had nothing to fear, this old man decided. However, in the first days of December he was to experience for himself all the "pleasures" of sharing the town with the soldiers.

One evening five hefty and already drunk men in masks burst into his house on Zelyonaya Street. They were contract soldiers with the Interior Ministry, whose job it is to maintain law and order in the town. They beat up the *yut-da*, then locked him in his cellar for more than two hours. What were these degenerates after? First they demanded all the gold ornaments in the house. Then they wanted $1,500! They beat up Abdurashid because he would not meet their demands immediately.

Two hours later the conquering heroes relented: "Get the gold and collect the money from the neighbours, you're elder of this town, aren't you? We'll be back tomorrow. If you don't have it ready we shall send you to the filtration camp as a supporter of the fighters!" That morning the insulted and demeaned *yut-da* went to the military administration of the town and lodged a complaint, detailing all that had happened. It had only a limited effect. No military prosecutors appeared to pursue such criminal activities and no security men were there to protect him, but, nevertheless, the bandits in uniform did not return that evening to rob him. They didn't even shoot him down in the street, as his neighbours had predicted.

Unrestrained and open plundering is one of the main features of life in Chechen villages "after liberation". The most frightening figure in this war remains the contract soldier hired by the Interior Ministry: a law unto himself, he is desperately feared not only by the refugees and the "liberated" Chechens, but even by soldiers serving with units of the Ministry of Defence. If the soldiers and the contract men are assigned to man the same post, the army digs itself trenches at a reasonable distance from the "police" and unless there is fighting keeps well away from them. The contract men beat up the conscript soldiers, humiliate them, take their food and personal belongings, and send them into the village for vodka, which is strictly forbidden under present circumstances.

To the north of Assinovskaya is Sernovodsk, the very place where the 36 carriages full of refugees ended up. It is indeed not far from Ingushetia, but the two might be on different planets. Peacetime laws do not apply in Sernovodsk and "cleansing" of property by the Interior Ministry's units has become a normal and everyday occurrence. They took everything they could find on Lermontov Street and Mazayev Street, Ivet Bashigov tells me:

"We didn't have anything fancy at home, we're very poor people. But the contract men carried off an electric alarm clock before my father's very eyes. They didn't say a word and walked past as if he did not exist. If they'd asked us, and said they needed an alarm clock, we would have given it to them . . ."

Sixteen-year-old Ramzia Kharachuyeva cries as she listens to these words. Today this orphan is already back in Sernovodsk. I talked to her when she was still at the Sputnik camp. Like the rest she was simply dumped in Chechnya, after being denied her ration and effectively driven out of Tent No 7, Block 10.

Hers is a tragic tale. During the first war, the federal forces killed her father, then buried him themselves, not permitting the relatives to follow Muslim funeral customs. Afterwards – and she witnessed it all – they drove a tank back and forth across his grave several times in a fit of hatred. Those same soldiers then took everything out of the house and set it on fire. Her relatives helped Ramzia to build herself a "cosy dugout", the girl's own description, in Sernovodsk. This November when there was a new "cleansing" of the town, the dugout was pillaged and then destroyed.

Ramzia tells me: "I went back to see where I could live now. Soldiers were wandering around the market asking for vodka. If they don't get it for free then they bring sacks of potatoes or tinned meat and exchange it for vodka. Once they're drunk they start shooting. That's how Mohammed Esnukayev died, because he didn't give them vodka. But he didn't have any, he was a very religious man."

Ramzia clenches her fists: "The time will come."

Adam Aduyev, nephew of the humiliated elder Abdurashid from Assinovskaya, is living for the time being in Nazran with his family. Adam, 38, was director of the school at the Assinovsky collective farm, just outside Assinovskaya, and then deputy director at the technical college in Sernovodsk. He likes talking about their beautiful farm, the wonderful people who worked there, and how bright all the children were. This is his verdict on recent events:

"I shall only go back if they observe one fundamental condition: the local authorities must be in control, not the military. I'm an educated man. I don't need their insults. I cannot live where the federal forces are. I don't want my sons to grow up under the barrel of a gun, humiliated from the very first simply because they are Chechen."

The overwhelming majority of refugees say the same. Only perhaps ten per cent of those I talked to were totally indifferent to what was going on and simply wanted to shut themselves up in their houses and take no notice. Their argument: "Let whatever will happen, happen. We might as well die there as here."

Obstacle No 2 to their return is that they also want to avoid the unparalleled pillaging and humiliations that living with the federal forces would bring. Chechnya has been handed over to the "victors" for plunder and pillage and the generals are wallowing, with enjoyment, in these mediaeval practices. Their only disappointment now, it would seem, is that most of the villages are half-empty and there are too few people about. If only there were crowds, crammed and squeezed together, that they could now command and dominate! Then the adrenaline and blood would pulse through their veins. Like a diabetic in need of insulin, the generals acutely feel the lack of the Chechen population: too many of them are over the boundary in Ingushetia and there you cannot have much fun, because peacetime laws are still in force.

This explains the announcement to be found in Nazran, in the republic's own migration service, of a "list of population centres in the liberated districts of the Chechen republic allocated for the reception of those who were forced to leave". This numbers two dozen villages and towns throughout lowland Chechnya. It is signed by Colonel-General Kazantsev, commanding officer of the combined forces, and is further authorised by "Lieutenant-General Babichev, Commandant of the Security Zone, Chekalin, First Deputy Commander of the Russian Interior Ministry, Lieutenant-General Palkov, Deputy Commander of the Interior Ministry's Internal Forces, and Major-General Bayramov, Deputy Commander of the Russian Ministry for Emergency Situations".

Nobody cares that this is an open lie, since there is nothing left to return to. Samashki looks little better than a sieve; Valerik from the air resembles a moth-eaten old coat; the camp at Znamenskoe is inaccessible for the majority; and the authorities still refuse to investigate the tragedy at Alkhan-Yurt. (We were the first to write about the events in Alkhan-Yurt, but the Kremlin only turned its attention to the punitive nature of the "cleansing" operation there after President Clinton was informed of events by the Western media. They, in turn, got the story from us.) But the authorities could not care less about the old people, pregnant women and homeless children. It is time, they've decided, to put the collective punishment of the Chechens on a different footing. Now they intend to make everyone pay, even those whom they first accepted and saved in Ingushetia. It will be much easier, however, if all of these citizens are returned to their historic Motherland and then locked away there. Every journalist who has been working in the area knows that it will be much harder to find out what is going on in Chechnya than to visit the camps in Ingushetia. If the forcible return of civilians to the "liberated" areas continues, they will find themselves trapped and in close proximity to forces that behave as occupiers without a care for the consequences.

The Laws are Powerless

The Independent Expert Legal Council in Moscow, at the request of the Memorial Human Rights Centre, has recently provided its analysis of certain aspects of events in Chechnya. This voluntary group of lawyers, headed by Mara Polyakova, has spoken out firmly and clearly, as international law and Article 2 of our own Constitution ("the rights of the individual take priority over all other values") demand.

There can be no talk of a guilty nation that must answer for the actions of certain of its members. The Criminal Code and Russia's law "On the Struggle against Terrorism" both define a terrorist action as a specific event. An anti-terrorist operation is therefore an action taken against specific individual criminals. Any restrictions on the rights and liberties of the population as a whole can only be imposed by the law "On the State of Emergency". In this case, that law has not been invoked. Additional Protocol No 2 of the Geneva Conventions (to all of which Russia is a signatory) is expressed in even more uncompromising terms: "collective punishment for a specific crime is categorically prohibited".

Are we witnessing an anti-constitutional putsch? Without a doubt.

When you carelessly congratulate yourself that we have just had democratic elections to the Duma, stop and think for a moment. We are living under a Constitution that has in part been revoked and now functions only in those parts that continue to receive the approval of the Kremlin. If they then take a dislike to other articles they will toss them aside, just as they will quickly deal with any of us. Yet what will Chechnya look like in the year 2000? We are moving towards the creation of some anti-constitutional territory, a reservation jointly controlled by the harsh military rule of the federal authorities and the so-called police force of the Gantamirov band.[36] This reservation has been set aside for people of an inferior status, Russia's Red Indians of the late twentieth century, who are guilty of having been born in the Chechen Republic. Russia, it seems, cannot live without a Pale of Settlement.[37] At the end of the last century the Jews were thus confined and, as a consequence, they provided many of the young revolutionaries and terrorists of Bolshevism. By creating a reservation for the Chechens we are preparing an inevitable rebellion, led by the hot-headed youths who will grow up there.

INGUSHETIA-MOSCOW

36 A Dudayev ally until 1993, Beslan Gantamirov then aligned himself with the federal authorities and returned with them in October 1999 (see Biographies).
37 The nineteenth-century Pale of Settlement restricted Jewish residence to the Western provinces of Tsarist Russia (modern-day Ukraine, Belarus and Lithuania).

17

CONCENTRATION CAMP VILLAGE

A New Russian Type of Settlement

10 January 2000

The fate of ordinary people in Chechnya is now in the hands of someone like Isa Madayev. He heads the local administration and, at the same time, is military commandant of Chiri-Yurt, one of the largest settlements in the Shali district, located in the foothills below the famous Argun Gorge. He has limited power, but it is genuine.

Isa's story and that of his native village, Chiri-Yurt, is typical of contemporary Chechnya. He was deputy director of the local cement factory, a construction engineer and a colonel in the reserves. Throughout the first Chechen war he fought on the side of Jokhar Dudayev, but he refused to sign up with Maskhadov's forces. Nevertheless, at the beginning of the present war he revived the self-defence unit, made up chiefly of workers from the factory, that he commanded in the earlier conflict. At the end of November, 52-year-old Isa was elected head of the local administration at a village gathering (the previous head had fled), chiefly so that he could negotiate with the commanders of the advancing federal forces. The election took place after Chiri-Yurt had been heavily bombed for the first time and people were killed. It then became clear that the village could not keep out of the new war, even though there were no Chechen fighters there because the villagers had not let them in.

The negotiations were successful and the village suffered little damage. Officially Chiri-Yurt has been "liberated" for over a month, since 12 December. Yet life here can hardly be called normal. Neither war nor peace, neither food nor pensions, neither electricity nor calm. The old authorities of Maskhadov's time and the new administration of the republic based in Gudermes have shown no signs of activity here. Units from the Ministry of Defence and the Interior Ministry hold the village in a fortified ring and forbid any local inhabitants to leave. Meanwhile several thousand refugees from the mountain areas have gathered in Chiri-Yurt and their numbers increase daily. People need to be fed, clothed and given medical treatment. The hospital has been totally destroyed in the bombing and refugees are living in the school building. Despairing of support from the local authorities – of any political persuasion – Isa Madayev left his home village after the New Year and was able, despite many obstacles and delays, to reach Moscow in search of humanitarian aid. We met, and he agreed to answer my questions.

Q. **I don't entirely understand why you came to Moscow and not Gudermes? The permanent mission of the Russian President in Chechnya, headed by Nikolai Koshman, is based in Gudermes.**
A. The so-called new government in Gudermes, it seems to me, is afraid to go anywhere outside the town. Three weeks ago I sent a request, through the soldiers based around our village, for any of Koshman's colleagues to come and visit us. "If I am forbidden to go beyond your post," I told the commanding officer, "then bring the new authorities to us here in Chiri-Yurt: let them see for themselves how we are living. Why don't you get Sherip Alikhadjiev, the new prefect of the Shali district, whom you yourselves appointed, to come here?"

Nothing came of these requests. I still don't know what kind of man the new prefect is. Then Musa Djamalkhanov, Koshman's aide, arrived, typically, in an armoured vehicle. With him came various colonels. I asked them: "Do you fellows consider yourselves the new authorities?" They replied, "Yes." Then I said, "In that case, at least do something to help the refugees. You can see how difficult things are for them."

By way of answer Djamalkhanov for some reason thanked me for staying in the village and not going up into the mountains. Then he drove off in his armoured vehicle and since then I have heard not a word from him. What kind of civilian government is it that rides around in armoured vehicles? In our village people now say of Koshman and his government, "When there's money about they turn up very quickly. If you need help they're nowhere to be seen." After Djamalkhanov's visit, incidentally, I sent my people to Koshman several times with the same requests, but there was no reaction. They're still squabbling as to who gets what job and you can't find out who's responsible for anything. But people are hungry and cold and they can't wait for ever.

Q. **Has any aid ever been delivered to Chiri-Yurt? Have the new authorities sent flour or sugar or money?**

A. Nothing, absolutely nothing. They don't pay our allowances or send rice or bread. We survive as best we can. The only happy news in the month since we were "liberated" is that the commander of the Rapid Response Unit, Yura – he didn't tell us his surname, although he turned out to be a good person – went away somewhere and made them turn the gas back on: the villagers were forbidden to go outside the village to cut firewood to heat their stoves.

Q. **What explanation did they give for this ban?**

A. None at all. The soldiers simply said: "We have an order not to let anyone out." Everyone who tries to escape is turned back. We're truly held hostage there. After three weeks of that, I realised I'd have to go up to Moscow to ask for help. We won't survive otherwise.

Q. **If you had managed to see Koshman, what would you have told him?**

A. I'd say: "Your actions have resulted in almost 40,000 refugees becoming concentrated in the three villages of Novye Atagi, Starye Atagi and Chiri-Yurt. For us this represents a major catastrophe."

There are about 12,000 people in Chiri-Yurt today. About 7,000 are our own villagers, the rest are refugees. We share all we have with them, but this war is not like the last one, and since then the village has become much poorer.

Q. **Chiri-Yurt today is next to the most serious fighting. The refugees fleeing from the mountain villages pass through your settlement. Who is there to meet them? Are officials and employees of the Ministry for Emergency Situations and the Migration Service working in Chiri-Yurt? What are the reception procedures for refugees today, or is there anything of the kind? Who, for instance, explains to the refugees where they should go and where people are waiting to receive them?**

A. There is nothing like that. There's no system at all. No one is waiting for the refugees or explaining anything to them – or to me, the head of the village administration where they are forced to gather and collect. The only reason the authorities reacted to the outcry over the ultimatum to Grozny, in my view, and were forced to show that there were tent camps for the civilian population, was because the Duma elections were approaching. Now that 19 December is behind us and Putin is acting President there is no mention in the southern districts of Chechnya of any camps or civilised reception for refugees. People are coming to Chiri-Yurt to escape because the mountains are being napalmed. I gave the order for them to be housed in the school building. I told the villagers to take them food. That's how we're surviving.

Q. **Do you think the soldiers in the fortified posts around your village know where to send the stream of refugees from the mountain villages? Do they know how to feed them and find them a place to stay?**

A. Of course not. They exist in exactly the same vacuum and are surviving on what there is to hand. The soldiers come to me, asking for the same things as the refugees: "We need bread and water, help us out."

Their supplies of food from outside are very irregular. We are baking bread for the soldiers in our village bakery! We did agree, though, that it was only with the flour they themselves brought us. We couldn't manage otherwise.

Another example. The OMON men didn't have anything to carry water in. I gave them some cisterns. But I asked them to leave them behind when they go. The policemen here from Vladivostok don't have a single car to get around in, and they're fighting on foot. When their commander said, "Isa, give me a car," I gave it to him and also supplied a guide to go with them. I'm always ready to help if they will leave my villagers alone. All I want to do is save this village, that's my goal at the moment, not to make any contribution to the geo-politics of the North Caucasus. Hence my relations with the soldiers, but only with those who are based around our village. We try to reach a good agreement with all of the officers. As a result, in response to our kind deeds, the army behaves itself properly towards the village.

For instance, one night two soldiers ran away from the Interior Ministry battalion. They told us they'd had a fight with the bullies in their post and were afraid to return. To escape they came to the school. The refugees living there gave them tea, somewhere warm to sit and the next morning came to me: "Isa, there are two soldiers stay-ing with us. What should we do?" I ordered them to bring the soldiers to our offices and dozens of people saw this happen. I registered their description of the incident, wrote a report to the Red Cross section so that they, in turn, in accordance with the international conventions, would inform the deserters' families what had happened. Then I called in the commander of the Rapid Response Unit and told him: "There's been some trouble in the battalion. Here are the soldiers, now write me a note that I handed them back to you, alive and in good health, and that you will investigate their complaint." Everything went off peacefully.

At night-times, incidentally, our self-defence group patrols the different areas of the village. We have a duty rota just like you did in Moscow after the explosions.[38]

Q. **But no one is allowed to move around at night. Aren't you afraid that the soldiers will open fire on your patrols?**

A. I told the commanders quite frankly that we would be happier if we had our own fortified posts, then we could protect ourselves from the fighters, the military, and possible provocation and acts of treachery. I said: "If your men don't fire on them, our men won't shoot at your positions."

Q. **Did it work? Were there no unpleasant incidents?**

A. Not once. When the military had only just arrived outside our village, two armed soldiers came for plunder under cover of darkness. I detained them. To be honest, all they'd taken was food, home-baked bread and cheese. They told me, "We're starving." The next morning I went to their commanding officer and requested: "If you need anything please say so during the daytime, so that no one comes into the village bearing arms at night." Our villagers for the most part are patiently waiting for some political solution to the situation, but not everyone in the village is that reasonable. The men in my self-defence detachment, of course, have things under control, but you can never tell whom the soldiers might come across at night. Since they're armed someone might kill them just to get their weapons. An automatic rifle is selling for $300–350 in Chechnya today.

Q. **The commanding officer understood what you were saying?**

A. Yes. They didn't have to fight to take my village, so why shouldn't they understand? You can always reach agreement at the local level. I consider that only the higher ranks like General Shamanov are eager for blood. The company and battalion commanders are responsible for their men and they don't want to lose them.

38 For several weeks after the explosions residents of apartment blocks organised themselves into shifts round the clock to monitor any suspicious activities in or around their buildings.

Q. **What are you doing in Moscow?**

A. My aim is to find money from charitable foundations and kind individuals, and use it to buy sugar, flour, rice, oil, and groats in Ingushetia. Then, having first reached agreement with President Aushev, it will be transported to our village in vehicles of the republic's Ministry for Emergency Situations to feed the refugees there. I'm the only one in this country who is taking any interest in them. By the way, the people I'd like to give a bloody nose, like a Chechen, like a proper man, are those representatives of the new administration in Chechnya! That new prefect for the Shali district for instance. It's possible to reach agreement with the military, but quite pointless dealing with those people.

Q. **What do people in Chiri-Yurt want? Who do they want to win? What kind of future do they want to see?**

A. People are in such despair today that they only want one thing: to be left alive. What did people dream of in the concentration camps?

Q. **Of surviving.**

A. It's just the same for us. Each village today is a concentration camp. Inside you can move about more or less freely, but you mustn't go beyond a certain point. People may enter the village only between the hours of 12 noon and 4 p.m. Someone issued such an order. Who exactly, no one can say. If the refugees arrive before noon or after four they do their best to keep their heads down. I keep asking the soldiers: "What's the sense in this rule?" They have no answer.

Q. **But in the long run what do the people of Chiri-Yurt want? Just for the military posts to be removed and to be able to move freely again?**

A. For the time being I'm trying to gain only one thing: a corridor for aid to move freely from Nazran to Chiri-Yurt. I don't want anything else apart from to feed the refugees. There is no single centre of power in Chechnya today and I must help my village to survive and those who, through force of circumstance, also find themselves there. I've got to hang on.

Q. **So who is controlling Chiri-Yurt today? The federal forces or Chechen forces?**

A. Ours is a Chechen village. I answer only to my fellow villagers, no one else. Neither Mozdok, Moscow nor Maskhadov. That's because I value the views of my fellow villagers over everything else. When I die I know they will come to my funeral, and there won't be any Koshman, Maskhadov or Putin there.

Q. **You seem to be contradicting yourself. You said you were living in a concentration camp, so that means you are totally in the power of the military.**

A. No, we are simply adapting in order to survive. The officers with whom we are forced to live as neighbours understand perfectly well that this village is controlled by Chechens, that we do not like them, and are only tolerating them because we have to. The officers know that they are not the real power here. Sometimes they simply tell us they are protecting us from the fighters.

Q. **Is that true?**

A. I consider that the fighters are bandits and the federal forces are a punitive mission. Cars travelling from one village to another are being shot up. Buses carrying refugees are being shot up! The soldiers under General Shamanov's command behave sadistically towards the civilian population; those commanded by General Troshev behave normally. Everything depends, in other words, not on politics, but on the attitudes of different generals.

MOSCOW

18

SENTENCE HAS
BEEN PASSED

6 February 2000

Before I wrote the following report I wondered whether I shouldn't now spare the reader. Perhaps it would be better to leave you all thinking that the army and the new authorities were settling down and we could be optimistic about the future. However, when the intensive psychotherapy of political expediency to which the Russian authorities have subjected us wears off, it will already be too late. Hundreds of decent people will have died because we lacked compassion. And we cannot avoid the consequences or return to our pleasant and carefree existence.

The Sernovodsk Nightmare

A stout, elderly woman in filthy rags crawls with great difficulty on her hideously swollen legs along the stinking narrow corridor. It is crowded with people in old clothes. She is wailing and imploring everyone who catches her eye to help her die: "I can't stand it any longer! There's nothing to eat, nowhere to live! Nowhere to die even . . ."

"Who are you?"

"I'm no one. Valentina Yefimovna Silova from Grozny. All my life I taught the youngest classes in the school at Cheshki. What did I ever do wrong?"

The old woman falls on her side. People make room for her, but no one has the strength to lift her up and help her to a bed. The crowd just weep over her body. Indifferent to everything apart from pain, hunger and cold, she clambers upright against the wall and moves on – though where she is going no one knows. Her thickly matted vagrant's mop of hair shakes above her trembling back, covered by a coat several sizes too large. Valentina is in Ward 6 (just as in Chekhov's story of madness!) of what used to be the Sernovodsk agricultural college. She has a temperature of 40°C and it shakes and tosses her from one wall of the narrow corridor to the other.

Sernovodsk is a small Chechen town. It has long been within the "zone of security", supposedly, and as a consequence there are thousands of people here who fled from the pogroms and fighting. They have all been forbidden to travel on to Ingushetia. No one has any money. They are in the grip of cold, flu, lice, heart attacks, TB and psychiatric illness.

"Do you have any children, Valentina Yefimovna, who might take you away from here?"

"I shan't tell you. I just want to disappear."

Finally it becomes clear that she actually has two sons, one in Bryansk and the other in Rostov-on-Don. Like a partisan being interrogated, she refuses to give their names so as not to make things more difficult for them.

"But you're dying!"

"Yes. Thank God, I am."

That is the most horrifying reality of the refugee camps in Russia today, that people who have been driven to extremes of despair are now readily pronouncing their own death sentence. (I call on her nameless sons to ignore Valentina Yefimovna's wishes and to quickly get in touch!)

A diminutive old man runs up. He has a crazy look in his eyes, he is dirty and dishevelled, and the ear-flaps of his hat wave about. No, he isn't an alcoholic, there's been nothing to drink here for a long time and no money to buy anything. He's just another demented person.

"Valya," he calls her, "I've found it." Paying no attention to anyone else he prods the indifferent body of Valentina Yefimovna with a small book he's carrying. He was looking for something about Stalinism in the college library and has found it. His name is Nikolai Semyonovich Sapunov, but it is pointless asking him any questions. He doesn't answer or even look your way. His elderly mind has been so oppressed by months of hunger, cold, anarchy and shooting that it is kinder not to insist and overexcite him. The only thing that interests Nikolai Semyonovich now is a comparison between the present killing of those who live in Chechnya with Stalin's similar activities in the 1940s.

Suddenly he returns from his own imaginary world to the present and reality: "I want to eat. Nothing else. I don't want to hear or know about anything else and I don't want to see anyone. I just want to eat! If you can't feed me then get out of here!"

So I left. An impoverished country which I, in some sense, represent started this war and now it is unable to feed the elderly who have worked for it all of their lives. By irresponsibly unleashing this war, the authorities have condemned Valentina Yefimovna and Nikolai Semyonovich to almost certain death. The Kremlin issued those orders. As I hope you've noticed, the former schoolteacher and her husband are both Russian. Perhaps that detail will help some people to show a little feeling.

Ward 5

I leave the corridor and go into the wards where dozens of refugee families are squeezed together. Finally I reach Ward 5. Here the crowd is made up of people who are lying down or can barely walk. Squashed in side by side, 39 people lie there without any consideration of infection or privacy. Twenty grown-ups and nineteen children, from infants to grim-faced teenagers. A very handsome man stands out against this background.

"My name is Saikhan Bazayev. I'm 44 and I have four children. I come from the Shatoi district. I have TB. They've removed my left lung and it's actively spreading in the right lung. There's no medicine and even if there was ... In my condition I need to eat properly six times a day. Here all I get each day is half a tin of corned beef and two pieces of bread."

Saikhan is not at all nervous. He is very calm and thoughtful, with no sign of excitement. He doesn't long for death like Valentina Yefimovna, he simply knows that it is not far off and that he will achieve nothing more in his life. His children will be left destitute, since his house and orchards were destroyed by the war. Even if they could escape this nightmarish refuge, they have nowhere to go.

"It's hardly decent for me to complain, you know," Saikhan continues, his shoulders shuddering with the fever that does not leave him for one moment. "I just feel so sorry for those around me. I'm passing on my infection to the children all of the time. Our living conditions here make it impossible to isolate me from the rest. Even if they survive the camps and go back to some kind of home in Chechnya they have little hope, I've signed their death sentence. For instance, I pleaded with the people from the Migration Service to give me a separate basin. They said that was against the rules."

His wife Malika is weeping next to him: "Just look at us, we're real terrorists."

"What are you hoping for in life?" I ask. "Everyone in order to live, must have something to hope for."

"We have no hope."

It may seem to you, my readers, that your continuing support for the war gives you the right to pass sentence on another human being. Yet when you imagine that you can obtain if not happiness then at least peace of mind at the cost of another's life you are making a tragic mistake. I can only say that no one's peace of mind is worth the death of another human being. Retribution is sure to come. Moreover, it does not come to us together, which would be easier to bear, but to each individually. Then we have to face a single choice: either we end this war or it will be the end of us.

Into the Carriages!

On the far outskirts of Sernovodsk there is one more appalling place. To the right of the railway track is a military compound and to the left is another. This means that every night there are gunfights, drunken soldiers, disturbances and uncertainty. On the night Yeltsin abdicated, for instance, rounds of ammunition were joyously fired straight at the carriages and everyone lay on the floor, not daring to make the slightest movement. For between the two compounds sits a train of 47 carriages in which 2,250 refugees are living. It was shunted here from Ingushetia under strong pressure from Deputy Prime Minister Nikolai Koshman. It is crucial, he thinks, for the future of Russia that those who fled to Ingushetia from Chechnya must be forced to return as quickly as possible, and he has persuaded acting President Putin and Minister for Emergency Situations Sergei Shoigu to support his policy. The rationale is that finance for the refugees will then flow directly from Moscow to Gudermes and pass only through his hands. There must be no more diversion of funds to Ingushetia. The results of his policy can be seen only on the ground. From ministerial offices in Moscow you see very little of what is really going on.

Rosa Djabrailova from Carriage 16 and Yakhita Dudayeva from Carriage 15, both from Grozny, insist they are only 40 years old. The two women look nearer 60. Circumstances have forced them to forget about themselves, but they beg us, for the sake of the children and old people, to pass a message to someone at the top, and to take them back to Ingushetia. There is no water and nothing but hunger, lice, filth, and a desperate cold in the carriages. Since early January there has been no fuel for heating their miserable refuge. Rosa clings to my sleeve and begs me not to leave. It's easy to understand. As soon as the carriages were moved to Sernovodsk journalists were forbidden to go there, so that the complete elimination of the refugees could proceed in profound concealment from the world. The decision was taken at the headquarters of the forces in Mozdok, by those same generals who are implementing a policy of mass liquidation of the civilian population.

However, we must keep working, even when access to information has been totally denied. Journalists secretly reach the carriages by employing all the guiles of the partisan: wearing different clothes, lying their heads off, and, in some cases, giving various forms of bribe to those at the federal checkpoints. It's very unpleasant to behave in this way, but people are begging for help. How does this square with the numerous assertions in Moscow that Chechnya is a part of Russia and that Russia supposedly wants it to live in peace? I think you know the answer.

As I am talking to Rosa Djabrailova, a young woman, Dina Saldalieva, crawls out to us. A week ago in the freezing carriage, on the filthy bunk, she gave birth to her daughter, Iman. Dina is sure her little girl will not live. In front of everyone else, and with no shame or embarrassment, Dina and Rosa tell of their gynaecological afflictions – the constant haemorrhaging, pain and inflammations they suffer. I ask them, why don't you at least lower your voices, as is usual when talking of such matters: it makes an extraordinary impression. They look at me with incomprehension and say, "When you're facing death you cease to fear such things."

I remember the dormitory at Sernovodsk. It was the same there. The women told me of the uterine growths and tumours, inflammation of the Fallopian tubes and the absence of obstetric stools without lowering their voices, standing in the middle of a crowded ward next to their own apathetic husbands and, most shocking of all, the husbands of other women.

Clutching her stomach Liza Elbieva, 42, from Grozny, staggers over to speak to us. She stayed till the very last moment, when even the basement had been destroyed. In early January the soldiers came and told her: "You have 40 minutes, run in that direction. After that the bombing will begin."

"What if someone can't get out?"

"That's their bad luck," the soldiers replied.

On Pitomnik Street, for instance, the Vagapovs, father and son, remained behind at No 16. The son was handicapped and confined to a wheelchair. In 40 minutes you could get nowhere safe with him.

As a result of all the shock and stress, Liza is now suffering a massive haemorrhage and it's noticeable, but I'm the only one to pay any attention to the spots of blood on the back of her coat. In the Kirov suburb of Grozny, an Uzbek soldier called Ural, who was at the checkpoint, also saw these blood spots. No one wanted to let the people fleeing from Pitomnik Street go any further, although they had been told to abandon their homes (so much for those imaginary "safe corridors" out of the city). The Uzbek came up to Liza and quietly said: "I'm also a Muslim. Let me help."

And he did. He was able to get her through the checkpoint and when Liza reached Sernovodsk she went to the local hospital, a small and poorly equipped place. The gynaecologist there refused to examine her and said indifferently: "Go to the market and buy me some gloves. Then I'll examine you. But in any case I have no medicine." Liza had no money at all.

I give her some money and beg her to spend it on herself, to buy the gloves and the medicine. She grabs the banknotes as if she were delirious. She has forgotten about her pain, she says, now she can provide for her children for many weeks if she uses all of the money to buy millet and prepares no more than 100 grams a day.

Walking past the carriages towards the crowd are four people of Russian appearance. They are the carriage conductors, it turns out, who were also shunted back into Chechnya in the carriages with the refugees without their knowledge or consent. Now they are virtually hostages. The Railways Ministry has forgotten all about them. The Migration Service and other government departments, of course, have no time to worry about their plight. They have even been forbidden to walk back into Ingushetia and phone home: the checkpoints are no more ready to let them through than the refugees. Lilya Bayazitova, Larisa Gavrilova, and Zhenya Kukushkin are all from Chelyabinsk.

"Remind them in Moscow that we're down here," they request, and comment: "Why are *we* here? We're totally bemused. Are we still at work? Or are we participating in some experiment in survival, together with the Chechens? Whatever for? We also have nothing to eat. All the medicines we had we gave to the children in the carriages."

Ruslan Koloyev, First Deputy Minister in the Ingushetia MES, is not used to showing his emotions. He is of a profoundly practical turn of mind and takes a rather sceptical view of the reality he faces today. He is not inclined to overreact to the horrors of the refugees' existence. At the same time, he cannot calmly observe what is going on:

"Sernovodsk is in the Chechen republic, it is not part of Ingushetia. Who should be in charge there? Who should be caring for those people? The answer is quite clear: the government of Chechnya, headed by Russian Deputy Premier Koshman and his people. I can't understand why they're doing nothing! Why are we the ones who have to take the most basic food to Sernovodsk every day? – which, strictly speaking, is an infringement of the rules. I'm ashamed to admit it, but we're sending dried milk and baby food to Sernovodsk and thereby depriving the refugees who are actually in Ingushetia. Because we can see what's going on there. Supposedly, the Migration Service is functioning again in Chechnya and they have put a certain Mr Kaplanov in charge and given him the responsibility for feeding 'his' refugees. But nothing has happened. We don't know where Kaplanov is or what he's doing. We merely see the results of his 'activities'. The tins of meat that very occasionally are sent to

Sernovodsk for 'Kaplanov's' refugees are bought for 20 roubles, when they should cost only 8. It's barefaced squandering of funds. Remember, the budget is paying out 15 roubles a day to feed each refugee. If a can of meat is sold for 20, then all that person will get is two thirds of the contents. Naturally, no one bothers about the regular transfers of funds and the result is nothing less than a tragedy."

A hungry person, who has no way of earning a living for months, endlessly waits for some aid from the authorities. Finally he gets one tin of tinned meat to last him a week. Can you imagine what that means?

CHECHNYA-INGUSHETIA

19

MY HOMELAND

March 2000

Picture a classroom. Children sit on their small chairs. One is scratching her leg, another picks his nose, while over there a boy in ragged sports trousers examines a gaping hole in his shoe as if no one else exists.

What can you expect? They've only been going to school for three years and are still little children by ordinary standards. They have just written a composition on the most universal school subject of all: "My Homeland". Which of us has not done the same, and committed the minor offence of filching wise words from some book or other?[39]

But as I read through this pile of papers I was horrified. This hackneyed subject produced a series of burning revelations. It proved so wounding and painful a subject for those gathered in that classroom that I could hardly bring myself to call them children, let alone small children. Outwardly eight or nine year olds, tragic circumstances had filled them with an adult and fully formed view of the world. Moreover, there were no exceptions, it affected each and every one.

But before you read about "My Homeland" I should set the scene.

39 The author and her readers wrote their patriotic school compositions about the Soviet Motherland, a multi-national state with a cosmopolitan ideal ("My home is not a house or street, my home is the USSR").

We are in Ingushetia on the outskirts of the village of Yandara, not far from the Chechen border, at a refugee camp called "Goskhoz" (State Enterprise). Tents, sheds and dugouts. Nothing to eat, nowhere to sleep, no clothes to wear and nowhere to wash, not even once a month. Nothing to provide any cheer. Yet the school is working and, an unbelievable luxury by local standards, it has been given several tents.

Officially we are in "Tent School No 8". Almost 500 children are taught by 21 volunteer teachers. Of course they are not being paid, though there have been a great many promises. The admirable young director, Minkail Ezhiev, is devoted to his profession and, until September, was Head of School 21 in Grozny. Today that school is nothing but ashes.

Class 3C. Russian Language. Composition. Jamila Djamilkhanova, the young teacher from Grozny, speaks a faultless literary Russian; she does not conceal her surprise and pride at the patriotism of her pupils.

There's nothing else to add. I did not select the best compositions. There were only twelve altogether because the classes in the school are small. The tents are not large and many children cannot attend regularly; they have nothing to wear. As a rule, one member of a family attends school today, and tomorrow a different child goes. No one complains if they miss their studies; no one calls in the parents for an explanation.

There is something else distinctive about these compositions. The girls are usually more lyrical, but the boys are severe, single-minded and uncompromising. It's frightening, isn't it?

The first important discovery: not one of the children said that the Russian Federation was their homeland. That's all finished! They have cut themselves off from us.

Second, and equally important: these texts are the work of small children and so they have made quite a few mistakes. Their teacher Jamila has given them all full marks, however, no matter what errors they made in spelling or grammar.

"In our situation could you possibly say to one of them: 'I'm giving you top marks for love of your homeland,' and tell another, 'You're only getting 3 out of 5'?" she asks. "I thought I could also learn some patriotism from them, and so could many other adults. Full marks are a very small reward for the suffering through which these children have learned to love Chechnya. Not one other child in Russia has had a comparable experience."

She handed me the twelve flimsy scraps of paper. Condensed emotion. Undeniable proof and material expression of their love. It does not get any more truthful than this.

And in the short interval before her next lesson we talked: you can still do something about hatred (for instance, by using superior force to overcome it) but, we agreed, there is nothing you can do about love. The only reaction is one of resignation and acceptance.

"I'm giving you these compositions," concluded Jamila, "with one purpose in mind: so that people in Moscow will finally understand."

And their authors seem to be talking to us; even in the pages of our newspaper you can feel how much they want to make us listen.

Abdelazim Makhauri:

I have only one homeland. Grozny. It was the most beautiful city in all the world. But my beautiful city was destroyed by Russia and together with it, all Chechnya and the people living there. The people that Russia had not yet managed to destroy went to Ingushetia, as I did. But I miss my home. I so terribly want to go home although I know already that my house has been bombed to pieces. All the same, I want to go . . . Why do I want to live at home? So I can have the right to do what I want, and no one would tell me off.

LEAVE US ALONE, RUSSIA. WE'RE ALREADY FED UP WITH YOU. There were only a few Chechens before you started. GO HOME and put things in order there, not in our country . . .

Ali Makaev:

I always wanted to see my country Chechnya free from terrorism. Now here I am studying in a cold tent while Russian children can work on computers in warm schools ... I do not know if Putin has a heart. But if he did he would not have started such a war. Putin thinks that human life is worth 50 kopecks. He is deeply mistaken. He is stealing these lives from people. I'd like Putin to know that we are also human beings. Until war came Chechnya was more beautiful than Moscow. I would like to go home and live there to the end of my life.

Bislan Dombaev:

My homeland is the most beautiful and richest country. I was born in Grozny. We lived in Chernoreche. Our village was very beautiful. But now when you look at our homeland you don't want to cry even, you no longer want to live. All has been bombed into the ground and destroyed. My kind, quite innocent little homeland.

Our country is being bombed. Its young people are tormented. Grown-ups and little children are being killed, one after another. What kind of lawlessness is this? What did our people ever do wrong? Why are we suffering?

Islam Mintsaev:

I very much miss my school, my friends and all that I know and love. We don't live badly here in Ingushetia. We go to school in a tent settlement. But Ingush children go to big schools, to a three-storey building like we had in Grozny.

At night I often wonder when this cursed war will come to an end and we can go home. Grown-ups say that the houses are no longer beautiful there: everything has been destroyed and each day young people and our furniture are carried away on APCs [armoured personnel carriers]. They take the young people to Mozdok and torture them there like in the worst films. When I hear the roar of aeroplanes I again feel terrified, just like when we were at home. Again they are bombing my homeland. How many of our relatives have died? And how many are left homeless?

Shaikhan Sadulaev:

My homeland is Vedeno. When I was in the first class at school we moved to Grozny, to the Zavodskoi district. I went to School 21. During the first war I lost my father. The soldiers took him away and he has not been found to this day. I thought then that the war had ended but on 1 September it began again, when all children should be going to school. But they did not let us study. On 21 September Russian planes began to bomb our homes, schools, hospitals and all that we needed. They flew over us, and scared us night and day. So we had to leave our homeland.

The soldiers from Russia are killing children, our sisters and brothers. They say they are bandits. But they are not bandits, they are defending the homeland. Because we love our homeland.

Zaira Magomadova:

My homeland is the most beautiful city on earth, Grozny. I loved the city. During school holidays I went with my parents to the village of Chishki. It is a fine, richly green part of my homeland. Many children from different villages and towns used to go on holiday there. Everything was fine but then the war came. It destroyed my city and all our dreams. It carried off many lives. Who was the person who thought up this war? He also has children, hasn't he? Good people, stop the war!

Petimat Mutsaeva:

My homeland is Urus-Martan but now there is a war there. I was so scared when they bombed Urus-Martan. The schools and the houses where we lived were destroyed. But we are also human beings! I love my homeland very very much and want peace to come there as soon as possible. I want to go to school and enjoy being alive.

Hadijat Djamaldinova:

When they gave us 48 hours warning we left Grozny for Zakan-Yurt. A month passed and we returned home. But on 22 September they again began to bomb our city and on 29 September we went to Ingushetia. I so want to go home! Although only ruins are left there. In Ingushetia it's peaceful and there's no bombing but each morning I wake up thinking about my home. It was bombed to pieces and then burnt. Perhaps there's only ashes left there but it's mine, my homeland.

[No name]:

I love my homeland, the village of Urus-Martan because it is the most beautiful village in the world. Now I miss it very much. At night I dream that I am running with my satchel in my hands and my girl friends to our own school.

Here in Ingushetia planes and helicopters often fly past and I get scared, as though I am at home again. During the last war the soldiers from Russia killed my father. Mum searched for him everywhere. Finally she found a dead, mutilated body buried in the ground. I was six then, my brother was eight and my younger sister was eleven months old. After everything that happened I thought, the war has ended for good. But in a short time it all started again.

Now every day I hear the grown-ups weeping and telling

of their murdered relatives. I would like to live under a peaceful sky! But will there be such a thing?

Aminat Sedieva:

I was born and lived in the capital of the republic, Grozny. Our city used to be very beautiful. I went to School 14. Our teacher was called Tamara Usmanovna. I would like to study in our school, in our classroom. But now we go to school in cold tents. We came here to Ingushetia because they bombed our city and it was frightening there. Now we have neither city nor school. I don't know when we'll go home.

Koka Musostova:

Because of the military operations we moved to Ingushetia. Here the military helicopters and aeroplanes of Russia fly over us. They almost come as low as the roofs. I want to go back to Chechnya as quickly as possible, to live, study, play and make friends. I very much love my homeland. Help me to do that.

Marina Magomedkhadjieva:

My city Grozny always radiated beauty and goodness. But now all that is gone like a beautiful dream and only memories remain. The war is blind, it doesn't see the city, the school or the children. All this is the work of the armadas from Russia, and therefore not only our eyes are weeping but also our tiny hearts.

Now we have nowhere to go to school, to play and enjoy ourselves. Now we run back and forth and don't know what to do. But if they asked us we would say: "That's enough bloodshed. If you do not stop this senseless war we shall never forgive you." Soldiers! Think of your children, of your own childhood! Remember the things you wanted in

childhood and what your children want, and you'll understand how sad and difficult it is for us. Leave us alone! We
want to go home.

                                        INGUSHETIA

THE DECISIVE BATTLE

20 March 2000

The fighting around the village of Komsomolskoe in the mountain foothills, now in its second week, will decide the fate not just of the war but of Russia itself. Our country's territorial integrity, independence and economic well-being depend on the outcome – or so the official announcements tell us.

Try as we might, we cannot square events in Chechnya today with what the authorities say. It is not just that reality is more complicated. Quite simply it does not correspond to the propaganda of either presidential aide Sergei Yastrzhembsky or of the combined forces headquarters.

Lema and Ruslan are 30 and 26 years old, relatives and members of the same *teip* or "clan". They are also Chechen fighters, and both in the detachment commanded by Ruslan Gelayev. (It was a condition of the interview that I did not give their surnames.)

We made no particular effort at concealment in order to talk. Yet Lema had come out of Komsomolskoe only the night before, during the most intensive fighting when federal forces had the village "completely" sealed off. His appearance leaves no doubt about his recent activities. Extremely thin, his face is black and he constantly scratches his head (lice). Ruslan looks much better. His commander ordered him to leave the group earlier. But Ruslan's story is virtually identical: he left the village of Shatoi then, surrounded by federal troops, took to mountain paths with the wounded, and escorted them to hospital (that was his assignment). Now he is being treated for the severe frostbite he suffered during that expedition.

Neither bothers to hide the fact that they are waiting for April, when the trees in Chechnya come into leaf. Then they will go back and fight again. Most of the fighters now resting or recovering are also waiting for those same leaves to appear, they say.

Before 1994 they were ordinary villagers. One grew maize in Naura, the other planted wheat at Samashki. During the first war Lema did not touch a weapon. Ruslan is more experienced; he fought then.

Q. **How could you get out of Komsomolskoe if it was completely surrounded by soldiers?**
LEMA: We came out at night, naturally. The sentries were on duty and the artillery shelled the place. The soldiers were coming under fire from their own side. They held their ground, but were terrified of everything – they want to live. In our case, the soldier was crouched beneath a tree because the bombardment was very intense. We walked past ten metres away.

Q. **Are you sure the soldier saw you? It was dark, after all . . .**
LEMA: I'm sure he saw us. Without a word, he cocked the bolt on his rifle and we did the same in reply. We "greeted" each other and parted. I think he knew: if he fired a shot we'd kill him straight away. But the soldier doesn't want this war, he just wants to live.

Q. **So you came out of Komsomolskoe bearing arms?**
LEMA: Of course we were armed. There were times when a group of up to 50 fighters walked past the soldiers and they saw us.

Q. **What was going on in Komsomolskoe when you were there?**
LEMA: They were firing every kind of heavy weapon at the village. The peaceful inhabitants had become hostages and many died. Sometimes

the soldiers tried to storm the place. Our main force is in the mountains, there's only a small group in the village. It's like this: we're in the village, surrounded by the feds, and around them is a ring of our fighters.

Q. **Did your group not consider leaving Komsomolskoe? No one, including boys more than ten years old, was being allowed out because of you. If you'd gone, the village could have been saved from destruction.**

LEMA: To begin with we wanted to do that, but then we were left with no choice.

Q. **Why? You've just come out. You could have taken people with you . . .**

LEMA: People wouldn't come with us, they're afraid of dying. We're moving at night, aren't we? Without any guarantees.

Q. **All right, you've managed to get out of Komsomolskoe. What next?**

LEMA: It's no problem to get past army posts in the night. I won't tell you exactly how we do it, though.

Q. **You mean you paid the feds on the army posts and during "cleansing" operations?**

RUSLAN: We never pay to get past their posts. But we do buy weapons and ammunition, of course, from Russian officers. The feds have a lot of the latest weaponry and they sell it.

Q. **When did you yourself last buy weapons from the soldiers?**

RUSLAN: About a month ago.

Q. **How do you make such a deal?**

RUSLAN: Through Chechen intermediaries. We hire those Chechens who are on good terms with the military. For instance, people in the recently created local administration. Usually we're buying large quantities and the military know perfectly well what it's for. There were times when they deliberately gave us ammunition for rifles that blew up in the sniper's face. But that doesn't happen often. Most of our ammunition and weapons, though, we get from fighting.

LEMA: I've noticed that in this war the soldiers are making wide use of Omnopon and, of course, Promedol.[40] They often go into battle drugged out of their minds and fear nothing. Our prisoners also told us that they injected themselves before a battle and then they weren't frightened of anything.

RUSLAN: Each carries a little yellow packet in his pocket, his own first-aid kit. We've seen them on the dead. We usually take painkillers from these packets for our wounded.

Q. **But people say just the same about your fighters, that they also take narcotics before attacking and that's why they're so reckless.**

LEMA: That's not true. We don't fear death because we shall go to paradise if we die on the battlefield. Some drug addicts did join our groups when we were in Grozny. But junkies are no good at fighting so we pushed them out.

Q. **How did you join the group?**

LEMA: Like everyone else. When the war began the lads in our village got together: "What shall we do?" We decided to fight. "Who will be our commander?" We agreed, "He'll do it." And off we went. We've been fighting since the battle at "Soviet Russia" village in Naurskaya district [i.e. since early October]. We weren't in Daghestan.

Q. **How many mercenaries are there in your group?**

RUSLAN: There haven't been any in our group. The mercenaries make up about 1–2 per cent of the total, no more, and they stick together. The military are lying when they say on TV that there are lots of mercenaries. For myself I haven't seen a single black or Chinese among our fighters.

Q. **Is discipline strict in your group?**

LEMA: At the moment there's a campaign against cigarettes, no one should smoke. A warrior of Allah should not smoke. As long as he's fighting he should give up all prohibited things – drinking, swearing, going out with women, stealing, lying . . .

---

40 Common painkillers in Russia that are widely abused as narcotic substances.

Q. **And if someone breaks that rule when you're out fighting, then they're beaten with rods?**

LEMA: Without fail. If you've been drinking you'll be thrashed.

Q. **You consider such a punishment quite normal?**

LEMA: Of course. It very much helps self-awareness. A grown person feels awkward when he's beaten with rods in front of others.

Q. **What is the monthly pay in your group?**

LEMA: I've never had a wage. The last time I got any pay was when I was 18 and working in a building brigade before serving in the army.

RUSLAN: Our system works like this. The commander keeps all the money. If I need help – I'm sick or something else has happened – then he gives me money. But no one pays me something every month, that's not the way. You don't expect money for fighting a holy war.

Q. **How do you regard yourselves? Are you partisans? Servicemen in the Chechen army? Guerrillas?**

LEMA: We're warriors of Allah. I am liberating my country from enemies and infidels. I see Chechnya as a free Islamic republic, and want it to become one. I'm not interested in what someone else in Russia may want. When the war ends and Chechnya is freed I shall cease being a warrior of Allah and become an ordinary person, a servant of Allah.

Q. **You follow Gelayev. Explain who gives the orders, and to whom, in your group.**

RUSLAN: Maskhadov is in overall charge. No one acts on his own. There are no independent initiatives, we're strictly centralised. Military councils are regularly held. I've taken part in several and Maskhadov was there.

Q. **When did you last see him?**

RUSLAN: It's now a month ago. I went to the council as the bodyguard of our commander.

LEMA: And I heard Maskhadov's voice over our radio in Komsomol-skoe. All there obey his orders without question, and he knew exactly what was going on. It's nonsense that no one knows where he is.

He's in good health and not wounded.

Q. **In your opinion how many warriors of Allah are there now, in March?**

RUSLAN: About 20,000 who are fighting. How many in the reserve, it's hard to say.

Q. **What do you mean, the reserve?**

RUSLAN: Those who are resting in the villages until someone tells them it's time to go back.

Q. **What are you fighting for?**

LEMA: For the sake of Allah. When we're attacked we rejoice because the gates of paradise are opening.

Q. **Do you consider yourself Wahhabites?**

LEMA: No, we're just Muslims.

Q. **Do the people of Chechnya support you?**

RUSLAN: Some do, others don't. And anyway, people are too intimidated for them to talk of their support for us.

Q. **You know that in those villages you passed through whenever you broke through federal lines there were very harsh "cleansing" operations and numerous victims. It doesn't make you stop – the thought that you are putting your own people at risk?**

RUSLAN: But we aren't doing it on purpose. War is war, and casualties are unavoidable. No matter if they destroy villages and murder people, we shall not stop fighting. Because even if we do call a halt they won't leave the Chechens in peace, they'll carry on with their extermination. That's what our prisoners, both soldiers and officers, told us. They have been given a spoken, unwritten order to kill as many as they can, and it doesn't matter whether they're fighters, women, children or old men.

LEMA: That's why this war will never end. Even if the troops leave, they won't escape our vengeance. There've been so many victims . . .

Q. **Do you believe that the troops will leave Chechnya?**

LEMA: Of course. You can't predict how Russia will behave. Today it has one policy, tomorrow it'll have another. And we won't tolerate any permanent garrisons on our territory.

AN ESSENTIAL POSTSCRIPT

Take note of two things in this interview:

(1) I was talking to Chechen fighters on territory that, if one believes the official statements of the combined forces headquarters, has been completely under the control of the federal troops for several months. But Lema and Ruslan were calm and not particularly secretive. Only once in a while did they flick their eyes from side to side, barely turning their heads. This was more a habit acquired as guerrillas in the forested areas, however, and not in response to any danger – for none indeed threatened them. There were all kinds of people around us. Soldiers and their officers walked past. There were certainly FSB men among the latter, since the front-line area is crawling with them today. Only a few dozen metres away stood an army post. From Moscow this picture must seem incredible. Here are soldiers with automatic weapons, here are refugees and beside them both is Lema, a follower of Gelayev, who has come straight here from Komsomolskoe. Yet that is the present war in the North Caucasus, where double standards rule and each day claim another victim.

(2) Both sides support the same ideology: neither one nor the other has any pity for the civilian population as it is driven and harried across Chechnya. They both consider the numerous civilian deaths to be some unavoidable accompaniment to their own "work". And in this sense they display no double standard at all.

That is why I must state the obvious yet again. This kind of fighting can go on without end and always provide serious arguments on both sides of the barricades. In other words, the madness must stop – and now!

SOUTHERN CHECHNYA

*

On 26 March the citizens of Russia voted to elect a new President. Two of the candidates had stood in 1996 against Yeltsin and repeated their achievements of that year: the liberal candidate Grigory Yavlinsky retained his steady 7 per cent of the vote; the Communist challenger, Gennady Zyuganov, maintained a 34 per cent share. The newcomer Vladimir Putin, contesting his first ever election, won outright. He was supported by 52.9 per cent of those who voted (the turnout was 70 per cent).

At that moment, the Chechen fighters were on the brink of defeat. Almost a year later a representative of Aslan Maskhadov frankly admitted this: the Chechen side suffered very serious losses during 2000, and in Komsomolskoe alone 841 fighters were killed during March. Speaking in Paris to Pavel Felgenhauer (Moscow News, 6 February 2001) Hussein Iskhanov said that the Russian military saved the situation. Their treatment of the civilian population in the "liberated" areas rapidly turned opinion against the federal forces, creating the conditions for a classic partisan war.

PART THREE

RESTORING ORDER

May 2000–January 2001

Q. But the war really will end and then everyone will have to adapt and live according to peacetime rules.

A. You know what, let's finish the war first. Then we'll see by whose rules we are going to live! Things are not that obvious in Russia today. Our self-awareness, which is gaining a stronger hold on us, means that if the rules are holding us back they must be changed.

LIEUTENANT-GENERAL VLADIMIR SHAMANOV
JUNE 2000

The nation must no longer be left stranded half-way; no longer must it be deceived by this "independence" and "liberty" that no one has ever actually given us and never will. Freedom, in fact, is something the ordinary man – and I count myself one, I come from a very modest peasant family – does not need. He needs work and in return a wage and security.

AHMAD-HADJI KADYROV
JULY 2000

Soon a year will have passed since the atrocity in Novye Aldy, a Nazi-style massacre of modern-day Russia. There has been no investigation. During the entire eleven months since it happened, the witnesses have not once been questioned. No one has presumed to create photofit pictures of the criminals, though certain of the killers did not hide their faces.

ANNA POLITKOVSKAYA
JANUARY 2001

21

A REDUCED CITY

Plans to Rebuild Grozny

18 May 2000

Just before the long-drawn-out May holidays – this year combined with the "inauguration" of the new President[41] – Putin and Prime Minister Kasyanov received a report on Grozny. The government had sent a commission to investigate the state of the Chechen capital, and it had worked very hard and rapidly to produce this document. Albert Marshev, First Deputy Chairman of the State Construction Committee and head of the commission, submitted several proposals that ought now to be transformed into a government decree, establishing the priorities in restoration work. A decision cannot be put off any longer. Without such a decree there will be no funds and Grozny might face winter in its present devastated condition.

What exactly has the Marshev Commission requested their lordships to consider? If truth were told, it isn't very ambitious: it asked for funds to restore accommodation for a mere 20,000 people. It did not make sense to restore the city to its pre-war dimensions – it then had about 420,000 inhabitants. The commission members concluded that since so many people had either died or fled it should now be reduced to about 230,000. By the end of this year the commission

---

41 As in Soviet times, the holidays begin on 1 May (May Day) and continue, with little pause for work, up to Victory Day on 9 May. Inauguration is one more Western neologism introduced into Russian public life over the last decade.

predicts that the population will barely exceed 100,000. And that is where the figure of 20,000 comes in.

"I think that the Chechens will make apartments and homes for 30,000 people using their own resources. So, together with our contribution, that already adds up to 50,000," says Marshev. "Add the houses that have survived and you've got another 30,000–40,000. By winter, 90,000 people would have permanent dwellings." The man who rebuilt Grozny after the 1994–6 war, Marshev knows the city like the back of his hand. Now 64, he graduated from the construction engineering institute in Kazan and has spent his whole life in construction, starting as a site foreman and ending as a highly placed government official.

This is all very fine, but we know only too well that the authorities, especially in Russia, always try to reduce the scope of their responsibilities. The commission's arithmetic is neither accurate nor decent in human terms. To a very great extent it is dictated by political considerations. Judge for yourself: they are already talking about a deliberate reduction in the population of Grozny. If the commission's proposal is accepted, some 100,000 of the city's former inhabitants, who now live in the refugee camps of Chechnya and Ingushetia, will be "written off", and will face the coming winter in the same destitute condition as now. Not a word is said about them in these plans and proposals.

And then there's the money. How much will it cost to rebuild Grozny? As any thoughtful person can see – because of the constantly renewed outbursts of fighting, raids and the laying of minefields – no one can answer that question for the time being. If someone gravely names a specific sum, don't believe them.

Government decrees are written according to other principles, however: demand as much as you can, then quickly pass the buck. According to Marshev's commission, before the cold sets in the basic restoration work in Grozny will require about 100 million roubles [$3.4 million, Tr.] in public funds. This will cover the following work. First and foremost the water supply must be restored: no more than a quarter of the town is provided for at present, and that is only because water continues to drain out of the reservoirs, thanks to gravity. Second, the sewerage system must start working again. Third, rebuild the hospitals. Fourth, be ready to open the schools by 1 September. And only last come homes for people to live in.

It's a pragmatic approach and, indeed, what sense is there in putting up housing if there won't be water, heating and a sewerage system for those apartments? What will people do there? Merely confirm the "victory" of their return to the place where they lived before?

The last point in the Marshev plan, the rebuilding of homes, has stirred the most powerful outbursts of official passion. It stands a strong chance of being turned down. Putin, as we all know, is particularly concerned about appearances, and this often works to the detriment of the job in hand. The presidential staff intends to oppose the restoration of Grozny in stages, as proposed by the commission. This is all in order to impress the West: the first thing we're doing, they'd like to say, is to build houses for the people of Grozny.

"Some of the residential areas have survived," continues Marshev, "but the water supply and sewerage system have been totally plundered. And I mean exactly what I say! Only the shells of the former pumping stations and part of the underground structures have survived. Everything else has been stolen. Bombs fell only on the Starosunzhensk reservoir (the transformer was hit) and on the only sewage pumping station No 1 in the city (but no more than the electrical works there were affected – a couple of weeks to repair at most). It will take months, though, to make good the damage caused by this barbarous plundering.

"When I saw it I almost burst into tears. I would never have believed that people were capable of doing that to themselves. All the twelve pumping stations in Grozny and the second-level booster pumps have been stripped and plundered. The generators have been destroyed, all the copper has been stripped out. All the transformers have been ripped apart. The contact wires and all the aluminium from the high-voltage cables have been removed. Water won't rise by itself: there are 6,000–10,000-kilovolt lines running up to the water reservoirs!

When we were examining the Chernorechensk reservoir we caught four marauders red-handed. They were smashing the two remaining "operable" generators with sledgehammers in order to steal the copper windings. As a result, it will need from 70 to 100 million roubles just to restore the sewerage system – and that's only to ensure the most basic minimum. It's the good fortune and salvation of Grozny, I believe, that it is one of the few cities in the world where the water reservoirs are higher than the city itself: they are at 232 metres while Grozny itself is at 80 metres above sea level. Water can reach the city simply by gravity. I honestly cannot understand how people could destroy what their fathers and brothers and sisters built – it should all be working for them! To my mind it's like the behaviour of field commander Ruslan Gelayev.[42] How could he ever think of taking the war home, to Komsomolskoe, knowing in advance that his own home and village would be destroyed! Evidently he has no sense of honour or conscience, either towards his fellow villagers or his clan."

There is, of course, quite another side to life in Grozny and Chechnya today. Some certainly continue to rob themselves in this way, but others are working day and night to make life more bearable for those around them. Highly experienced construction engineers have already returned to Grozny and, without waiting for decrees to be issued or funds released in Moscow, they are now saving the city: Elmurza Ismailov has been appointed to head the revived Chechen construction department; Aidi Aliskhanov is chief engineer for the city's water supply system; Abu Sugapov and Curie Bataev are experienced gas engineers and Mansur Bakaneev is responsible for the city's electricity network. They are passionate about their work

42 See Chapter 20, "The Decisive Battle".

and are labouring selflessly. They weld pipes, venture out across mine-fields, and take every conceivable risk in order to bring water, gas and light back to the city.

A separate and highly sensitive issue in the present rebuilding of Grozny is the way in which compensation for lost property and housing will be paid. There has still not been any mention of payment or how it is to be made. The plan is that the majority of people will receive building materials from State reserves and will begin to restore their own homes. The Marshev plan pursues the same ideology: it is more sensible to give people compensation in kind – since the affected families have so many problems the money could disappear in any direction and as a result a wrecked home might remain without a roof or doors this winter.

Lastly, the most important question of all. What deadlines is every-one working to? The special commission sent to investigate Grozny did the impossible and in the space of eight (!) days worked their way painstakingly across all the city's ruins. They understood that the speed with which funds for the restoration work began to flow depended on the rapidity with which they submitted their report. In the capital quite a different picture is to be found in those corridors of power that must utter the final approval.

"Many people ask me: Is it possible to restore Grozny within a year or two?" comments Marshev. "I say: It's possible. It could also take 20 years. Even now everything else we need is already happening in Grozny: people are trying to rebuild the schools, and gradually the hospitals are re-opening. But things must start moving much faster. The tragedy is not behind us. Four months will pass in no time. We must hurry and reach a decision."

Alas, if the new president must be inaugurated and a new govern-ment chosen, there is little time left to think about rebuilding Grozny or signing some decree! Of course not. While the State's highest officials were celebrating and, at the same time, nervously waiting to see if they would remain in office, these crucial documents lay unread and unconsidered. Thousands of dispossessed and homeless people were waiting with baited breath for Moscow's reaction. But in the capital serious work was set aside yet again, because no one wanted to miss out on the parties and celebrations.

22

THE NAME'S SHAMANOV

Russia's Youngest General

19 June 2000

The war in Chechnya has now reached the stage of a steady, long-drawn-out guerrilla campaign. How long it will go on, God alone knows. For decades, perhaps? There is one thing, however, that we already understand all too well. Thousands of men, from privates to generals, are quietly returning home but do not find the long-desired peace in our company. It's difficult for them, away from the fighting. They have altered dramatically and are now strangers to friends and family. People shrink from them and fear them. Some are even openly reproachful: "What can you do, apart from kill?" Those who survived the fighting, it seems, must not show their faces anywhere.

So how will the latest Chechnya veterans settle back into society? And how does the first among them feel today – Lieutenant-General Vladimir A. Shamanov, a decorated "Hero of Russia", former commanding officer of the Western group in the North Caucasus campaign, and now in charge of the 58th Army?

Vladimir Shamanov, 43 years old. Graduated from the Ryazan paratroop officers' college, and from the Frunze Military Academy and the General Staff Academy in Moscow. Served in Pskov, Ryazan, Moldavia, Azerbaijan, Ulyanovsk and Novorossiisk. Wounded during the first Chechen war. Now commands the Ministry of Defence's 58th army, with headquarters in Vladikavkaz. Married, with a son and daughter. Has had two heart attacks and suffers from an ulcer and chronic insomnia.

Q. **All the country now refers to the two generals who led the latest campaign in Chechnya as "kind Troshev" and "cruel Shamanov". Don't you find that hurtful?**

A. No. For me it's praise.

Q. **But haven't you wondered about the consequences? Perhaps it was precisely your intransigence, your determination to wage war with such brutal methods, that has left soldiers so disturbed that they cannot settle back normally into a peacetime existence. What they witnessed in Chechnya was surely an unbearable burden for 18–20-year-olds. As their commanding officer, how much are you to blame for what they are going through today?**

A. It is society, above all, that is to blame. We've accumulated a rich experience of military operations in so-called localised conflicts – Angola, Mozambique, Ethiopia, Egypt, Korea, Afghanistan and the various "trouble spots" [of the Soviet Union] – but there is still no well-organised system in Russia for the psycho-neurological rehabilitation of those who take part in such campaigns. Yet I am convinced that when a person returns from conditions of extreme stress to normal life, he must go to such a rehabilitation centre and undergo a process of re-adaptation under medical supervision in specially maintained conditions.

Q. **Do you yourself feel the need for such rehabilitation?**

A. Unquestionably. I'm just like everyone else. I'd like to say, you mustn't shift all of the blame on to the commanding officers. The decisions that I took during the war were intended to create the maximum conditions for preserving the lives of my subordinates and minimising their psychological stress during battle. Sometimes it proved possible: the armed clashes were of short duration. But when we began Operation "Wolf-Hunt", for instance, to lure the Chechen fighters out of Grozny, there were eight days and nights of continuous fighting. As commanding officer I managed no more than 30–40 minutes sleep and only by days five and six did I sleep for one-and-a-half to two hours. But the privates and junior officers, up to and including battalion commanders, did not even have that much rest. It's hard to withstand that kind of pressure.

Q. **But it's not just a question of serious physical stress, is it? It's more the problem of uncontrolled looting and the deaths of innocent civilians. When you destroyed the bandits you were also destroying ordinary people?**

A. That's all been much exaggerated by the media.

Q. **What about the tragedies in Alkhan-Yurt and Novye Aldy?**[43]

A. I wasn't in Novye Aldy. It did not come within the territory for which I was responsible. As far as Alkhan-Yurt is concerned, the premise is totally false. Four commissions have proved and confirmed that we gave the civilian population the chance to leave before the fighting began.[44] Furthermore, the corridor was open for the entire week, not just one day.

Q. **But you know very well that in Chechnya far from all the inhabitants of besieged villages use such official "corridors". Indeed they can't leave. People are afraid to abandon their cattle and houses.**

A. All the commissions confirmed that we only fired at those locations in Alkhan-Yurt that we had identified during the week the corridor was open. The houses were hit in which the bandits were located, and those basements in which fortified weapon emplacements had been established.

Q. **But there were ordinary people there as well as the bandits. Didn't that disturb you?**

43 In early December 1999, at least 18 civilians were killed by federal soldiers in Alkhan-Yurt, not far from Grozny (see Chapter 14). On 5 February 2000 no less than 62 civilians were killed by soldiers in Novye Aldy, a village-suburb of Grozny (see Chapter 38).

44 Deputy premier Nikolai Koshman visited the village and on 23 December promised a rapid inquiry but no results were made public. An investigation by the military prosecutor's office was soon closed.

A. After a week of the open corridor that was already their choice. Incidentally, when the commissions later requested that the graves be opened, only 20 bodies were found. Of those, 12 were bandits. Six weeks later the prosecutor's office issued a finding about the remaining eight bodies: they were people connected in one way or another with the bandits.

Q. **What does that mean, "connected in one way or another with the bandits"? In your view, who is the wife of a Chechen fighter?**

A. A female bandit.

Q. **Why?**

A. If she's not a female bandit then she should leave him.

Q. **Vladimir Anatolevich, your reasoning is applicable to Russians.**

A. What do you expect? They're living in Russia.

Q. **They have their own laws and customs: she can't just leave him.**

A. But what if "their" laws are immoral? We want to do everything with clean hands! It won't work. And it never will. Kindness must always have its limits. I don't agree with turning the other cheek. If the bandits do not understand our code of ethics they must be destroyed. If someone falls ill, they hurt the patient by removing the affected organ.

Q. **But they don't operate on relatives in that case! Is the child of a bandit also a bandit?**

A. Certainly. Tell me something: how can you tell someone's wife from a woman sniper? It's all very well for you to discuss things, sitting clean and comfortable here in Moscow, gazing at the TV screen. But for me, down there . . .

Q. **Don't you get the impression that the ordinary soldiers don't always reason that way and don't even share your point of view? That's why, later on, they commit suicide.**

A. I know no soldiers of that kind! The ordinary soldiers and I understand each other perfectly, we have clear visible goals.

Q. **Probably, they simply don't talk to you about it.**

A. I don't know. I spent 50 per cent of my time during the war in the trenches with the soldiers. That's why today they call me "the trench general". And it's my credo to be at the front line, to know what's really going on, and how those risking their lives feel. In the Western group of forces there was no gap between the commander and his soldiers, but a perfect understanding and I'm proud of it. I conclude that from the following indirect examples: when the CO appeared or another of the commanding officers, their subordinates did not run off and hide or look grim, they smiled! And you can't buy a smile like that, especially in those circumstances.

As concerns looting, it does of course take place and a string of criminal charges are now being brought. However, the roots of this shameful phenomenon lie not in the army itself but in the situation created by the presence of contract soldiers. As you know, the people who join the army as contract soldiers are those who have not found a place for themselves in normal life, so they go off to war to improve their material well-being. Looting is one of their ways of doing so.

Q. **Were many contract soldiers under your command during the war?**

A. At various times they made up from 3 per cent to begin with, rising to 15 per cent.

Q. **Don't you think that it's wrong to create a professional army by inviting contract soldiers to serve?**

A. Undoubtedly. You won't find a single officer who would oppose a professional army. And we don't need the kind of army that we're trying to create now. From the outset contract solders have false premises. They are not thinking of their duty. Drunkenness. Looting. A low level of professionalism. Elementary human laziness – living life "just to get through the day". Meanwhile the military machine is in operation and the lack of one bolt can cost us dearly. An organism that is potentially 100 per cent effective is reduced to 50–70 per cent. I personally don't need such a "professional" army.

Q. **But what kind do we need? Do you have your own ideas about that?**

A. I'd like to get $5,000–10,000 a month, like an American general. I'm paid $180.

Q. **Does that seriously affect you? After all, you are an army general, a "Hero of Russia", and the State probably pays all your costs: food, medical treatment, transport and so on.**

A. Where do they feed me? In the trenches. The rest of the time I buy the food and I feed myself.

Q. **But perhaps, as a hero, you have other possibilities? You probably have an excellent apartment. And not just here in Moscow.**

A. To this day I am a general without an apartment. I have my service accommodation. Just imagine, I am a lieutenant-general, commander of the 58th army and I don't have a flat of my own! Not since 1993.

When I was studying at the General Staff Academy from 1996 to 1998 I felt totally humiliated and powerless. For months on end they didn't pay our allowance. I was already a general by then! I felt terribly ashamed in front of my family. In order to buy a packet of cigarettes all those in one class – three generals and seven colonels – had to chip in. There were other colonels and generals who were using their own cars as taxis to earn money in Moscow.

Q. **Why didn't you do that? For the sake of your family.**

A. I didn't criticise the others, but I couldn't allow myself to do that. It's a matter of convictions. I'd rather eat dirt . . . There've been generals in Russia before me, and there'll be others after me, and we mustn't dishonour the uniform. If the country has given me my stars then I have no right, no matter how hard I find things, to turn myself into a taxi driver. And if this humiliating position does not suit me I should resign my commission. Then I shall be free to do what I want. I've never understood those officers who want to go into politics, who try to pass comment and instruct others – that's not part of the profession. If you want to do all that then hand in your resignation, take off your uniform and do whatever you like. If you've remained under arms, then please live according to the rules established by previous generations. No one has the right to betray traditions, they must be cultivated and upheld.

Q. **Is it true that your entire family is now scattered across the country?**

That your wife is living under one surname in one town, your children in another, while you are in Vladikavkaz?

A. In part that's true. I have been obliged to take certain precautions: there is firm proof that Chechen fighters are looking for my family.

Q. **But that's no kind of life, without home or family. If you're a hero then you ought to be living like one. If you're certain, that is, that you acted properly. Was it really worth it? To fight as you did in Chechnya and then not be able to live a normal life?**

A. Yes, I do have doubts that I've chosen the right way of life. I feel guilty towards my family. Since 1990 when I was made commanding officer of a regiment in the area of the Karabakh conflict [Armenian enclave in Azerbaijan, Tr.] all my time as a soldier has been spent in the struggle against Evil. Still . . . Someone had to do the job.

Q. **The feeling of guilt towards your family isn't growing? Doesn't it make you want to turn your back on it all and get out?**

A. There have been moments. Once I was ready to give it all up. Twice my wife said we couldn't go on like that any longer. We'd had enough. We were going to give it all up and live a normal life for as long as was left to us. But I couldn't take the final step. I'm 43 and since I've chosen to be a professional soldier I want to leave something behind me when I die. That's what's most important, and not that I've been made "Hero of Russia". Heroism isn't an end in itself. I never aimed for that. Four times during the first campaign [1994–6] I was put forward for the title, but they didn't give it to me. But after that both my pupils and my fellow officers felt more warmly towards me. I can say with pride that I have reared seven "Heroes of Russia".

Q. **And you became a hero after all of them?**

A. Yes.[45] But, actually, I didn't do anything particularly heroic – I just did my duty.

Q. **I suppose an army general is not up for Alexander Matrosov's type of feat. Generals don't take part in attacks, do they?**

45 On 28 December 1999 President Boris Yeltsin presented Shamanov with the "Hero of Russia" medal (see page 118).

A. Why not? I did. I saved the *spetsnaz*.

Q. **But that wasn't your job, was it?**

A. If your subordinates are dying and there's no one to lead them, then you must go out there yourself and sort things out. That happened near Sernovodsk when a senior officer sent in the *spetsnaz* and they were ambushed. The weather was filthy. I had no radio contact with them. I set off in a helicopter. I'd decided to fly out to where they were fighting and assess from the air what their prospects were. The lads, it turned out, were badly placed and further fighting would lead to pointless losses. But they didn't realise that.

I took a decision: the military helicopters would open fire and I'd go in under their cover. There, in the ambush, I saw a major who had lockjaw from nervous stress and the soldiers were demoralised. There was nothing left for me to do but take off my jacket – it has no general's shoulder-straps (that's how I usually walk around) – so that they could see they had the general with them. The scouts had flown in with me and they opened fire, giving me cover as I walked about, sorting things out and giving orders. Twenty minutes later the fighting began to ease off. Reinforcements arrived, the five dead and one wounded were evacuated, and I flew away.

The second attack I led was at the Tersk ridge in the middle of the war. We were pursuing the bandits. It was afternoon, about 4.30. There were still about 800 metres to the crest of the ridge. I noticed that the troops had stopped and couldn't move any further. We had to take that ridge! If we attacked at night it was ten times more likely that we would be ambushed. But the troops were tired and sitting down: some were chewing bread, others had opened tins of meat. No words would help. So I just said: "OK, lads, I understand how you feel, but I'm ashamed and I'm going to take that ridge myself." I jumped into an armoured vehicle and drove off. The road could have been mined. The officers who rode with me still shudder when they recall our journey. I'll admit I was also very scared. But I knew one thing: if we took that ridge before evening we would minimise our losses tomorrow. When I got to the ridge, however, I was only 15 seconds ahead of my men. They were in such a hurry – you should have seen them!

Q. **How do you feel after all that when you find yourself back in Moscow?**

A. I feel out of place here. Most of all I'm depressed by people's thoughtlessness. They don't understand that their well-being is not assured by the city's Outer Ring Road but by what is happening on our southern borders, in the Caucasus. I'm disappointed that I constantly have to repeat elementary and self-evident truths about many of the problems of the Chechen war. People just don't understand. I don't feel happy in Moscow.

Q. **And where do you feel at home?**

A. Among my colleagues. Fellow officers. My friends. I'm quite choosy about who I select as my friends and comrades and that's why, perhaps, none of them has ever betrayed me.

Q. **How many friends do you have?**

A. I have one very close friend. He was in the armed forces, but now he's resigned his commission. I've a couple of dozen comrades. No more. For me that's enough.

Q. **Do you today feel that our State has treated you badly?**

A. Not in the slightest. I'm aware that my country is in a bad way today. Now's not the time to rake over the past; and I feel an enormous urge to make a contribution, so that people don't talk badly of my Motherland. I always remember that although I came from a large and very ordinary family I was able to go to school and enter higher education three times, get a master's in sociology, and become a lieutenant-general and army commander.

Q. **To which of your parents do you owe your harsh character?**

A. Many of my qualities come from my mother. She's a Siberian and I was born there, in Barnaul. Mother was always winning the regional championship in cross-country skiing, light athletics and cycle racing. Her striving for achievement formed the main component in my character: never be satisfied with what you've achieved, but always move on, conquer one summit and immediately set yourself the next goal. I've passed this on to my children. When my son still lived at home my wife would say to me: "You're not bringing him up, you're behaving towards him like a fascist."

Q. **She was joking, of course.**

A. No. She would say that when she was really fed up with me. I'd reply: "Time will tell." I think that being a man means saying little and making sure your words and deeds don't contradict each other; the ability to withstand any blow; not to make a tragedy of your defeats but draw lessons; always move forwards. If you've started a family then you must provide for it; if you've got a child you must bring it up.

Q. **You're like a robot.**

A. I'm no robot, but I've set myself limits and a framework.

Q. **So what's the next summit?**

A. For now I'm taking a breather. Today I'm the youngest army general in the Russian armed forces and I find it quite difficult to get on with people who are over 50.

Q. **They treat you like a boy?**

A. Not directly, but I feel something like that under the surface.

Q. **But you're quite capable, aren't you, of telling them: "You haven't led an army into battle, so I don't have to take orders from you."**

A. That's happened, and more than once. I've suffered for it.

Q. **What does it take to make you that outspoken?**

A. Gossip and intrigue. For instance, the rumours that I'm supposedly a heavy drinker – you mentioned that yourself earlier. The intriguers among us are those with no professional or campaign achievements to boast about: they've spent their time behind a desk, working to please their superior and have earned the right to whisper in his ear. In recent years there have been quite a few like that in our armed forces. Several times they've dropped hints to me in Moscow that the war's one thing, but it will soon end; then we'll be living by their rules.

Q. **That's probably right. But the war really will end and then everyone**

will have to adapt and live according to peacetime rules.

A. You know what, let's finish the war first. Then we'll see by whose rules we are going to live! Things are not that obvious in Russia today. Our self-awareness, which is gaining a stronger hold on us, means that if the rules are holding us back they must be changed.

Q. **Don't you find it odd, that the anti-terrorist operation has now been going on for so long, almost a year?**

A. How long have the Turks been fighting the Kurds? What about Northern Ireland?

Q. **Am I right to think that you intend to remain in the army, a fighting man, for the rest of your life?**

A. I would gladly not have fought a single day. Believe me.

Q. **I can't.**

A. It gives me much greater pleasure to see soldiers on training exercises and manoeuvres, and know that all of them will come back alive.

Q. **Nevertheless one gets the impression that this war could not have been timelier for the army. No matter how much you now assure me you would happily never have fought.**

A. We gave a worthy reply to the sceptics in the West who had written off[46] our army: there is no one stronger in this world than the Russian soldier. This isn't an abstract idea, the Russian soldier, but quite specific. You will not find anyone less demanding or more devoted, self-sacrificing and capable of adapting to difficult conditions than the Russian fighting man.

Q. **But you can't hide the truth behind lofty phrases. There is a war going on inside this country. The losses are enormous. Is it worth paying such a price to prove to the West that we are still strong?**

A. Someone had to do it. It's fine to have these dilettante discussions, sitting here in Moscow. Things are as they are. I'm not saying that

---

46 In Russian Shamanov uses the idiom "buried" (*pokhoronili*), cf. Anatol Lieven's assessment, *Chechnya: Tombstone of Russian Power*, 1998.

because I'm a fatalist. Nevertheless the first and most important task has always been to preserve the life of our soldiers and minimise the risks.

Q. **You're afraid for your family. Do you yourself fear the vengeance of the Chechen fighters?**

A. Not in the slightest. I've already stopped being afraid. After the other war, I was very concerned to begin with. But you can't remain in a state of constant fear. That leads nowhere. So I said to myself: "Shamanov! You're an upstanding citizen. From this day on, don't you fear anyone else." That was in October–November 1996.

Q. **But many officers behave quite differently after fighting in Chechnya. They feel unsure of themselves, change their names, and don't tell anyone who they are.**

A. I can only answer for myself. I am Shamanov. It's quite possible that I might be physically eliminated, but I'm not afraid of that. Twenty-one years with the paratroopers have left their mark. Starting with the first jump, you must constantly overcome your fear, leaping into the void with nothing but a small bundle of nylon on your back and, to some extent, simply trusting in fate. You confront your fear every time you jump.

Q. **When did you last make a jump?**

A. With my son. He was on his first jump. It was the 153rd for me. Summer 1996.

Q. **Why did you jump then?**

A. It was my son's first jump. I thought it a father's duty. Everyone must respect the main principle of the army: do as I do.

Q. **You were there to protect him?**

A. No. I jumped first, he went after. You can't protect anyone in the air, anyway.

Q. **Where did you get such a strange surname?**

A. Honestly, I don't know. My father grew up in a children's home. He left our family when I was still little. Since the second Chechen war several other Shamanovs have written to me. In two cases there's some hope that they're relatives. I've now realised that's something I need.

Q. **In your view what would count as victory in the war?**

A. That I could go and visit my friends in Chechnya without any fuss or worry, that the buses were running and life went on as usual.

On 15 June the "Fighting Fraternity" of the airborne troops held an event in the Podolsk Palace of Youth, not far from Moscow. Former paratroopers gathered at the rather oddly titled "Anti-Sniper" evening, remembered those who had died in action, and watched the visiting dancers and singers.

Shamanov sat for a long time on the stage, shoulders slumped, hands hanging loosely, as a guest of honour. He sat motionless, as though he was tired and ill at ease; behind him there was a large poster advertising alcoholic drinks. There was movement and bustle all around, frantic noise and flashing lights enticing people to relax and enjoy themselves. Once in a while the former paratroopers in the hall wiped a tear from their eyes.

Shamanov's sturdy, powerful figure expressed nothing but his total and irreversible loneliness. It was painful to look at him.

MOSCOW

*

In December 2000 elections were held to pick a new governor for the Ulyanovsk Region. Shamanov stood for the post and won. This gave him considerable local influence and a seat in the Federation Council, the upper house of the Russian parliament, where he joined the other regional governors and republican presidents.

23

THE ORDINARY MAN DOES NOT NEED FREEDOM

Chechnya's New Leader

24 July 2000

On 8 June 2000 Ahmad-Hadji Kadyrov was appointed by President Putin to head the provisional administration of the Chechen Republic. Born in Karaganda, Kazakhstan, in 1951 he studied at the agricultural college in Sernovodsk (Chechnya) and at the construction institute in Novosibirsk, but failed to graduate from either. In the 1980s he received a religious education in Central Asia, attending the *medresseh* (Koranic school) in Bukhara and the Tashkent Institute of Islam. Since 1991 he has lived in Chechnya, becoming the republic's deputy Mufti in 1993 and Mufti in 1995.

Q. **There have been many different leaders in Chechnya over the last ten years – someone, you might say, to suit everyone's taste: Dudayev, Zavgayev, Khadjiev, Maskhadov and Koshman. Now you. Every time a new leader arrived, the people heard enticing words about the happy future that was just round the corner. But it never came. Instead, they faced poverty and violent death. What are the main tasks of the new Kadyrov regime?**

A. My task is to save the Chechen nation from the path that it has repeatedly been deceived into following for the last 300–400 years. Each imam who came to our land, once every 50 or 100 years, would incite the Chechens to begin a jihad.[47] He'd promise them paradise on earth, then abandon the nation before it ever reached this goal. I speak from experience. I was drawn into such a jihad. We shall gain our freedom, I thought, develop our republic and start to live well.

And at first everything indeed seemed to end in victory for the Chechen people. In 1996 the federal forces withdrew, we held elections and President Maskhadov had all the power in his hands.

I did a great deal to ensure this happened and consider his election to be my personal achievement. Without me the elections would never have taken place. After that all Maskhadov had to do was preserve the reputation the Chechens had won after the first war; the Arab and Muslim world were then simply in raptures over us. But Maskhadov failed in this, as in so much else. Gradually people lost confidence. He allowed ordinary people to be robbed. He should have sent away all the mujahedin who had come from abroad, but he didn't.

Q. **How could he? If you fight in a war you always expect your share of the booty.**

A. It's very simple. He should have told them: "If, as you say, Allah led you to join us then we are very grateful. We owe you nothing, and you've already stored up enough wealth in paradise. Off you go." Instead we let them take enormous liberties, gave them oil wells and they brought criminals here from all over the world. Finally, the assault on Daghestan began and the federal troops entered Chechnya. Once again Maskhadov did nothing to stop the war, though he was given the chance: I appealed to him, and so did Moscow.

I personally witnessed the phone conversation between Voloshin, the Head of the Presidential Staff, and Alsultanov, then Chechnya's Deputy Premier, who was actually in Maskhadov's office. "If you make an announcement that you condemn terrorism," said Voloshin, "then

---

47 An allusion, in particular, to the Imam Shamil, a religious and military leader from Daghestan, who led a protracted guerrilla war (1817–59) against Tsarist forces in the Eastern Caucasus. The Chechens rebelled in 1825–6 and joined forces with Shamil in 1839.

a meeting with Yeltsin can take place." Maskhadov replied: "I won't say any such thing. It's only the Russians, only Moscow, who need me to say it." It is my conviction that Maskhadov abandoned the Chechen nation after the first war.

Hence my main goal today: the nation must no longer be left stranded half-way; no longer must it be deceived by this "independence" and "liberty" that no one has ever actually given us and never will. Freedom, in fact, is something the ordinary man – and I count myself one, I come from a very modest peasant family – does not need. He needs work and in return a wage and security.

Q. **That's just what no one here, apart from yourself, possesses at the moment. You have a job, you're paid a salary for doing it and your personal security is assured by your own bodyguards, supplemented by members of the Alfa group [elite FSB commandos, Tr.] disguised as Chechens. You're taken by helicopter to work in Gudermes from your home in Tsentoroi village and then flown back again. Meanwhile Grozny is stricken with hunger and infectious diseases; there is no water, gas or electricity but a great many mentally disturbed people. In the villages entire families are now suffering from tuberculosis.**

A. That's the price you pay for phoney freedom.

Q. **You're saying that as long as you're in power the idea of an independent Chechnya will never be discussed?**

A. There will be no discussions, no ideas of that kind. Today all that people want is an end to the shooting. Simply not to be robbed or killed. Of course, when everything settles down they'll want to get back to work. And they'll need jobs and wages. That will be freedom for Chechnya. I take Ingushetia and Daghestan as an example. They're also Muslims and they're in no hurry to go anywhere else; they don't let themselves be deceived. But we Chechens, I wouldn't say we're stupid, but we are more warlike than other nations and have allowed our warrior instinct and ourselves to be exploited. Now I want to obtain a document from Moscow that guarantees that we'll be left alone for 40–50 years.

Q. **You want some kind of "safe conduct" from the Kremlin?**

A. That's right. All we have been doing for the last 300–400 years is to devalue our worth as a nation. The best and bravest people, after all, the most honourable, the real patriots, are the ones who go off to war. They are offered ideas, deceived by them, and they perish. I must stop all that. In this document it must state that our people are the main treasure of the nation and no ideas should be allowed to lead them off to war. This document is necessary so that, at any moment, any new leader who wants to start a war could be told: "You mustn't get us involved, we have lost so much already."

Q. **But you're hardly a pacifist, are you? You yourself declared a jihad against Moscow. What now? Are you revoking it? Are you going back on your vow to Allah?**

A. I declared a *jihad* during the last war. And it finished of its own accord with the Khasavyurt Agreements in 1996.[48] That's my view. When the war ended and we decided to build an Islamic State we had no right to fight with anyone else and infringe the rights of neighbouring nations. However, we invaded Daghestan, thereby going against Sharia law. That's why I have said we are guilty of starting this war. And in 1999 I did not declare a jihad. So there is no jihad today.

Q. **In the future Chechnya for which you now bear responsibility, what place is allotted to Islam?**

A. All Chechens are Muslims. But Chechnya should not be an Islamic republic. I consider that Islam should occupy the same place with us as it does in Ingushetia and Daghestan. They have as many *medresseh* and mosques as they need and no one is oppressed. To call it all an "Islamic republic" is unnecessary. We once described ourselves in that way and did everything that goes against Islam. What good did it do us, marching under a green flag? Did we help Islam? No, in fact we were driving Muslims away from Islam! We were pushing the nation towards extremism. All these Taleban, Wahhabites and other

48 See Chronology.

tendencies are against Islam. They were deliberately encouraged by those who wanted the world to equate Islam with terrorism.

Q. **Have I understood you correctly? You're saying that what Aushev has done in Ingushetia is a model for you?**

A. Yes. At a recent meeting with the governors from the Southern Area, attended by both Kazantsev and Aushev,[49] I said just that in front of everyone: "Aushev is a very clever lad. When he understood in 1991–2 what Jokhar [Dudayev] wanted to do in Chechnya, he broke away. Today Ingushetia is flourishing and we're a catastrophe."

Q. **Do you see Aushev and talk to him?**

A. Not since the beginning of this war.

Q. **Public opinion considers you to be fiercely opposed to Aushev. You are always running him down in public statements.**

A. Aushev must understand me. I want to save my nation.

Q. **But Aushev is also saving the Chechen nation. When do you think those several hundred thousand refugees now in Ingushetia will have enough confidence that you are really in control to return to Chechnya?**

A. Some figures, first. Aushev constantly talks about 214,000 refugees. But I sent my own commission to Ingushetia and they found no more than 115,000 refugees there.

Q. **Does that really make any difference?**

A. Before winter I want to move all refugees to my own territory and set up temporary tent settlements for them in the Sholkovskaya and Naurskaya districts. I'm confident that Moscow will provide serious and rapid aid. Not the present kind of support. Every day for us, after all, is like a year.

Q. **How are you going to deal with what people call the "Wahhabite" problem?**

A. There is no alternative but to root it out.

---

49 In May 2000 Putin appointed seven presidential plenipotentiaries to each supervise a group of regions within the federation. General Kazantsev was put in charge of the group embracing the ethnic republics of the North Caucasus and the predominantly Russian regions to their north.

Q. **But you can't destroy a single idea in someone's head, except by decapitating him.**

A. Exactly. Anyone who will not admit that he is wrong and will not turn back, will meet such an end. Anyway there are no convinced ideological Wahhabites in Chechnya, only people who have been misled or have sold their support.

Q. **What about the suicide-bombers? They're not ideological?**

A. They aren't fundamentalists but zombies. They've simply been hypnotised and stuffed full of drugs. No normal person would do such a thing. Islam strictly forbids suicide. Unending punishment by Allah awaits the suicide-bombers until Judgement Day: every time they blow themselves up, they will be brought back to life so as to be blown to pieces again.

Q. **Who is explaining this to people today after a series of such terrorist attacks?**

A. I told the nation this on television. [The television broadcasting station in Gudermes, where Kadyrov's official residence is located, broadcasts only to the population of that small town, AP.]

Q. **What are you today? A mullah or an official?**

A. I would like to consider myself a human being. But since I now head the administration of the Chechen Republic, I am an official.

Q. **Who is the present Mufti of Chechnya?**

A. No one as yet. I have already summoned all the imams and said: "I cannot be both Mufti and head of the administration. Choose someone new." For the time being they have not agreed on a single candidate. Personally I would like to see Ahmad Shamayev, the imam of the Shatoi district, as Mufti. His greatest merit is that he will tell everyone the truth. If need be, Putin himself. Every day he says what he thinks to those who walk past him, fully armed, knowing quite well that they could kill him as they murdered the imams in Urus-Martan and Alkhan-Kala.

Q. **Are you trying to talk to Maskhadov now, to make him change his mind?**

A. We don't talk directly: he fires a missile, I fire one back. We don't meet face to face.

Q. **What's stopping you?**

A. He wouldn't understand my reasons even if I asked him to meet. But if he wants to meet me, I shall not refuse.

Q. **Why don't you take the first step? What's the problem?**

A. What good is he to me? He controls nothing. Basayev acts on his own, Khattab acts on his own, and so does Maskhadov. He's got money but no power. The field commanders are a law to themselves. They come to me and we talk about them giving themselves up.

Q. **But when will Turpal Atgiriev give himself up, for example? It's now two weeks since you supposedly agreed that he and his 200 followers would lay down their arms.**[50]

A. I heard that I'd reached such an agreement from the television. Turpal's people certainly came to me and suggested a meeting, but I refused.

Q. **Why?**

A. I don't trust him.

Q. **What should he do to make you trust him and include him in the amnesty?**

A. He must not turn people against me.

Q. **Which other field commanders, if not Atgiriev, have already surrendered to you?**

A. Brigadier General Ali Sultanov from Shali. At one time he was Maskhadov's deputy premier. Ali was seriously wounded and went abroad for treatment.

---

50 Turpal-Ali Atgiriev and his men took part in Salman Raduyev's January 1996 raid on Kizlyar (see Chapter 3). He also headed Maskhadov's election campaign in 1997.

Q. **How many fighters did he bring with him?**

A. There was no surrender of weapons as such by his group. He simply came, we talked and he made an official announcement.

Q. **So his detachment continues to fight?**

A. Today there are only very small detachments. Only the big names remain. Even Mohammed Khambiev, who was Maskhadov's Minister of Defence, has less than a dozen men. If Khambiev announces that he's surrendering and we tell him to bring in his fighters he'd have no one to bring. And Khambiev himself has hardly left home since the fighters withdrew from Grozny. Atgiriev does not have anyone either. Yesterday evening people from Vedeno came to see me at home and said: "A detachment of 50 men in our district wants to surrender." I said, "Let them come." Because I know they're not Wahhabites.

Q. **They're part of Basayev's brigade?**

A. Of course. At the moment many of our fighters are waiting for a guarantee that if they surrender the federal soldiers will not infringe the amnesty.

Q. **However, there should be a guarantee on both sides, not just from the federal forces. Can you guarantee that the fighters will not go back to war again?**

A. There are no guarantees. Only words. Only trust. We have to trust people.

Q. **But no one wants a bullet in the back!**

A. What do you suggest, that they should sign something? Even if they gave me such a document it would solve nothing. For instance, I know that Atgiriev very much wants to end this war, he's tired and has been weary for a long time. He did not make any announcements of this kind earlier because then it was Koshman's administration here. Atgiriev and the others will be drawn by the name of Kadyrov.

Q. **If you are so sure of yourself then why do you fly home to Tsentoroi every night from Gudermes? Who are you afraid of?**

A. No one. It's just that my home's there, and I like it.

Q. **Are you hoping for a mass reaction to the amnesty and that many will surrender their arms to you?**

A. Yes, many will surrender because of me. But I won't intercede for some with the federal authorities. There are about 20–30 per cent that can only be destroyed. I can name them: the Akhmadovs from Urus-Martan and the Tsagaraevs.

Q. **And Maskhadov?**

A. Maskhadov is quite a different matter. He is neither a Wahhabite nor a Sufi. He's no one. Maskhadov must officially renounce his post. That's all we ask of him. If only he'd say: "Forgive me, I could not cope" – and then go and live with his son in Malaysia for good.

Q. **And they'd let him go?**

A. I think so, yes.

Q. **But who wouldn't they let go?**

A. All those whose names are constantly being mentioned. I don't want to repeat them and give them another free advertisement. They are in the media all the time, as it is. But they're just like the rest of us, they're mortal. They show Khattab with long black locks, armed to the teeth, and apparently invincible, but he fears death as much as any of us. He's not made of iron. Khattab also wants to live and that makes him weak.

Q. **What do you think will happen to him in the near future?**

A. I think he'll run away.

Q. **And Basayev?**

A. He'll stay, I think, and fight to the last. If he decides to take up arms again then it will be his last uprising.

GUDERMES

POSTSCRIPT

This interview left a strange feeling. On the one hand, it all made sense: Kadyrov is on the side of the truth and ordinary people. On the other, literally every word was tinged with petty untruths. This is clear to anyone who has spent a couple of days driving round Chechnya as it is today and talking to people. Ask anyone in any part of the country "Who is in charge round here?" and no matter whether you're in Chiri-Yurt, Argun, Shali, Grozny, Oktyabrsk or even Gudermes, the answer is the same: "No one is in charge." "But what about Kadyrov?" "If he were in charge we would at least have seen him."

Having taken Koshman's place in Gudermes, Kadyrov never leaves there. He is afraid to. He does not drive or walk anywhere. It is pointless to ask him anything about the economy. He cannot answer the most elementary question of that kind – for instance, how many enterprises there are in Chechnya and which of them are working today. Kadyrov is wholly engrossed in political feuding, in his hatred for Maskhadov and his urge to show that he has won and can draw the field commanders to his side. And he displays a fatal absence of ideas about how to ensure the most important thing of all, a peaceful existence for his republic.

Once you realise that, you can no longer accept his fine words about the "Chechen nation" and how it "must not be deceived any more".

24

A RETURN TO NORMALITY?

Elderly Victims of Government PR

24 July 2000

Only the very strong in body and mind can endure Grozny today. The survival of the fittest, and no one else. Everywhere there are ruins, filth, hunger and hordes of thin, homeless puppies digging in the ruins of what once were houses and finding nothing there. This is no place for children, old people or the sick.

Someone from the crowd calls out: "Did you know that the old people's home is back on Borodin Street? And they've brought the weakest of them here. They just want to boast that the war is over and now people can live normally again."

"What do you mean, the home is back? Whatever for? Who decided . . . What right did they have . . . ?"

From October last year *Novaya gazeta* engaged in a titanic struggle to persuade our government bureaucrats that they must immediately take steps to save the inhabitants of the old people's home: the hundred scared, hungry and totally impoverished old people on Borodin Street in Grozny needed to be evacuated to escape the bombardment of the city.[51] (The home was, moreover, also serving as a residential home for those suffering from chronic mental diseases.) Of course, no one wanted to do anything about them. Every official in Moscow cited the fighting as the obstacle; it was impossible to reach

51 See Chapters 9 and 11.

agreement with the military, they said, to create a safe corridor. The Chechen fighters then in control of the district kept raising the price. Time passed, the bombs kept falling and every now and then disturbing news about the dreadful conditions in the home would reach us. It became clear that if we did not act immediately then quite probably there would be no one left to save.

It took until mid-December before we managed to wear down the government officials and generals. Our newspaper gathered the money needed to pay the drivers and guides and to buy the petrol for the coaches. Brave officers from the Ingush republic's organised crime squad received the necessary orders. They inched their way towards the home, as bullets and shells continued to fall around them, and brought the old people back to their own front-line republic.

And now we learn that the old men and women have again been returned to face the bullets in Grozny! Someone just couldn't wait to report back to the Kremlin that "civilian life was fully restored in Chechnya"! On 26 June the inhabitants of the home were brought back to the Chechen capital, and back to the fighting that has never ceased here. They did not want to go and resisted, but the matron, Tamara, used every argument to get them to go back. (We already knew her all too well: she repeatedly deceived and misled everyone who had worked to evacuate the old people the previous autumn and winter.) Before they set out, she assured all the old men and women: "The building has been fully repaired and restored and everything is there again – water, light and food." They gave in. The first group of 19 returned to Borodin Street where, it turned out, there was no electricity, no water, no gas and no food. There were not even any staff there.

"Thank God they gave us some supplies for the journey," said a tearful Auntie Lucia. "We still had some noodles and pearl barley. Otherwise we would have died of hunger straight away. But that is a month ago now." Lucia (Lyudmila) Petrovna Malyshkina is one of the old women from the home. We were sitting on a bench out in the courtyard and did not dare go into the building. Empty windows gazed down at us; all the glass was gone.

"What did you eat for lunch?"

Auntie Lucia keeps silent.

"And just now, what did you all have for supper?"

"I boiled up some tea in a saucepan. And I handed out the last remaining bits of bread."

On the boards stands a filthy saucepan, found in one of the nearby ruins. Filthy hands, filthy metal mugs. It's almost unbearable to sit among the inhabitants of the old people's home, even out in the courtyard, even when there is a light evening breeze. In all likelihood they have not washed since they arrived back on 26 June and the stench is unbelievable.

We enter, through the gaping hole where the doors used to be. On the floor and the narrow metal-frame beds lie those who cannot get up. Someone's mother or father lies there absolutely bedridden. A blind old woman who doesn't remember her own name (she is in a small room marked No 7) immediately reacts to an unfamiliar voice and asks: "You're not a doctor, are you?" Without listening to the answer, she hurriedly demands, "Have you brought the medicine?" A paralysed old man lying nearby, Uncle Isa, pleads: "I want to die. Give me something, a pill, an injection."

I have no medicines with me, either to save life or to take it away. The old woman bursts into a flood of silent tears. No one has been here. Neither the cheerful new mayor of Grozny, Supyan Makhchaev, who is constantly shown on all the main Russian TV channels, nor Beslan Gantamirov, who is struggling ferociously to undermine all the others fighting for control of Chechnya today.

No one has any need for these old people who are no longer of any use to anyone.

Somewhere not far off heavy artillery is firing. Shells whine past us. Bursts of automatic gunfire can be heard but no one pays any attention. That is how night comes to Grozny.

Is this the secure old age they were always promised?

Only a sadist could have dreamed up this return to Grozny. There is just one question to ask Valentina Matvienko, the deputy premier in the Russian government who is responsible for social policy. Can she tell us how she assesses the situation: these old people, who are totally in the care of the State, were taken to a city where even generals on active military service prefer not to show their faces too often. She has the ultimate responsibility for all old people's homes. How does she explain this transfer, compounded by a failure to provide them with food, water, or clothes, when everyone knows perfectly well that they cannot work or find food and clothing on their own?

We have a word for it – but it's not one you can print. There are cuts everywhere in welfare payments. The country wants as few dependants as possible. But in pursuit of that goal it forgets that there are a few tests that very clearly reveal the moral health of a nation, i.e. how it treats the incurably ill, the destitute and the elderly. The history of this latest war shows yet again that we do not pass these tests. And it is a failure, furthermore, not of oversight but of our conscious decisions and convictions.

As we were leaving we suddenly had a hopeful idea. There is an army post not far from Borodin Street. Surely they could help? Policemen from Vyatka were on duty there. I appealed to them: help these unfortunate old people, share some of your food with them, give them the leftovers of tinned meat and bread. These food products can always be bought at army posts at prices lower than those in the improvised markets that most people in Grozny use. But the policemen stubbornly and persistently refuse to understand our request. Gradually we see that they are ready to sell, but not to give things away.

I pull out my last banknote and offer money. "Take this and go to the market," I say. "You'll be going there anyway, so buy something for the old folk: they can't move themselves."

But they refuse to do that as well. They have no desire to go to the market – for anyone else. For themselves, they'll go. Of course, the Vyatka policemen are not obliged to worry about anyone but

themselves and their own survival in Grozny. Of course, their commander has not ordered them to help the old people. Of course.

The Vyatka contingent told us to try a detachment of the Sofrino
brigade of Interior Ministry soldiers, a group from the Moscow Region
who are stationed a little further away. There was now no time left
to reach them, however: the curfew was approaching inexorably and
the army posts were preparing themselves for night duty. So nothing
is left but a direct appeal through our newspaper to Lieutenant-
Colonel Vyacheslav Tikhomirov, the commander general of the
Interior Ministry forces, and Stanislav Kavun, his deputy: Please, order
your soldiers who are manning the post in the Staropromyslovsky
district of Grozny to share at least something edible with the old
people. They'll die otherwise.

From this day on, meanwhile, our paper is collecting aid for the
elderly inhabitants of the old people's home who were so treacher-
ously carted back to Grozny. Readers who want to take part in this
effort to save them should record their offers on pager number
232-0000, #49883. Volunteers with experience in caring for the
elderly are desperately needed; they should bring everything they
need with them (from sleeping bags to water), to come and help in
Grozny. It would be so good, at the end of this saga, to say proudly,
"That may be the way others behave, but we are still human beings."

As we drove away, simple Maka ran after us, as far as her
deformed, trailing leg would take her and kept crying something to
us, raising her hands to her teeth. A filthy nightdress covered her
emaciated body and her head had been shaved to clear the lice. To live
you must eat and you must drink: that's what Maka was telling us,
though not a word was intelligible.   GROZNY

POSTSCRIPT

After we had left, I'm glad to say, the commander of the Vyatka
policemen, Kuznetsov, sent formal instructions, at our request, to his
subordinates in Grozny. They fed the old people. Thank you.

25

WEIGHT 300KG, VALUE 0.00 ROUBLES

24 July 2000

A real war has its own bitter and proud symbols. Like May 1945. Like the words of the songs that little grandsons know today. Like Grasshopper's eyes in *Only the Old Men Go into Battle*.[52] This war has nothing. We don't even know if it's a real war or not. We already know that there will never be a victory. It's like some crazy, broken merry-go-round dangling little zinc coffins instead of horses.

In December 1999 I went with Galina Matafonova to Paveletsky Station in Moscow to meet her son Lyonya. All that remained of this young man over six feet tall were some ashes in a little box no bigger than the palm of my hand. We met an empty wooden crate, in other words. Perhaps I should have written about it then. But at the time I was writing about another boy who died in Mozdok: he had been shot by one of our lieutenants and then they lied to his mother that the Chechen fighters had killed him. Six months later a letter from Galina arrived at *Novaya gazeta*. We had both wept at the station, but I doubt if she remembered where I worked. Evidently, she had written to the newspaper because every mother needs to preserve such memories.

---

52 In the 1975 Soviet film, lanky "Grasshopper", a teenage conscript, is waiting for his chance to fight the Germans but only the "old men", those with a year's service, are allowed to go off to battle.

"My name is Galina Nikolayevna Matafonova, I'm the mother of three children.

"My eldest son Alexei was taken into the army on 15 May 1998. He went out of a sense of duty and served for a year and a half. Every fortnight he wrote home. Suddenly there was silence for two months and I began to fret. I was afraid he was in Daghestan, but I reassured myself with the words of [Prime Minister] Putin: our boys would not be sent off to fight, he said, without their voluntary agreement.

"After two months a letter nevertheless arrived. He wrote to me as they were on their way to Mozdok. He told us he had been shown how to drive a military reconnaissance vehicle (MRV) four hours before they set out. He wrote:

> I don't know what will happen next. There was neither the time nor a good reason to get out of it. We only learnt where we were going when we'd been travelling for 24 hours. You know, Mum, I've only now realised that there's nothing worth doing in the army. It's just shameful. There's a young lad who's only served two months and he's travelling with me. He doesn't even know how to shoot, so how's he going to fight anyone? They're proud and fearless, though: "We'll show 'em," that kind of thing . . . the number of my death warrant is F-926411, MRV No 110, Convoy No 10115. Love to everyone.

The letter arrived in September. He had just over a week left to live.

"I went up to Moscow. There they told me that two women would soon fly to Daghestan to demand the return of their sons. I was to call them on 15 October. But the day before, I received a telegram that my son had died. The coffin and body did not come back for a long time. The boys from Alexei's unit told us how they were forced to sign a formal declaration of their agreement to fight. They were brought to the banks of the Terek River and told: 'If you don't agree, hand back your weapons. You're free to go. You can make your own way back.

You're Russian soldiers, wearing uniform, and you won't get back alive . . . It's that or sign up.' The coffin turned up in Rostov-on-Don at Forensic Laboratory No 124. I then first learnt of this terrible place.

"In Rostov I met with the parents of Andrei Pyrlikov from the Altai Region. He and my son died together, when their MRV went up in flames. Our boys were tall six-footers, but all that remained of them could fit into a small plastic bag. They wrapped camouflage shirts around these little bags, and added trousers and shoes, then sealed the lot in a zinc coffin.

"I left without waiting for the representatives from Alexei's unit, who, according to army regulations, should have been at his funeral. On the baggage slip that accompanied Lenka's body (that's what we called him at home) to Moscow was written: NATURE OF CONSIGN-MENT: COFFIN WITH BODY OF MINISTRY OF DEFENCE SOLDIER. WEIGHT: 300 KG. DECLARED VALUE: 0.00 ROUBLES.

"Galina Matafonova, Tver Region."

A Book of Memory

We continue to publish a list of the dead. Our *Book of Memory* already contains 1,396 names of those who have not returned from the second Chechen war.[53]

240. Sidorov Roman, lieutenant (Moscow Region), died 14.08.99.
241. Gafitulin Alexei, private, died 22.08.99.
242. Rakhmedov Ramil, private, died 19.08.99.
243. Alexandrov Roman, private, died 18.08.99.
244. Batrutdinov Ilsur, paratrooper.
245. Derevensky Sergei, private, died 16.08.99.
246. Zatselin Alexander, private, died 19.08.99.
247. Pyzhyanov Alexander (*b.*1981), died 18.08.99.
248. Stepushkin Alexander (*b.*1980), junior sergeant, died 22.08.99.

53 The full list can be found at the *Novaya gazeta* website:
www.novayagazeta.ru/actions/memory/memory.shtml

249. Chumak Yury, sergeant, died 19.08.99.
250. Marusev Dmitry.
251. Marienko Vitaly, senior lieutenant, died 22.08.99.
252. Shorokhov Andrei, private, died 25.08.99.

If you know people whose children have died in the Chechen war please give them our address: 101000 *Novaya gazeta*, Moscow, Tsentr, Potapovsky pereulok 3, or our e-mail address:

gazeta@novayagazeta.ru.

In the letter or telegram indicate name, age, unit number, home address, and the circumstances and date of death (if known).

MOSCOW

26

NETHERWORLD

Tales from Grozny

27 July 2000

The Courtyard

Klavdia Anufriyeva, 73, is blind and lives in apartment 85 at house No 46 on International Street. She has not washed for a long time, and her hair is uncombed. Today is a happy day for her, she tells me: there were two pieces of bread for lunch.

"But where do they take you to wash?"

The old woman does not want to say that she is not taken anywhere to wash. And the toilet is out among the anti-personnel mines. Going there several times a day is like playing Russian roulette.

"Why don't your relatives come and get you? Where are they?"

Klavdia tries from memory to repeat the Moscow telephone number of her one and only son who, it turns out, is in charge of the fire brigade at Mytishchi near the capital: "But you must say that everything is fine."

"I'll tell him what I saw."

"Not under any circumstances! He'll be upset. And he's a very important man, always at work and that's why he can't come to get me."

Klavdia Anufriyeva's fate is typical of Grozny today. Tens of thousands remain here because no one has come to take them away or even invited them to leave. Our old woman is living on what is a most typical courtyard in contemporary Grozny. (Just round the corner is Minutka, the city's famous central square. These days it's like a firing range.) In the courtyard they let down a bucket on a rope through an inspection cover into a hole where everything liquid gathers in such a heat wave, and they use what they find there as water.

In the middle of their courtyard is an enormous pit. It appeared several days back when unknown people dug up a body there. Now the children swarm at the edge of the open grave. For them it's like a sandpit. They make pies there and their parents are not shocked.

Unexpectedly Klavdia turns harshly: "O do shut up, Volodya! I'm fed up with your whining."

Vladimir Smola, a tiny dried-out figure on stiff reedy legs, stands on top of a pile of rubble. Above him the sky and under him, his mother. Seven months ago that heap of bricks was apartment 24, his apartment. "Don't shoot!" he yells. "I'm 51, I want to live!" He looks up into the sky above Grozny and just as we might wave away persistent flies from a pot of jam he tries to bat aside the military helicopters flying overhead. Back and forth energetically, left to right . . .

Mad? Yes, Vladimir no longer remembers that helicopters are not flies. He used to be an electrician. He gradually went out of his mind, beginning on 15 January 2000 when the third staircase on which he lived was directly hit. He survived, but his mother and two of her old women friends were buried in the rubble. Since then Volodya has lived on this common grave.

At first he searched everywhere for an excavator to dig them out. Then he went mad.

"Don't get the wrong idea, before this war our Volodya was quite normal." Maryam Barzayeva from 55 Lenin Street, is talking. "Let's go and pay our respects to Auntie Amina, Auntie Katya and Auntie Rosa."

We set off and behind us runs a crowd of the local children. They listen to this talk about graves and dead people and do not show any reaction at all, as if it were normal that the corpses of three old women lie only a short distance away and no one has dug them out; with the temperature around 50°C the smell is predictable. The children whisper to one another: "Go and call Yura."

Here he is. Yury Kozerodov. Swollen from hunger, his age is uncertain and if he did not carry his passport opened in front of him (as everyone who wants to stay alive here has learned to do) you could not tell his sex. In order not to go mad at the beginning of the siege of Grozny Yura thought up the fairy tale that he was guarding the city's MacDonald's.

"Where is it then," I ask, "the MacDonald's?" It's hard to imagine that this ploughed-up corner of the earth has room for a fancy fast-food outlet.

"Over there," Yury points at a door. He didn't even go down in the basement but remained guarding the door he had chosen. It is still intact, but leads nowhere. Yura, though, is now just another crazy person in the courtyard.

"Yura was quite normal before the war. He was a very good man. But it was hell here," explains Zinaida Mingabiyeva. She was once an "Honoured Stockbreeder" in the USSR and lives in the same courtyard. Zina is convinced that her mind, at least, has not been affected at all by the war, but three times she repeats exactly the same story: what records of milking production she achieved at the collective farm and how many times they sent her abroad to learn from the experience of milkmaids in the GDR, Czechoslovakia and Hungary. "I grew to hate eating meat then. Now I don't remember when I last ate some meat. How I want to eat, all the time."

I turn to Yury Kozerodov. "Yura, do you have any relations?"

"Near Tikhoretsk, but they call me a 'Russian Chechen' and don't want to take me in."

"And you, Volodya?"

"Near Smolensk, but they won't take me either."

"What about you Zina?"

"I'm even less welcome."

That's just one courtyard in Grozny. I picked it at random, by chance. It was to ensure that this courtyard lived in peace that they began the "anti-terrorist operation".

The Factory

Before the [1994–6] war there were 34 large industrial enterprises in Grozny. Some of them were working very well and employed thousands of people. What's happened to all that activity today? Where are the workers?

"I want to make steel, like I've been doing for the last 25 years. Tell that to Moscow. I'm no bandit. There's nothing I want apart from to make steel again, and then go home, tired after a day's work."

Said Magomedov heads the trade union committee at the machine-building plant, Red Hammer, one of those 34 enterprises I mentioned, none of which is now operational. Red Hammer was a State-owned enterprise, so it still exists only because the workers have taken the initiative and are determined to preserve it whatever happens.

Today Said is on duty at the plant. With him are two cheerful old men, Medi Saidayev and Selimon Tokaev, respectively a turner and a milling-machine operator. Each has worked for more than 50 years at Red Hammer.

"Lady!" asks 70-year-old Medi flirtatiously, tipping his pale blue skull-cap at a jaunty angle, "what is an honest Chechen to do? There's no one in charge, apart from the thieves, that is. So we're on guard here. Ourselves."

Said shows me the duty rota. Since 3 April this year, 80 of the 5,000 formerly employed here take it in turns each day to protect the plant from looters. Until last summer its eleven workshops were turning out heavy equipment for the oil industry. On Stakhanovites' Street in the Lenin district where Red Hammer is located, the fighters came on 1 November and the workers dispersed to their basements.

Then, for several months, the military bombarded the workshops with predictable results.

"Has anyone in authority talked about the prospects for getting the plant working again?" I ask.

"No, of course not. No one shows the slightest interest." Said becomes exasperated. "The plant belongs to Moscow, but they've not shown their noses round here. We demanded to know, 'Tell us, is it yes or no?' Hopeless. No reaction. Up there they're only concerned about who gets into power and controls the money for rebuilding the country. But we want to have a clear idea what's happening in the near future. So far it's our impression that the authorities don't realise that without jobs there's no way of saving Chechnya. The plant must work and that will be the best cure for banditry."

Said likes to speak his mind and find out the truth. But is there anyone today who still believes that what has happened here has done anything to stop the bandits? Strolling through Grozny quickly convinces you of the contrary: everything is being done to make the bandits feel at home and make life unbearable for everyone else.

Said strides along like a real worker, proud, strong, at ease – just the way workers were shown in Soviet films about the proletariat. Each morning he walks round the remains of the eleven workshops. But before anything else he visits his own steel-making shop at the heart of the plant.

"Look at this and remember it all your life." If Said knew how to cry he'd probably howl. "There was kilometre after kilometre of industrial estate here, packed with equipment. Dynasties of workers who won medals and decorations; it was all alive. Now, there's nothing. We're digging out the ruins by hand and making an inventory of all that's survived."

"What for? Did someone ask you to do that?"

"No. We know it should be done."

And this is also typical of Grozny today. Nothing now is being rebuilt in the city. Absolutely nothing. It is a silent ruin. All that talk

in Moscow about restoration work and rebuilding is no more than
an extravagant PR exercise, put on for the rest of the country. No one
here has seen it. "Work is proceeding," the TV assures us, but there
is no work. Or only to the extent that a TV report requires, in order
to convince the "necessary people" in Moscow that "everything is
in hand".

Do you remember at Easter they showed us the generals standing
in front of the Orthodox church in Grozny, which "had been restored
in record time"? If you could only see that church today. All the
"repair work" stopped as soon as the cameras turned away. And if,
driving past the endless ruins of the city, you were not told, "There's
that church the generals promised to rebuild," then you would not
even realise it was a church building. And do you remember those
stirring images on 9 May when a Victory Day parade was organised
in the Grozny sports stadium? The rest of the country was told: "The
stadium has been restored." The stands were full of invited spectators.
Hoorah!

Now here they are, those same stands. And here we are with
Mohammed Khambiev, a former construction-site foreman who, like
everyone else, has to beg in the city to survive.

"We were all herded in here the day before and they said, 'If you
work, you'll be paid. Start with the stands,' they ordered us. Then we
put some paint on the main building. The TV cameras came and
they filmed. The day after the parade everything went into reverse. The
builders came to the stadium, expecting the work to continue, but
no one was interested any more. The military didn't show up. Work
stopped. With only a few days notice we had been asked to work round
the clock and afterwards they didn't pay us one rouble."

It's hard to conceive today that the stadium was recently repaired.
It looks more like it was plundered. After the parade, those inhabitants of Grozny who are trying to rebuild their homes before winter,
without any assistance from outside, came in and took what they
could for building materials. Foreman Mohammed is one of them.

There are nuts, hinges, bolts and other fixtures in his bucket. First he screwed them in and now he has ripped them out. Do as you have been done by.

The Hospital

Nothing can compare, however, with the powerful PR surrounding City Hospital No 9 in Grozny. Every leading official of the health service has given numerous press conferences about the hospital's restoration after the storming of Grozny and the provision of the very latest in medical equipment.

Hospital No 9 is the only accident and emergency hospital in Grozny. You come here to be saved or to die. All emergencies end up here, from appendicitis to a stab-wound in the chest. Most of its patients, though, are people wounded by mines. Not a day passes without an amputation, because the main scourge of the city are the anti-personnel mines that were scattered everywhere and today turn up in places where they were not to be found yesterday. During June there were 41 amputations, not counting the patients who did not survive. Ilyas Talkhadov in Ward 3 was blown up on a route he had safely used the day before, driving to collect hay from the "60th October Revolution Anniversary" collective farm. The six neighbours travelling with him were torn apart. Both Ilyas' legs are broken and his hip joints were smashed to pieces. The only hope for him is Hospital No 9. However, there is nothing here today apart from healing hands and souls. Nothing that could distinguish a hospital of the early twenty-first century from a rural dispensary of one hundred years ago. The only modern equipment is an X-ray machine that works one day in two because the electric current is unreliable and the machine itself is old.

A diesel engine roars fiercely outside the office window. The military donated it so that the hospital could occasionally have some electric light. Abdul Ismailov, deputy chief surgeon of the hospital, explains why the engine has just started: the relatives of a patient have finally found some fuel and the doctors have begun to operate.

Another way of operating is described by Salman Yandarov, a middle-aged and highly qualified specialist. Today he is the chief traumatologist and orthopaedic surgeon of the Chechen Republic, having recently returned, after appeals from his colleagues, from St Petersburg where he had everything: a professorship, students, respect and a very good position in a famous clinic (not to mention a salary).

"This is my native country, so I gave up everything. But what can I offer people who are blown up by mines every day? The hospital is not functioning, it simply exists," he says. "For instance they often bring in someone who has lost both legs and needs urgent amputation if they're not to die. I carry in the battery from my car, connect it to the X-ray machine and take an X-ray. Only then do we operate. When the relatives don't have any money to buy diesel I again go and get my battery, rig it up to my car-lamp and operate. It's shameful . . ."

"But they've surely been bringing you some equipment from Moscow?"

"Yes," replies the doctor, who has the hands of a pianist and the manners of a gentleman. "They donated three operating tables. I can tell you, they are so out of date that no self-respecting hospital in Russia would accept them today."

To begin with I thought how senseless everything happening here was. If you look at it from the State's point of view, why scatter a vast number of mines around the city and receive in return an astronomic growth in the number of disabled people, who require tons of medicine, artificial limbs and so on? And then scatter more mines. And again ferry in medicine, etc. Now it's clear what the State is up to. Its concern for the situation is purely virtual; the only reality is the scattering of mines. No matter how much we want to believe the reverse, or attribute everything to our chronic disorder or thieving, the reality is that the inhabitants of Grozny have been sentenced to this fate. Evidently, the ultimate aim is to ensure that as many people in the city as possible are either left without legs – or dead. Perhaps this is a new stage in the "anti-terrorist operation", an unhurried punitive mission directed against one ethnic community, which now requires hardly any more ammunition, just the patience to wait for the inevitable outcome.

It all fits together. Why bother to rebuild if there is no fundamental need to rebuild? Why feed people if there is no fundamental reason for them to be fed? The only working excavators in the city I was able to find were those digging out deeper trenches around the army posts.

GROZNY–MOSCOW

27

OIL RULES

A New Division of the Spoils

31 July 2000

What's the fighting in Chechnya really about? If the subject comes up most people say, "Because of the oil." Opinion polls show this view is widely held. For the last ten years, with a majestic indifference, the Chechnya pipeline and the country's oil wells have ruined and remade a hundred thousand human lives. He who controls an oil well dictates the rules. Dudayev gave those who fought on his side their own oil well. Those loyal to Maskhadov also received oil wells. And what about those who have just been fighting now?

The tradition is being faithfully observed. The winners get their share of the spoils: the oil wells and those desirable leaks in the pipeline. The most important Chechen "cake" is rapidly being shared out. And the victors, the federal forces, are supervising the process and keeping order.

The Field of Miracles [54]

It appears no more than the modest entrance to a local collective farm on the far outskirts of Argun. An unimportant road leading across the fields. In the distance a tractor distracts curious eyes. There is even a man gathering something out in the fields.

54 Name of a popular Russian TV game show, taken from Collodi's tale *Pinocchio*, and often applied to the entire country in the Yeltsin era of pyramid schemes and other scams and rackets.

Now we see what could well be the gatekeeper at a collective farm. He raises and lowers a rope hung with red bunting. Parked next to his miserable hut is an ordinary *Zhiguli*. Nothing unusual, except that the car is full and four pairs of attentive eyes follow our vehicle as it passes. We shall soon find out who's here and what they're up to.

Actually, we already know where we're going. The road that once led between old pear trees to a farm takes us straight to the local "goldfield". After a rough ride of two kilometres we arrive at the Argun field of miracles. The Baku-Novorossiisk pipeline has been dug out of the earth and sprouts illegal offshoots in every direction. Day and night the oil gushes from holes of various calibres. It pours into natural settling tanks, pits dug in the earth to a varying width and undefined depth. In the local slang they are "barns". It is there that the gas is removed and the primary refining of the stolen oil takes place.

Standing here you can observe the evolution of the entire process. Over there are the old "barns", which are now dry and recovering. Further away are the newly dug and still empty "barns". It looks as though someone has been moving earth and several days must pass before the ground settles again. Then the "barns" will be brought into use.

The main "barns", though, are full. The oil there has a bright green tinge. This means it is ready and at any moment the oil tanker will come to load up. We are not fated to witness that moment, however. Our "farm" gatekeeper has only allotted ten minutes for our tour. The quiet of this remote spot, which shrouds the mysterious pits, is broken by helicopters. They circle above the exposed pipeline and our experienced guides advise us to end our provocative visit and leave now. The helicopter won't ask why we're examining this oil "hideaway"; it will simply open fire. There's too much money at stake to bother asking questions: it's easier to kill us.

That's not the end, though. A few hundred metres away we encounter the local minders. They are Chechen "policemen", disbanded followers of Beslan Gantamirov, who drive a white jeep without number plates but, of course, carry automatic weapons. The doors of the jeep are already open and they're about to fire. The *Zhiguli* had gone to call the police.

Thank God, a miracle happens. Probably it's just too hot for everyone. The policemen let us go and we speed past the gatekeeper, who looks after us in amazement: why are they still alive?

Such fields of miracles can now be found all over oil-rich Chechnya. The history of oil in the country today is above all a story of theft. The summer of 2000 is no exception and by now everything is back to normal. The pipeline illegally pumps out as much as you have the energy to cart away: this kind of illicit oil extraction and processing is well organised. Yet the most desired object is an oil well. The main battles rage around the wells. Perhaps that's why they didn't kill us for touring the Argun collective farm: it's very insignificant (by Chechen standards, of course) and only for the impoverished.

What is the Chechnya Fuel and Energy Complex?

Officially it is made up of nine branches, all of which are nationalised and belong to the republic:

1 Oil and gas extraction
2 Oil-processing
3 Oil by-products
4 Oil transport
5 The gas sector
6 The energy sector
7 Ecological technology
8 Solid fuels
9 The oil and gas research institute.

However, none of the above is working today. Or, to be more exact, they are not working to the benefit of the public purse. The entire complex is now illegally owned and operated. Oil is still being transported, but the pipeline is in the hands of a variety of criminal groups and their interests are protected by the Chechen police together with the federal forces. Those entrusted to guard the parts of the complex that are not working get rich by pillaging them and selling the parts off at fantastic rates. Although all the oil-refining plants are half ruined, the dismantling of the remaining equipment continues.

The usual pattern is as follows. At night when the curfew is supposedly in force and army posts should fire without warning at any moving object or vehicle, trucks loaded with the dismantled equipment and bearing Chechen number plates drive to North Ossetia and the Stavropol Region. Usually the columns carrying stolen State property are protected by a convoy of contract soldiers from the federal side. As is well known, they couldn't care less what they sell so long as there's a profit. This teamwork is believed to be very well established already.

This combination of federal forces and Chechen thieves not only scares off those in the Chechnya administration who answer for the fuel and energy complex, it also deters soldiers from other military agencies. The companies of the Grozny military commandant, for instance, are responsible for protecting the enterprises on the territory under their control, but they are scared of being caught in someone else's gunfight (something that has happened many times already).

Naturally, the official Chechen authorities have not just looked on gloomily all this time as the plunder flourished and grew. They tried to get the economy working again and make it function within the framework of the law. In November 1999 when the military were more or less firmly entrenched in Chechnya, but the fighting for Grozny continued, the Provisional Directorate for the Oil-Extracting Complex was set up. On 25 May, with Koshman installed as the main Chechen administrator from Moscow, the directorate was transformed into a State-run body, Grozneft. It encompassed 26 plants and 776 oil wells. There were attempts to bring all these enterprises under its control. They were unsuccessful. The local military commanders did not support Grozneft and, therefore, they did not support State policy towards the Chechnya fuel and energy complex.

Today the officially appointed head of Grozneft is Andrei Gusak. Yet he controls absolutely nothing and, since the end of May when he was appointed, he has not once visited Chechnya. He stubbornly refuses even to come to Gudermes to formally take charge of his assignment. Gusak is linked to Zia Bazhaev, the Moscow-Chechen businessman who died in a plane crash this spring, and also to another well-known Chechen figure, Salambek Khadjiev.[55] As the generals, among others, bluntly explained to Gusak, if he appears in Chechnya he should fear for his life. After battling tooth and nail, no one is going to surrender their gains without a fight.

The Flaming Torches of Tsatsan-Yurt

All the oil wells in Chechnya are today controlled by someone else, even though on paper they belong to Gusak. Depending on their real owners the wells are of two types: those that burn and those that work normally. Certain wells suddenly catch fire, at others the fire is put out, while others keep working steadily. In the last case, it's quite clear what's going on. If nothing happens then the owner is a respected wealthy man who can afford his own security forces and no one disputes his right to the property. The rest are daily the focus of an uncompromising struggle, in which firearms come into play.

If you travel south-east from Gudermes towards the Kurchaloi district, where Ahmad Kadyrov, the present head of Chechnya, comes from, you immediately understand where the capital of the local illegal oil market is. There is not a road in Chechnya where you cannot buy home-refined petrol, but in this district the oil tankers and stalls stand at every road junction and before each home.

---

55 Briefly Soviet minister for the oil industry, Khadjiev has opposed Dudayev since 1991 and for a year in 1994–5 was in charge of the Moscow-supported administration in Chechnya. In his early 40s, Bazhaev for several years headed Sidanko, the new Siberian-Far Eastern oil company.

We are driving along a concrete road towards a roaring torch. This is oil well No 7 (its official name) outside the village of Tsatsan-Yurt. For two months now it has been casting its evil orange-yellow flame into the atmosphere day and night. The nearer you get to No 7, the more people there are at the roadside selling petrol and paraffin. They are also to be seen in Kurchaloi, the district centre, and in Novaya Zhizn, a settlement in the foothills of the mountains, and the market is flooded with petrochemical products in quantities that greatly exceed the local demand.

Finally a heavy rumble grows ever nearer, comparable in intensity to the roar of a jet engine. Any normal person would see that you couldn't live next to this elemental force. However, the houses around are filled with adults and children. They are poor families and have nowhere else to go, even for a short while.

The burning oil wells are the fiefdoms of those bands that are not fully in control of their acquisition. When it becomes clear to the owner that he is not strong enough – usually his security guards are too few – then he sets the well on fire (not with his own hand, of course) in order to deter any others from pressing their claims. No one worries about the people who live next door to the well or the children growing up there.

Usually it is the federal forces that start the blaze. The villagers who live next to these flaming torches are convinced that they are encouraged to do this, or simply ordered to do so, by Chechen criminals. After the job has been done, the clients drill a new well a mere 100 metres away and set up their own "field of miracles" there. If the fire service come and begin to put out the blaze the locals take it as a sign that a new owner has appeared. He has either beaten or bought out those who were muscling in, and has even been able to order the fire to be extinguished – which costs ten times more than starting it.

Some statistics. In November–December, when there was fierce fighting, only three oil wells were burning in Chechnya. When the fighting moved up into the hills and the time to share out the booty

had come, there were 11 such fires. Later still, there were 18. By spring
the total had reached 34. Now it's only 22, but during the last few
weeks the numbers have again been increasing. Every day these
burning wells emit up to 6,000 tonnes of oil into the atmosphere, to
a total value of $1 million. How many tens and perhaps hundreds
of millions must be accumulating in those criminal coffers, if they
don't mind losing a million, treating it like so much small change?

The super-profits made by the illegal Chechen oil market are also
indicated by the fields of burnt fuel oil that surround all the wells
and by the "samovars" (mini oil refineries). After the petrol has been
siphoned off, as we all know, there remains the fuel oil, one tonne
of which is worth 3,000 roubles. But no one in Chechnya has any
interest in fuel oil and so it is either poured on the ground or burned –
they don't mess around with it. Naturally, these thieves have no
thought for the ecological damage they're doing, that's not their style.

The road from oil well No 7 is crowded with "samovars", small
mini-refineries that, like a distilling apparatus, consist of two cisterns,
with a burner under one and several small tubes. From time to time
the military raid these tilting structures outside the village houses.
They blow them up, shoot holes in them and wreck them. Impressive
reports are sent back to the General Staff about operations to curb the
illegal oil business in Chechnya. The generals applaud. The power
ministries announce to the public their latest success in the battle
against "international terrorism".

In reality it's not like that. The federal forces do not touch the oil
wells, the source of the bandits' lawless rule. They stubbornly fight
against the consequences and just as persistently leave the cause in
place. Perhaps they have their own interest? Are some among them
taking a share? You must agree that if this were not the case and the
military were ordered to set up posts next to all of the oil wells and
to only give Grozneft employees access, then . . .

The special oil interests of those in uniform are also indicated by
the lack of fighting around the wells. There are no destroyed buildings

here. Each side has protected these settlements, both the feds and the Chechen fighters. The federal forces would come here for "cleansing operations" only when there is popular indignation at the barbarity of these criminal groups.

For instance, in Tsatsan-Yurt the leader of the village is considered to be Ali Abuyev, former head of the local administration. During the last "cleansing" operation the federal forces took him away. Before his arrest, the men of the village, under Ali's direction, capped the accursed No 7 with an oil tank sawn in half. Ali is not a Wahhabite or a Chechen fighter; he is neither for Kadyrov nor for Koshman. He was his own man and was defending the right of his village to a normal life. A brave and decent person.

But listen to what the Chechnya police colonels have to say about him! He was a very devil from the Wahhabite hell, and a friend of Khattab, they tell you. So he will stay in prison for as long as the war continues. When you ask for evidence, they reply: "We had special reports from our agents." In other words, anonymous denunciations by scoundrels who want to reduce Ali's efforts to naught. And that was how things turned out. Ali was arrested, the well was set on fire, the land around was dug up for "barns", and "samovars" appeared. Life in Tsatsan-Yurt was brought under the bandits' control.

Finally, we reach the last link in the illegal Chechen fuel and energy complex. As you leave Tsatsan-Yurt, you find that the famous oil market has resumed its work outside the eloquently named Islam Café, just as before the war began. This is a transit point. Oil and petrochemical products are brought here and sold to wholesale dealers – right under the nose of the nearby military post.

Who is Getting Rich?

One of the newly appointed Chechen officials (he asked me not to mention his name) comments: "Every night thousands of tonnes of oil and petrochemicals are illegally transported out of Chechnya – and we can't afford to buy paperclips." Chechnya today is one constant and bloody battle for control over oil wells and illegal refineries, but the republic itself does not benefit one jot from all this. It has the resources neither to restore its industry nor to build houses for the homeless. Its oil is helping all kinds of people, but not Chechnya itself.

The crisis is intensified because not only has the economic chaos in the republic been artificially created, it is also energetically supported from Moscow. There is still not a single functioning bank here. Not one solitary legal source of finance. All the oil money is either stuffed under the bed or kept outside Chechnya. Even the attempts to organise a financial system are frustrated by the frank sabotage of high officials in the federal government. Moscow benefits not only from the lack of banks in Chechnya but also from the absence of tax authorities, courts and a civilian prosecutor's office. The super-profits from the oil business must keep flowing in the right direction, and no State cordon can be allowed that might impede the funds or divert them to the Treasury.

It is quite clear that everything I describe could continue only if two conditions were met. One, people running these deals must have protection. (The federal forces provide that.) Two, the bodies officially appointed to run the Chechnya oil complex must be unable to work. (Also achieved.)

So if someone assures you that the lawlessness in the oil sector is entirely due to the temporary inconveniences caused by a change in regime, don't believe them. The real problem lies in sabotage and a chaos that is directed from above. Thousands of lives have already been sacrificed so that the only things that change along the pipeline are the faces of the owners. Many lives have yet to be sacrificed on the altar of the oil revolution in Chechnya. How many? The answer can be measured in millions of dollars.

28

I WANT TO STAY ALIVE

How the Soldiers Survive

Locked Up

Fortification work is furiously under way at an army post in one of the most dangerous parts of Grozny, not far from Minutka Square. Military trucks energetically deliver one load of brand-new concrete blocks after another. The crane rumbles and the excavator squeals. The inhabitants of the neighbouring ruins quietly gather round, but no one approaches the army post. They prefer to keep their distance, sitting in silence on mounds of broken brick and distorted building panels.

Everyone feels uncomfortable: the soldiers working under the mute gaze of the onlookers; the people among the ruins as the barrels of automatic weapons point their way.

"I've only got one task here," says Yury Sidorov, the post commander from the Petersburg OMON, "to protect the lives of my lads." As he directs the work to strengthen their position he casts a weary glance at the gaping windows of the half-ruined buildings opposite.

"There's nothing else you're trying to do?" I ask.

"Nothing else. I've no wish to die."

Who does?

Evening descends. I must find somewhere to spend the night – there isn't a single hotel in Grozny now. We ask to stay at the post at the end of Staropromyslovsky highway, on the city outskirts. It turns out the Archangel Rapid Response Unit is based there. To begin with the commander is welcoming, but soon he has second thoughts and categorically refuses to shelter or feed us. He doesn't need any extra responsibilities.

"Fine," I say, "in that case give us somewhere in one of the protected houses nearby." The post is located on raised ground and below it stands a group of private houses that have not all been destroyed.

"We have no control at all over those buildings!" he answers. "How could I put you up there?"

Why did they fight this war then? It is now a year since the "anti-terrorist operation" began. Thousands of combatants have been killed or crippled. Tens of thousands of civilians have died or fled and vanished.

You can spend a long time discussing the logic of all that has occurred in the North Caucasus, but this is what it has come down to: each post in Grozny only controls its own immediate "territory".

Every army and police post must keep going independently and rely on itself alone, like a tiny State surrounded by enemies. All the posts taken together are like the water-tight bulkheads of a submarine. Camaraderie is all very well, but if one compartment catches fire the others must seal it off and have no right to come to the aid of their neighbours if the rest are to survive.[56] After seven or eight in the evening, every post in Grozny is locked up as tight as a bank vault.

Then the city stops pretending. Unidentified armed men come out on to the streets. There are a great many of them and they are everywhere, in their tracksuits and running shoes, without uniforms but carrying automatic weapons. Who are they? Whose city is it?

Well, some are the newly created "Chechen police", for the most part self-appointed. There are also the looters who now dominate

56 The *Kursk* submarine sank on 12 August 2000, nine days after this report.

Grozny's summer nights. Yet this is not the most important thing in a situation that is already difficult enough for an outsider to fathom.

"Why don't you catch them?" I ask the policemen from Vyatka who now man the post on 8th Street in the Staropromyslovsky district.

"I've no wish to die," says one.

There it is again, the catchphrase of the present war.

You will hear those words everywhere, like a password, a dozen times a day in Chechnya. From military men of any rank, with every award and medal, at any post and in any branch of the armed forces. That is the true Constitution for people in uniform who find themselves in Chechnya. That is the unwritten Statute that guides their actions from A to Z.

Do people think that way when they feel safely at home? No. Chechnya is not a part of the same country. And it won't be for some time.

So, you ask, what are we to make of those impassioned streams of patriotic rhetoric that assert the contrary? Don't pay them any attention. Let he who is not afraid to lie say such things. However, when you fly from Chechnya to Mozdok, back to headquarters and to peace and quiet, the officers meeting your helicopter joyfully greet you: "Welcome back to the Motherland."

That is the truth. And we must get used to it.

The Argun "Ministry of Foreign Affairs"

"We're foreigners here, aren't we?" many federal soldiers serving in Chechnya frankly admit.

Naturally, they are speaking "off the record" and don't give their names. The overwhelming majority hate the Chechens and are ready to repel their attacks any time of the day or night. Even when they see their colleagues, the newly re-established Chechen OMON, they mutter insults through gritted teeth. The life of the military in Chechnya is riddled with such ambiguities. But what happens next?

"International relations officer. The name's Zobov, Anatoly Borisovich. Deputy commander of the Chelyabinsk police combined unit," says the young man, by way of introduction.

"An international relations officer?" At first the phrase comes as a shock. You think to yourself, that's going a bit far. "What 'international relations' exactly are you monitoring here? With whom? The Chelyabinsk policemen with the Arab mercenaries on the other side?"

"No, with the Chechens, the civilian population. Our relations now are, in essence, international."[57]

Calmly disregarding my irony, Major Zobov tells me what his job is. He is not overly insistent, but he is completely convinced of the necessity of his work. Day after day is spent talking to the inhabitants of Argun where his unit is based. He goes to the market place, the local administration, and simply walks about the streets, although this is hardly a safe thing for him to do.

The major is not trying to change the minds of the local people: he realises that is impossible. He's just trying to restore bridges that were dismantled long ago, make some contact no matter how shaky, get acquainted with people, to establish ties, perhaps even make friends, if possible.

In other words, this really is the Ministry of Foreign Affairs in its purest form.

In such local conditions Zobov's ultimate goal is highly original: a softening of attitudes and behaviour, even if it is only within a single small Chechen town. Let them see that we're also human beings and then we'll all find things easier, since we've been thrown together in this way.

To anyone not living next to a war zone such efforts may seem something of a joke. Stupid, even. Naive and a little crazy.

Don't rush to conclusions. The introduction of an international relations officer is above all an honest response. It is a recognition of

---

57 Chelyabinsk is a city in the Urals; that is, a thousand miles northwest of Chechnya.

life as it actually is, not as the General Staff want it to be, and without any of Manilov's window-dressing. It is something our army desperately needs today. People have pushed aside their ideological blinkers and have realised that this is not Moscow, where you can chatter without fear of retribution. In order to survive down here you must not only dig deeper trenches, but also reach agreement with the people on the other side of the barbed wire.

Major Zobov's new job is one example of how the military, driven to the brink by fear, have themselves begun to seek ways out of the Chechen impasse. Paradoxically, and in spite of all the martial rhetoric, the path they have been tracing is unmistakeably political.

Never say never, indeed.

The place where we meet the major deserves to be described. Recently the temporary police department in Argun, to which the Chelyabinsk policemen are seconded, suffered the heaviest losses of any in the combined forces group in the North Caucasus. It was here this June that a suicide-bomber drove a truck crammed with explosive into the building at full speed. That's why the major is so convinced of the necessity of his work: it has been paid for by the blood of his comrades and he must do all he can to prevent a recurrence of that tragedy.

Unfortunately this local Ministry of Foreign Affairs is the only one of its kind in Chechnya. Zobov is unique. So it's too early to speak of achievements or results. But it represents a breakthrough. The officers have taken stock and realised that even if they pile up concrete blocks to the sky itself, that will not protect them if someone is determined to kill them. All it requires is enough explosive. So there is only one way out. You must look people in the eye, listen to what they say, and persuade them to try and revoke that death sentence.

Alas, the overwhelming majority of units are still very far from so thoughtful a response. A harsh and vengeful atmosphere predominates. An armoured train was blown up outside Gudermes and that very night the military carried out an operation to pacify and intimidate the population. Stupid and incompetent as always, because those it "pacified" did not cause the explosion. Others suffered merely because they happened to be nearby and, the soldiers argue, it doesn't matter, they're all bandits. Such a war will be endless. The victims of pacification will inevitably thirst for revenge and the next armoured train will fly skywards.

Meanwhile there is some chance, at least, for the men from Chelyabinsk and the people of Argun. I'm sure that Major Zobov finds his job a hundred times more difficult than those who take refuge in uninhibited vengefulness. For he is trying to change the course of a river, while Sidorov from the Petersburg OMON is merely riding with the current and heightening the fear all round.

School

We didn't just bump into Sidorov, by the way. We were sent to talk to him by the women living in the courtyard opposite his post in Grozny. They themselves were afraid to go. The Petersburg men are billeted in School No 18 and the mothers asked us to find out if they would leave the building before term begins on 1 September. The OMON men had no intention of going anywhere, but their commander was quite ready to "live" alongside the educational process in the school.

As proof of this, Sidorov invited us to tour the entire three-storey building. Whereupon it became clear that no co-existence of this kind would be possible. The former classroom walls were now a mural of soldiers' comments. The kindest of these read: ALL WOLVES DESERVE A DOG'S DEATH. The rest were obscenities from floor to ceiling, outlining in graphic terms what should be done to finish off the Chechens. It was a vivid textbook of ethnic hatred, past which Sidorov had marched as proudly as if they were tapestries on display at the Hermitage Museum.

The section of this textbook the pupils would pass in the school corridor as they went to their classrooms was especially elaborate and vicious. So children from Lenin Street in Grozny will not go back to their desks this autumn.

We discussed all this with Sidorov. He shrugged his shoulders and tried to persuade us that he was only a minor figure in the war and not himself to blame. But it's a matter of choice, isn't it? If we choose, we may find ourselves in an ambiguous position. It's up to us. We can also choose to find a way out.

CHECHNYA

29

STILL A CAPTIVE

Ongoing Trauma of a Hostage

10 August 2000

Magomet Tsaroyev sits on a chair opposite me, his face quite still, like someone who has made a final decision. He gives a welcoming smile and repeats: "I don't want to work or to study."

"Then what are you going to do?"

"Track them down and hang them, one by one."

"With your own hands?"

"Of course, that's the only way."

To anyone who doesn't know him, Magomet is a normal, modest youth. He is so like the rest that you don't notice him. Nothing would catch your eye if you passed him in the street.

Q. **What's the matter with the courts? Don't you trust the police?**

A. Not at all. I trust them, and they are now looking for this gang. Two are already in prison. But that changes nothing. Whatever happens, I must be the one to hang them.

[Every time he says "I" there is a particular emphasis, AP.]

Q. **But why?**

A. Because they'll have a soft time of it in prison. They'll never go through what I felt when they held me captive.

Q. **And you want them to experience that?**

A. That's all I want.

Q. **What will you do then, after you've hanged them?**

A. I'll live like everyone else. Like I used to, before.

Officially Magomet is only 16, but he has the eyes of a man of 40, as though a crippled older man has taken possession of him. He does not go to the cinema or the disco, he doesn't want to. For days on end he sits in a locked Moscow flat belonging to someone else; his mother found it in the hope of saving her son from the vengeful spirit that has possessed him. Rosa Tsaroyev secretly took Magomet away from Nazran in January after he caused a fight there: Magomet went out on the street and viciously beat up the first Chechen he met.

However, their hurried departure for Moscow, where the majority of the population hate Chechens just as much as Magomet, did not change anything substantial in his way of life. Whatever he talks about or describes, all his words radiate such a colossal hatred towards the individual CHECHEN that it makes you uneasy: just supposing he went out now, and the first person he met was a Chechen woman with a child . . .

No one would be there in time to restrain this young Ingush, Magomet Tsaroyev, whose family once owned homes in Grozny and Nazran. Everything was fine then and he liked strolling around the Chechen capital. His sister married a wonderful Chechen from a mountain village.

And then the catastrophe happened.

During the summer holidays in 1998, Magomet, a 14-year-old schoolboy, set off for Chechnya from Nazran. After the first war his parents had moved to Nazran, their shop was doing very well and the new house was already half built.

Actually, Magomet also had a purpose in going to Grozny. Like many another Vainakh[58] youngster he had been invited to train at Khattab's camp near Serzhen-Yurt.

He spent two weeks there. He learned how to handle an automatic

---

58 "Chechen" and "Ingush" are Russian names. The two nations refer to themselves, respectively, as Nokhchi and Galgai and jointly as Vainakh.

weapon, became familiar with a mortar – and then was given a short break before the next course of training, in sabotage and subversion. He did not go back to Nazran from Serzhen-Yurt, but to Grozny, invited by a friend who was also attending Khattab's "pioneer camp".

One evening he was watching an action movie at home. When it was quite dark his friend said: "Go to the store round the corner for some bread, I'm starving." When Magomet entered the building again four young men were waiting for him. Today Magomet comments: "So Khattab's people were even kidnapping their own. The only important thing was whether your family was rich. Nothing else mattered. I was set up: he told the gangsters about my parents' financial situation – my best friend at the camp!"

Then the car into which he was bundled drove into a courtyard and the boy was squeezed into a low basement cellar where he could only sit or half lie down. Life came to a halt.

During the daytime they beat Magomet, they tore his fingernails, slashed him with knives and burnt his body and, most important of all, demanded that he tell them how to put pressure on his mother "who didn't want to pay". At night he could not sleep for the hallucinations that hunger induced.

"They tormented and starved me. Starved me and tortured me. Nothing else happened," says Magomet.

Things were no easier for Rosa. The kidnappers, in contact with the family through intermediaries, demanded $1 million. The Tsaroyevs reported this everywhere: they told the prosecutor's office in Ingushetia, the organised crime squad, the Ministry of Internal Affairs and the republic's branch of the FSB. It was no good. There were a great many promises but hardly any action. Meanwhile, time passed and the gangsters' demands over the telephone became harsher and more relentless.

Realising that they would never raise $1 million, Rosa, who had six other children, tried twice to commit suicide. All this time the thugs were living somewhere very close. They knew everything that happened and when Rosa was brought round the second time they kindly reduced the pay-off to $200,000.

She rushed off to Chechnya. Several times she spoke on the main Grozny TV channel and pleaded: "Give me back my son." She walked through the towns and villages and met everyone who worked in the republic's new Sharia Security Service.[59] Finally, it was they who told her: "You have two choices. Either you give us money to conduct an investigation or you buy up another gang yourself. They'll free your son from his kidnappers and it'll cost far fewer dollars than the ransom they've set."

That was how the family lost their home, the dream home they'd been building in Nazran. It went for $17,000. They also sold off their car. The younger children went to live with relatives. None of the children were allowed out to school because the Tsaroyevs now lived in a world of constant threats: "If you don't pay tomorrow, we'll kill the little boy/girl." Rosa's husband could not stand the strain and had a heart attack followed by a stroke. Later he even began to show signs of TB.

Rosa herself tried to keep going. She travelled back and forth between Nazran and Grozny, taking whatever money she acquired in instalments. The senior investigator of the Chechen Sharia Security Service, Ruslan Akhmatov, alone received $11,000 from Rosa "for conducting the investigation". Another $5,000 went to one of Maskhadov's bodyguards who was pointed out to her as being very influential in those same gangster circles.

Everyone who took her money, of course, swore that any day now Magomet would reappear in Grozny. Rosa gathered up the younger children, and took them with her to Grozny, where, with the remaining money, she rented an apartment in the Zavodskoi district and hired bodyguards for the children on the advice of figures in the Sharia Security Service. She waited.

59 The Chechen security services (formerly DGB) were so named in 1997 as Chechnya began to redefine itself as an Islamic State.

I ask her why she had to move back to Grozny.

"So that my son would find me more quickly when he was released," she says.

The "investigators" (there is now no doubt that they were in direct contact with the kidnappers) made a show of taking Rosa to basements from which Magomet had supposedly only just been removed ("We've missed them!"). In her presence they enacted negotiations and bargaining. For as long as the trusting Rosa's money lasted, they kept up this appearance of strenuous activity.

Later it became clear that they themselves owned the cellars where they kept their own hostages, one of whom was Magomet.

When all the dollars were finished, her bodyguards withdrew, and they stopped taking Rosa out on such tours. She began to realise that they were leading her by the nose. Then in January 1999 there was an announcement one evening on Chechen TV that the body of a teenager had been found at the Central Market. All interested parties were requested to go to Hospital No 9 to identify the corpse. Rosa remembered nothing for four months.

"Suddenly I saw it all quite clearly: since I had no more money to give them, they'd return a dead body to me."

Yet it was not Magomet but another boy-hostage, whose parents had been unable to reach agreement with the kidnappers. Meanwhile, Magomet's conditions of captivity "improved". When Rosa lost her memory, his jailers even began to feed her son frankfurters. Perhaps, in their own way, they felt sorry for him. They certainly realised that there was no more money to be had and his mother had nothing left to sell.

It soon became obvious what was going on. They were trying to get Magomet off their hands, and feeding him up to ensure a good sale.

One interesting detail of the hostage-taking business. The very day Rosa lost her memory, Magomet was told what had happened to her. It was clear that those "looking" for him and those holding him captive were all part of the same gang.

In April 1999 a much-weakened Magomet was driven to Argun. The hardest period of his captivity, when he was held in a basement for five months and three days, was over. During that time he had been bought and sold four times and among his "owners" he saw many famous Chechens.

In Argun he was kept in a five-storey apartment block where the new gang owned several flats. From time to time Magomet was moved from the ground floor to the fourth floor and back. Occasionally he was allowed to walk around the room; his legs grew accustomed to walking again.

It was a sign that this gang were less tough and would demand less money that Magomet had only two guards, one of whom, moreover, liked to drink. This was the saving of the young Ingush. On 11 June one guard drank more than usual and the other said he was going to get some bread. Magomet realised this was his chance. He waited for the drunken man to fall asleep and jumped out of the window. He was helped to hide from the pursuit – they drove around in jeeps, firing their automatic weapons into all the surrounding bushes – by Isa, a young lad from Argun. He led Magomet to an abandoned construction shed and passed a note to his relatives. Soon they took him back to Nazran. His eleven months as a hostage had ended.

Now the mental torment took over.

Rosa put her son in hospital. His sight and hearing were poor and he had difficulty walking. For day after day, not trusting anyone else, she massaged his atrophied muscles, gave him herbal remedies to drink, and tried to distract him from his terrible memories.

By the onset of winter Magomet was back on his feet again. He played with his younger brothers and sisters, and walked about the apartment that Rosa had rented in Karabulak. She thought her son would now plunge hungrily back into his former life. Nothing of the kind. Magomet became more and more withdrawn. He felt worse, not better. In the meantime the family had been traced and the frightful notes began again. It was clear that Magomet's life still hung by a thread and that the gangsters would not leave the fugitive in peace – he had damaged their reputation by running away.

Once again the younger children were locked into their apartment (none of them had been to school now for two years!). Rosa used every ruse she could think of to raise money. But their life was hell, whatever she did. Realising what the gangsters were still doing to his family, Magomet told Rosa: "I'm telling you, I shall punish my tormentors. Both the guards and the kidnappers. I'm also going to find those who took all our money and did nothing. I shall make them give it back. I hate all Chechens. I shall kill them."

The first day he went out in Karabulak proved he meant what he said. It was then that he beat up the first Chechen he met.

Rosa wasted no time. She grabbed Magomet and brought him to Moscow, to save him. As a last resort she appealed to the Main Department for Combating Organised Crime and they understood her plight. The only people today who are really helping Rosa and Magomet are two officers from that department. For as long as they could, they kept mother and son at the police hotel and gave them money. Most important of all, they began to treat the xenophobia with which the young Ingush had become infected.

They are the only ones trying to return Magomet to a normal existence. They constantly talk to him, to instil in him those basic truths that he lost on his way back from captivity and to prove to him the elementary fact that not all Chechens are to blame for his misfortune. Two officers from the organised crime squad, and no one else. Two votes in the whole country for a genuine war against the gangsters.

Of course, psychotherapy does not form part of their duties; their job is to catch criminals. Who else, however, understands the reality of the situation? Another hostage is released and the whole country sees him on television; everyone applauds and celebrates the defeat of another gang, leaving the hostage alone with his broken soul. No one needs him and no one cares what happens to him now. The country is defiled by hostage taking and despite the war this profitable business goes on. There is, meanwhile, no service to rehabilitate the unlucky victims and return them to a normal life.

Yet no matter how hard these two officers try, it is difficult to imagine a worse situation than that of Magomet today. His family has nothing left to live on. Often Rosa and Magomet spend the night begging at train stations. Rosa has spent more than two years on the brink of a nervous collapse, she is homeless and sick, and she has left her younger children in the care of strangers in order to save her eldest son. She grasps at any straw, and often these hopes of salvation exist only in her imagination. Today she is convinced that she must get $600 somewhere. Then she could fly to Syria where very rich relatives of the Tsaroyev family live. They would certainly give several thousand dollars. She'll return to Moscow, buy a flat (but tell no one the address), bring all her children there and at last they'll be able to go to school. Magomet will come to life again and begin to work or study. Rosa is convinced their only chance is to never go back to the North Caucasus, and avoid living anywhere there are many Chechens.

And then? They'll try to blend in with the Moscow population. "We won't react when we hear Ingush or Chechen spoken," says Rosa. "We'll try to forget that we are Vainakh." Magomet nods in agreement.

A new happy life will begin? "Yes, and we shall gradually forget the nightmare that started in the autumn of 1998," she asserts. "All I need is $600, but where am I going to get it?"

MOSCOW

30

WE'RE DISPOSABLE

For the Attention of the
Prosecutor-General's Office

14 August 2000

Millions of my fellow citizens stubbornly refuse to understand what is going on today in Chechnya. It bears no relation to the propaganda in Moscow. The army is not being reborn, but collapsing. Ordinary soldiers are fleeing ever more brutal mistreatment from their officers – even "battle bonuses", now handed out each time they fight, are not enough to hold them.

Every week the Kremlin officially announces the number of men killed "in the fighting". On examination, however, this proves misleading. At least 85 per cent of these deaths should be attributed to other causes, such as when our soldiers in the North Caucasus kill each other.

Where does this figure come from, you rightly ask? These are the unofficial statistics from the combined forces headquarters in Mozdok. Moreover, I was urged by those who wear generals' uniforms to make this figure public: they themselves cannot do so for fear of repercussions.

What follows is only one of the proofs that this "85 per cent" figure is real.

On 7 August four soldiers, sent into the reserves, passed through Moscow on their way home from Chechnya. They had made a promise to their comrades who had remained behind near Kalinovskaya village as part of the 72nd motorised infantry regiment, 42nd army division, to make the Chief Military Prosecutor's office react to certain outrageous incidents, and save the lives of those still based in Chechnya.

With them they brought the following declaration:

TO: Chief Military Prosecutor's Office, Russian Federation

We request you to investigate the death on 29 July 2000 of Captain Andrei Katradjiev, commanding officer of the maintenance and repair company in Unit 42839.

On the evening of 28 July, Captain Katradjiev was in his tent with other officers of the company. Late that night the deputy commander (technical) of the regiment, Lieutenant-Colonel G. V. Borisov, entered the tent with soldiers of the reconnaissance company, woke up Katradjiev and took him away to their quarters. The next morning Katradjiev was taken from there in a coma to the medical company. When they started to treat him a dark fluid came from his mouth. He died as he was being transferred by helicopter to the military hospital. We believe this was cold-blooded murder.

Furthermore, on 30 July a conscript soldier was beaten half-dead in the reconnaissance company's quarters. The surgeon who gave him emergency treatment summoned a helicopter to take him to Mozdok since his condition was worsening. The regimental head of staff, G. Rezayev, categorically forbade this, claiming that the soldier was not unwell. Despite these prohibitions the beaten soldier was nevertheless sent to the military hospital. During the flight he suffered two clinical deaths. Since then nothing more has been heard of him. Such instances of brutal maltreatment of soldiers are not isolated.

The reconnaissance company in our regiment are acting like sadists and their behaviour receives the approval and protection of the commanding officers. Soldiers are being brutally beaten with crowbars, spades, etc. In some cases reconnaissance officers fire at the beaten soldiers using automatic weapons with silencers. A specific instance of just such an "execution" is that of Private Ilya Streletsky (2nd company, 1st battalion). Private Vladimir Demakov, a driver-mechanic in the engineers company, was beaten on his arms with a crowbar and bears the marks of an army belt on his back.

A new contingent of conscripts had just joined the regiment and they were handed over to the reconnaissance company for "re-education". Seven of them deserted the unit to avoid this bestial mistreatment. In recent weeks such desertions have increased. Lieutenant-Colonel Borisov himself repeatedly took part in these activities, but has not once been punished for his behaviour.

SIGNED: Former soldiers of Unit 42839: Vladimir Murashkin, Igor Koshelyov, Larisa Klimova and Victor Khmyrov.

In conversation they added the following.

Katradjiev's death was merely the logical result of everything that had been happening in the 72nd regiment (commanding officer, Colonel Igor Yegiazarov). The reconnaissance company are constantly out on active service and when they return to Kalinovskaya they believe they have a duty to keep all the remaining soldiers and their officers in a state of fear. The pattern is very simple. If the reconnaissance men see anyone drop a cigarette butt or leave their tent for a smoke, wearing only underwear, they drag that person off to the "cell". Between the tents where the reconnaissance men are billeted stands a welded cage like something you might find in a zoo. Offenders are kept there for several days in the blazing sun – this summer the temperature in Chechnya is around 50°C. The aforementioned Private Demakov spent 15 days in the cage after writing a report to his commanding officer about the mistreatment meted out by the reconnaissance men. Captain Katradjiev's misfortune was that he could not resign himself to the state of things in the regiment and constantly voiced his indignation. He paid the price.

"The senior officers tell us: 'It's because you're disposable'," adds Vladimir Murashkin. "I told them 'I'm not disposable', and decided to leave Chechnya. Others stayed there, however. Please, help them to survive. Stop this anarchy."

One very important footnote. These men come from the 72nd regiment. Formerly this was the famed Koenigsberg Regiment, which was awarded the "Red Banner" and was part of the Taman Guards Division. At the beginning of this year when it was re-formed it was assigned to the North Caucasus Military District. In other words, the 72nd is what they call a regiment with traditions, its own history and military distinctions. Not even these guardsmen can withstand the kind of war being fought today in Chechnya.

CHECHNYA

31

ELECTIONS IN A BATTLE ZONE

On 20 August a by-election was held in Chechnya to fill the republic's empty seat in the Duma or lower house of parliament.

24 August 2000

Kasim Getiev's eyes reflect his horror. He is both director of School No 2 in Chiri-Yurt (Shali district) and head of the town electoral commission.

"We are in a total state of shock," he says. "The night's events have stunned us all." It is difficult to meet his distracted gaze: his eyes are those of a tormented and persecuted man. "To be honest, what kind of elections can you hold immediately after a battle? You must understand . . ."

It is midday, 19 August, twelve hours before voting is due to begin, and twelve hours since the town was shelled during the night by every type of heavy weapon. Thousands of refugees from the ruined nearby villages in the Argun Gorge are still crowded into Chiri-Yurt. What they and the town's inhabitants experienced on the night of 18–19 August is described below.

Djamulai Djamulaev used to work at the cement factory. He is 40 years old and lives in one of the five-storey apartment blocks on the outskirts of the town. "I haven't slept at night for a long while," he says, "because of the shooting. This time I was out on the balcony having a smoke. There's nowhere for me to sleep anyway: there are 24 refugees from nearby Duba-Yurt in my two rooms. About 1.30 a.m. several men in masks carrying automatic weapons passed our building. They shouted out in Russian: "Everyone get inside. You there, stop. Lie down!" They were running checks on everyone before the elections. Federal soldiers, in other words. They went through the entire area. Most people were already asleep and in a panic they rushed out into the street. About three minutes after the soldiers had disappeared at the end of the street, a hail of gunfire began from all sides. This went on until dawn. You had to keep your head down all that time. Women screamed, children cried, everyone ran back and forth, trying to get to a basement in one piece. No one had any idea who was firing, what they were firing at or why . . ."

We speak outside the local polling station. Several dozen people wander around, all in a state of shock. Their eyes are wild and their reactions and movements are hesitant and slow.

"How much longer are they going to keep tormenting us?" asks Aimani Gabaeva, a refugee with four children and a disabled husband to look after. She is living in the same school where the voting booths stand, but she does not intend to vote.

"Why?"

"I don't understand any of what's going on in Chechnya. Not one of the candidates has come here to see us, to tell us when this accursed war will end and what he intends to do to stop it."

That is a typical response from a Chechen voter. The night-time tragedy in Chiri-Yurt is typical of the present election campaign in Chechnya. A wave of explosions and shootings has struck most settlements there, and no one knows why it began or where it will end. People frankly admit: We're scared to go and vote; the shelling could begin again at any moment.

The candidates share these fears. To visit voters in certain districts is to risk almost certain death. One of the candidates, Aslanbek Aslakhanov, is currently in neighbouring Novye Atagi. He had intended to reach Duba-Yurt, at the mouth of the Argun Gorge, that evening but was forced to change his plans. During the afternoon of 18 August the road from Chiri-Yurt to Duba-Yurt became extremely dangerous, exposed to gunfire along its entire length. No one knows who planned or carried out the night-time shooting in Chiri-Yurt, but it is now being used as a pretext for a new large-scale operation in the Argun Gorge. The roaring of helicopters drowns out all other sounds. There is a constant stream of rocket attacks on the mountains and the flames that leap up after each explosion are the main decoration in the run-up to the election. It's an appalling spectacle. Everyone is nervous and rushing about; the panic is obvious. At the last army post before you enter the gorge the officers sincerely advise us not to go any further: they're doing us a favour, they say, since the helicopters open fire on any moving targets. Only a few hours remain before the elections.

We can turn round and go back to peaceful Gudermes. But what about all the voters in the Argun Gorge (those in the Shatoi and part of the Shali districts)? Tens of thousands are entirely cut off from the outside world. How will they vote? How will their votes be counted and who will do it? Neither candidates nor observers can get to them. Only helicopters and armoured vehicles.

No one, though, can be considered fortunate in Chechnya. Those who have been sent in to "maintain order" at the polling stations seem little different to the bewildered and crazed local population. At the entrance to the school in Chiri-Yurt, which became a dormitory for refugees almost a year ago, young soldiers shelter behind their APC, filthy and scared. This is one of the companies of the Interior Ministry's 100th division. They have only just arrived to "guard the polling station". But they are a frightening sight. In their eyes you read horror and a total lack of understanding. The soldiers admit that none of their commanding officers has told them what happened here during the night. But they can tell from the way people behave that something dreadful occurred and that, as a result, their own lives are in danger. "We must stay here two nights," say the soldiers, "but we've no wish to die."

As I stood there, looking and listening, I kept thinking one and the same thing: where is our Constitution in all of this? What about the right to vote and be elected? To breathe and speak freely? To move about? Where is there the least sense, for the two days of this election, of normal life – of what the great majority of people long for, who have found themselves in this battle zone called Chechnya?

There is no hint of it. Nothing.

The situation on the roads in Chechnya is much the same as that in the mountain foothills. The main signal that this day of "free political choice" is upon us is that they have closed the roads throughout the republic. No one can travel anywhere even if their papers are in order – i.e. they have a valid internal passport and a residence permit: the army and police posts demand special passes that have not even been issued to the competing candidates or their official representatives.

The feeling of fear is most intense on the approaches to Grozny. The military invoked an order they had received not to let any cars through. Very occasionally they allowed someone to squeeze through the ring around the blockaded capital if they were prepared to go on foot. Since Grozny is a large sprawling city, the temperature is 40°C, and anti-personnel mines are scattered everywhere, there are very few takers. Those who do go have no choice – a dying relative, a child left in the care of strangers . . . Grozny is hardly the most welcoming city in Russia these days: today it has become a besieged and fortified election headquarters.

Don't imagine that these conditions are essential for ensuring "a normal situation in Chechnya". Quite the opposite – the strict controls actually reveal a complete lack of law and order. The proof is in the details. When roads into the republic were closed, for instance, they somehow "forgot" (at any rate that's how they explained this oversight) to provide people left outside with passes enabling them to participate as absentee voters. So how could anyone who was away from home take part in the elections? And where could people go to complain about infringements and abuses? Whatever is being said in Moscow, they haven't even begun to restore the courts in Chechnya. There is literally no one to go to if you have a legal complaint. The prosecutors today working in Chechnya (all of them military men) reject every application: "Appeals from citizens of Chechnya will be heard in the civil courts of adjoining territories." This is sheer provocation. The vast majority of Chechens cannot get to the neighbouring regions since they have no money and the roads are blocked. An ordinary Chechen stands as much chance of seeing General Babichev, the region's military commandant (who is personally in charge of all special passes), as some ordinary citizen from Tula or Perm has of meeting with President Putin.

Why do I mention the courts? On Saturday 19 August, the day before the elections when all campaigning was banned, Ahmad-Hadji Kadyrov arrived in Shali. The head of the Chechnya administration was accompanied by a guard of thugs, armed to the teeth. They surrounded him and trained their guns on the inhabitants of that small town, who had been called there to a rally. This travesty of democracy is easily explained: Kadyrov was offering his candidate to the people. He turned out to be Kadyrov's own nephew, Ismail Kasumov.

The high-ranking Russian officers who accompanied Kadyrov and Kasumov are fully aware of the law governing elections, but without the slightest embarrassment they urge the people to support the "head of the republic". This violation of the Russian Federation's Constitution by its "defenders" did not end there, however. Several hours before voting began, this performance in Shali was brazenly broadcast on TV that Saturday evening.

Whatever you say, our country remains a land of political slogans, whether we're being told to vote "Yes, Yes, No, Yes" in the 1993 referendum or to vote "with our hearts" in 1996 for Yeltsin. If you want to be as laconic about the Chechen elections in the year 2000 you couldn't choose better than the "Rape of the Constitution".

This mockery of human liberty cannot continue indefinitely. No matter how much they try to disguise the battle zone as an area controlled by the Constitution there will never be enough camouflage to hide everything. The settling of accounts lies ahead.

CHECHNYA

32

BREAD AND BULLETS

24 August 2000

Everything donated by our readers has now reached its destination. Several tons of clothes, food and medicine are today in Grozny in the almost completely devastated district where the old people's home stands.

"Now we'll survive the winter," says Sister Zinaida Tavgireeva. "We'll have the best dinners in Grozny."

"Could I take this coat right now?" asks Leonarda Zemchonok, her eyes twinkling. A tiny old woman in a threadbare dress, she has deftly plucked a gay red-patterned dressing-gown from one of the bags. What can I say? Yes you may? No you can't?

Most of the old people simply cannot believe their eyes as the soldiers carefully unload these unheard-of treasures from the army truck and APC. Ordinary people, just like them, had put together tons of donations – not the State which was directly responsible for their well-being and would have demanded several formal applications before sending a single dress.

On 18 August, about to leave Grozny for Gudermes, I call to say goodbye. Looking better and happier, the old women come out in their new clothes to meet me: they are about to enjoy their first lavish dinner: "Your rice and raisins, cooked in your oil." We embrace.

But I must mention some strange things as well.

*

The military base at Khankala is only half an hour away from Grozny. The trip from Moscow to Khankala takes time and required several hours of loading and unloading. Yet thanks to local attitudes it was much harder to transport our cargo on this last leg of the journey.

From our very first appeal to help the old people in Grozny we were supported by Anatoly Kvashnin, head of the General Staff, his deputy Valery Manilov, and the deputy minister of defence Vitaly Azarov. Thanks to their efforts our humanitarian cargo reached a military aerodrome in an air-force plane and helicopter. Major Gennady Dzyuba of the Ministry of Defence's press service was ordered to accompany our cargo to its destination.

Alas, the further we got from Moscow and from senior officials the more the emphasis shifted. Major Dzyuba did not have the faintest desire to go to Grozny. Every half-hour he did not fail to remind us, "Soldiers shouldn't risk their lives for your rice, let alone for you." Mockingly, he gave us a lecture on the "tasks of the counter-terrorist operation" which, he said, had nothing to do with the old people's home.

Finally he declared that my newspaper had only undertaken this operation, thereby burdening an officer "from the central apparatus" such as himself with our "foolishness", in order to boost its sales. It was a cheap and outrageous accusation and there was nothing to do but publicly call Major Dzyuba a "swine".

He hastily began preparations to fly back to Moscow and denounce us. He left for the capital without even entering the old people's home, thereby disobeying a direct order. "You won't forget me! I'll see you lose your accreditation here!"

Are we afraid of losing the right to work in Chechnya? Most certainly, because we know there are too many people there who need our help and can place no trust in the likes of Major Dzyuba.

So who did deliver our consignment? Officers and soldiers who had not received any orders to do so. They were moved by the plight of these lonely old people and saw that the inaction and insolence of the major threatened to wreck the efforts of hundreds of normal people. Many officers in Khankala and Grozny came up and offered their help. They had had no instructions from the General Staff, but simply learned what the problem was. While Dzyuba intrigued against us, they got on with the job. "What are your names?" I asked. "Tell me, and I'll publicly thank you in our newspaper." "We don't need any thanks," they replied.

In particular we have to thank Nikolai Ivanovich, military commandant of the district where the home is located, who became the guardian angel of our operation. He uttered no grand phrases about the "tasks of the counter-terrorist operation", but quietly and steadily worked beyond the call of duty. His military trucks and APC went to Khankala and brought back the supplies for the old people. His soldiers put their weapons aside and, under the command of Captain Dmitry Kharin, shifted tons of humanitarian aid without breaking for a cigarette or needing any encouragement.

As we left, the home's deputy director, Satsit Alieva, said with tears in her eyes: "Tell everyone who did this to help us that they will certainly go to heaven."

You think she's exaggerating? Not at all. It's just that no one brings anything to this home – apart from promises. Hunger, sickness and impoverishment reign here. The readers of *Novaya gazeta* are the only ones to provide these old people, abandoned by the State, with the bare minimum essential for their survival. If not me, then who? That's exactly the situation here.

GROZNY–MOSCOW

POSTSCRIPT

What brilliant mind decided to shift these lonely old people back to Grozny, you may ask, when even army officers avoid going there? Well, it was the idea of Nikolai Koshman, the former deputy premier

and plenipotentiary representative of the Russian Federation government in Chechnya.

When his own position as Moscow's chief deputy in the republic
was weakening he decided to engage in some PR. To show the
decision-makers in the capital that, under his wise leadership, civilian
life in Grozny was "getting back to normal" he sent an emissary to
Ingushetia: Magomed Vakhaev, the head of his administration's social
welfare department. Vakhaev assured the elderly that ideal conditions
had now been created for them in Grozny, and deceived them into
returning. They fell victims to a cheap trick in Koshman's struggle
to retain power. Koshman was replaced nevertheless and everyone
completely forgot about these starving old men and women.

33

BACK TO SCHOOL

28 August 2000

Ramisa Barzukaeva regards the world through the eyes of an incorrigible and determined idealist. "I hope you understand," she repeats several times, "if you promise children something then your word is sacred! How can you deceive them?"

With a gesture that betrays the schoolteacher in any crowd, she pats her immaculately combed hair (the sight makes it hard to believe there's a war going on), and sniffs back the tears of frustration that have begun to flow. "I can tell you agree. You must never go back on your word to a child."

She is categorical and insistent. Without pausing she adds, like a first-year schoolchild: "So you will tell them that in Moscow. How much longer must we put up with this?"

The Chelyabinsk Daydream

It would be hard to imagine a greater discrepancy between this lofty talk of sacred vows and the place and time in which I heard them. Ramisa is director of School No 1 in Argun. The scars of war and an atmosphere of heightened tension are everywhere. Argun is an uneasy town where the military, fearing mines, drive about at the same crazy speed as in Grozny. To go to school you must thread your way past

the concrete tank obstructions on which someone has written DJIHAD
(in Latin transcription) and the sour warning MINES. Of the three
buildings that made up the best school in the town, only the middle
block now remains standing in lonely isolation.

On 1 September, 1,070 schoolchildren will make their way past
the concrete blocks and the ruins. The rebuilding of Chechnya's
wrecked schools made a modest start in June, then stopped. The
teachers were informed that only 2.5 per cent of the funds to be sent
from Moscow, in accordance with government decree 1075 (27 July
2000), had been received. No building materials or salaries had
arrived. The workers hung around for a while and then disappeared.
The devastation remained.

Yet it was not this deceit of which Ramisa was speaking. Physical
surroundings, though important, are not the most essential thing. You
could become a renowned scholar, she is convinced, studying in a
cellar. What she has to tell is far more alarming: how the last bridges of
trust linking "us" and "them" are collapsing. On the one hand, there
are the young Chechens who have been brutalised by this war and
collectively labelled bandits; on the other, the country that with bombs
and missiles demanded their love.

In March the governor of the Chelyabinsk Region, Pyotr Sumin,
came to Argun, buoyed by the favourable political moment and the
imminent presidential elections. Chechnya was then getting an extra
spring feed from the federal authorities and heroic tours of the republic by the country's highest officials were in fashion. Chelyabinsk
would support and nurture the rebirth of Argun, Sumin loudly
declared. He was given a warm reception by the teaching staff and
older classes at School No 1 and the elders of the town were invited.
For several hours the boys and girls told the governor things he had
never heard on TV. Their chief desire was to have the right to study
like all other children in Russia, they said, to pore over the same textbooks, and not to remember how the shrapnel whistles after a mine
explodes. Governor Sumin was staggered by this reception, vowed to

the children that he would do everything to help and, before all else, would send all the equipment needed to start a computer class. The cameras recorded the governor's heroic face, the moved reaction of the elders, the tears of the girls and the thankful eyes of the boys.

By summer the governor had not yet managed to keep his promise. Ramisa patiently waited, however, and explained to her older students that it was a time-consuming, dangerous and tiresome business sending so much equipment to Chechnya today. That was the cause of the delay. But in July tragedy struck. A truck filled with explosives drove straight into the barracks in Argun where policemen from Chelyabinsk were stationed, and dozens died. Governor Sumin went on TV and declared: "I am terminating all aid to Argun." And this time, he kept his word.

"I wrote a letter to the governor," says Ramisa. "I wasn't particularly insistent. All I did was point out: 'Even the most disreputable Chechen would keep his word if he promised something to a child.' I won't pester him further, but you can see that any trust in Russia, of which little already remains, is being lost. And that's the most important thing of all. Whether there will be another war depends on how the children of Chechnya are raised. Will they grow up ready to fight or will they be strangers to violence? Why doesn't the Chelyabinsk governor realise this? And all the others? Russia has abandoned us again. There is absolutely no concern for schools or the next generation.

"We have been placed in a quite impossible position. No one, of course, gave us any particular authority in the matter, but we took it upon ourselves to tell our pupils every day that they are also the children of Russia. We know that if they are not aware of this, there will be no future, either for you or for us."

An Undecorated Heroine

There is no more astonishing group of people today in Chechnya than the teachers. There are about a thousand of them, and they are all obsessed by their mission to save the nation from ignorance, extinction and banditry. Ramisa is not alone.

In Moscow they were just beginning to think how to counter religious extremism in the Caucasus, and pretending not to see Basayev's "business" activities and Khattab's excesses, when this modest school director, Ramisa Barzukaeva, bravely and single-handedly took a stance against the insolence of the " bearded ones" flooding into Argun. Confronted by the fighters' automatic weapons, this small woman did not flinch but insisted on her pupils' right to a secular education. It was Ramisa, not the Russian minister of education who stood up to a dozen undisciplined fighters at the school entrance and said: "No, you are not going to get your way. We shall continue teaching in Russian and not in Arabic. The girls will continue to come to school!"

At a time when many men fled Argun and Chechnya rather than face this challenge, Ramisa stayed behind.

"But why? You have a daughter in Moscow, haven't you?"

"The children and their parents came to me and begged me to stay. They said: 'If you stay, so will we.' I couldn't abandon them."

For three years she has lived in danger of her life, for the sake of her students. She has shaped their thoughts and feelings and has brought all of her skills to bear on their distorted perception of the world. It was her duty as a teacher to give everything she had for the sake of the future.

Her heroism can be compared to that of submariners who contain the nuclear reactor at the heart of their vessel at the cost of their own lives. She personally saved hundreds of young lads from drifting into Khattab's camp, from becoming infected with rabid extremism and turning into cold-blooded killers. Who in the end was the most concerned to end the senseless slaughter? Ramisa, or the governor of the Chelyabinsk Region?

"I don't need any medals. I want computers for the children, and a decent school. So they have everything that others have in Russia today," says Ramisa. "I want my children to believe that they are not outcasts and are needed by the country. I want my pupils to try and get into Russian higher education when they leave school, and not go and study in Turkey. I think they just cannot appreciate in Moscow how very important that is today for Chechnya, and for the future of Russia! But, you know, I shan't now accept a single computer from Governor Sumin. He did not trust us then, though he put on a show of doing so. I want respect not humiliation. There's a world of difference between help and handouts."

The Omsk Cadets

Last winter Chechnya was shaken by a scandalous story.

The Ministry of Defence issued a challenge: select your 15 best teenagers and we'll give them places at the Omsk military academy. Chechnya really did send its finest youths to the distant Siberian city. The elders sent off their grandsons with words that anyone now capable of thinking in Chechnya ponders and repeats: "Study, and some day you will certainly be an honour to your homeland and prove that we are the equal of the other nations in Russia."

The Minister of Defence himself received this delegation of future cadets. There were many fine words, promises and wishes; parting advice, hopes and TV cameras. During his first days in Omsk, Amirkhan Shamurzayev wrote home:

> Mama, we are being very well taught here and the boys are well disciplined. Just what is needed. They've also given me my uniform. I'll come home in it and you won't recognise me!

Amirkhan is a typical teacher's son. He is more educated and well brought up than his contemporaries. His mother, Zulai Shamurzayeva, has taught Chechen Language and Literature all her adult life at School No 1 in Gudermes – she is as much a slave to her profession as Ramisa in Argun: "I don't talk about the war during our lessons. The children can see all that with their own eyes. I talk about friendship between individuals and nations, about justice and camaraderie."

Q. **And do your pupils understand what you're saying?**

A. I speak in such a way that they do. But it's going to be more difficult now, after this business in Omsk. I thought Amirkhan had been unbelievably lucky. He'd got out of this hell, I thought, and now everything depended on him. But soon the tone of his letters from Omsk changed. No one used our boys' names at the barracks but – if you'll forgive the expression – they called them "black-arsed . . ." – you know what I mean. No one even tried to wash away the offensive slogans in the toilet: NIGGERS OUT OF OMSK!

Soon most of the Chechen youths had returned home. Only four remained, among them my son. He said he would bear any insult for the sake of his education. And he was patient. But the evening before the end-of-year exams in May, the corporal called in these four and announced: "Whatever happens, Chechens won't study here!" And he wouldn't let them sit the exam.

Those young men had gone there with the best of intentions! They had a single dream: to be like all other children in Russia. On 25 May they were put on a train to Rostov, each given 165 roubles and sent back across the entire country without any papers. The boys only reached home on 9 June, because they were unable to leave Rostov without money or documents. They starved there, sleeping nights at the railway station, and asked the military commandant's office for help – but it was quite hopeless.

Recently the military commandant for Chechnya again spoke on TV: "Chechen lads are studying in Omsk. Now they're on holiday and soon they will return there . . ." Who was he trying to fool?

All three of my sons wanted to join the army so much. Now they don't. There is no way I can convince them that what happened to Amirkhan is not part of the system, but an unfortunate combination of circumstances. I tell them he just happened to meet bad people, the majority of Russians are kind – but my sons don't listen to me. They trust Russia less than they did during the war.

Q. **Has the business with Amirkhan changed the nature of your conversations with your pupils? Perhaps you won't begin the school year on 1 September with the "lesson about peace" and talk to them about friendship and justice?** [60]

A. I find it hard to bear, but I haven't changed. Chechnya's future lies only in friendship with Russia. I am hoping that on 1 September during the "lesson about peace" in Omsk the teachers will tell their children exactly the same: that the future of Russia lies only in friendship with Chechnya.

Q. **Despite everything that has happened?**

A. Yes.

So says Zulai. This woman who is living a semi-starved existence surrounded by the sound of gunfire every night, who has been mortally offended on behalf of her rejected and humiliated son, and who must borrow a pair of shoes from someone else on 1 September so as not to attend the festival of learning in her household slippers, possesses a certainty about the matter that I, for one, do not feel.

An Iron Response

We're walking down a long corridor, its walls covered with deep cracks left by shooting and bombardment. At the end is a small locked room where the equipment that has just arrived for the new school year is being kept. A pensive Vakhit Ganshuev, director of School No 1

60 The "lesson about peace" at the beginning of the school year was a Soviet innovation of the mid-1970s.

in Ilaskhan-Yurt (formerly Beloreche), and Khasa Baisultanov, the school's bustling manager, say I must not to be too surprised by what I see.

In accordance with government edict No 1075, as they are well aware, the salaries of Chechnya's teachers, a total of 1,445 million roubles, have been transferred via banks in Mozdok. So has their holiday pay of 1,209 million roubles; 23,325 million roubles for rebuilding schools; 7 million roubles for classroom furniture, and so on . . . So where is it all?

"There it is, our seven million," announces Vakhit Ganshuev with a cosmic sadness.

A child's hand has written THE LAST CRY OF THE TITANIC on the door that Khasa Baisultanov unlocks. Ganshuev gives an understanding smile and shoves the creaking wooden panel aside. There are 19 tables and 38 chairs in there. That is exactly how much the Russian government sent to Ilaskhan-Yurt and its 617 schoolchildren. That is not the full extent of their sorrow, however: poverty is not a vice, after all. It is the quite conscious mockery that is the true misfortune here. Without additional explanation a person would hardly realise that the unloaded pieces of metal, still in their paper wrapping, are indeed tables and chairs. Because these are only the frames: there is not a single wooden back, seat or cover.

"Nor did they send bolts, nuts or screws," adds Baisultanov.

"Our school was one of the worst affected. Our village was one of the worst affected. We've been through everything," says the director. "Half our children have developed heart problems since the war. They often faint. Why humiliate us with such handouts? They'd do better to send nothing."

The same picture can be seen in all of Chechnya's schools. Everywhere the directors, teachers and children have sad faces. Deep moats or trenches have been dug around the school playgrounds to keep out armed men and provide somewhere to hide. How can we cross that gulf?

*

On the eve of a new school year it seems almost inevitable that the coming generation will take Russia and Chechnya to war again in 2015. This dark lesson is imposed from above, from Moscow. The policy of central government seems obvious: to create as many uneducated, empty and amoral people in Chechnya as possible. The only people who are trying to hold back this tide are the Chechen teachers. But they may not prove strong enough.

And yet the appearance of well-being has been preserved. In Chechnya there is one decent school, No 2 in Gudermes. It was under the personal patronage of Nikolai Koshman. He liked to come there with TV journalists and, in front of the cameras, donated a fully equipped computer studies room. He brought textbooks and pencils and stroked the children's heads. It's now a habit to bring all the important guests from the capital here as well. They are greatly pleased and then give interviews in Moscow, saying that the public education system in Chechnya has been fully restored.

CHECHNYA

34

GUNS IN THE NIGHT

Making Enemies

14 September 2000

"What do you call it, when you no longer feel anything . . ." Ruslan Dachaev is not asking a question. He's simply talking aloud, to himself. "If you could only understand how we long to get back to work. How we dream that no one during the night will destroy what we've built that day. Every morning we assemble here to organise our day's work, surrounded by fighting, as though this were an ordinary construction site. Now it all seems a mockery . . ."

For five days without a break, as though they were Komsomol shock-workers of the 1930s, two dozen builders from the Chechen Republic's 9th Construction Trust have been erecting a new refugee camp on the outskirts of Argun. The administration of the republic had pleaded with them: we must bring our people back from Ingushetia and give our refugees somewhere to live on our territory. We must, somehow, resume our peacetime existence.

If we must, then we must. The builders set to and finished the job – without asking for any payment. Tenderly, as though cradling a newborn babe, they at last carried the panes of glass to the site; this priceless material had been transferred from another building site run by the Chechen civil construction agency. Ruslan Dachaev, who heads the production department of Trust No 9, personally directed the operation. If only they could now begin to live a normal life again, and get back to work. As they once did.

Alas, Ruslan and I are walking across yet another "carpet" of shattered glass, such as has countless times greeted the dawn here in Chechnya. Only the night before, the windows were whole and unharmed. Ruslan is a master builder who has seen much of life, but today his gloom is unrelieved. Once again, on the fifth night of their epic efforts, there was firing on the outskirts of Argun. Beneath our feet crunches this accursed powdered glass, a symbol of today's Chechnya. Everything has to start again from scratch.

Ruslan is empty, like a bell without a clapper. "I've nothing inside me," he says, "not anger, pain or vengeance."

"That can't be true."

Ruslan gives a hopeless smile. Long ago he graduated from the construction institute in Novosibirsk and for 20 years worked all over Siberia, completing one building project after another. He was happy then and only returned to his native Argun just before the war. His biblical lament over this lost glass is probably only comprehensible in Chechnya.

All our accustomed ideas about peace and life collapse in an instant here, just like the walls of buildings in Chechnya after a bombardment. Here windows are more precious than gold. That is why Ruslan Dachaev's lament is so heartfelt, as though he were mourning a dead relative. Anyone whose windows remain intact can confidently face the coming autumn and winter; if the glass is broken then it is a tragedy for the whole family.

Once again the Centre for Temporary Accommodation of Refugees, which was due to receive about 2,000 people in September and house them for the whole winter, cannot open. The cause is the usual, trivial event. The shots in the night were part of an insolent, cowardly and well-targeted action. Someone waited patiently until all the work was done, and the glass installed in every frame. Now not a single window remains intact.

We build and then we tear it all down again. That's what the entire "anti-terrorist operation" amounts to: a myopic, thick-headed running on the spot. But for some a profitable war, perhaps, is one where there is no end in sight or any restrictions.

"Who was firing? Do you know? Perhaps it's finally time to demand a strict judicial approach. Otherwise there really will never be an end of it."

"Judicial?" Ruslan grimaces and thinks out loud. "If they used heavy artillery then, probably, it was the Feds. They also get the benefit: 900 roubles each for every day. As long as there are 'battles' in Argun they continue to draw their daily battle bonus. As for us builders we couldn't really care which 'irreconcilable' foe was firing, the Feds or the Wahhabites. The result is the main thing. We have to start all over again – but we've used up our materials. And there won't be any more. They scraped them together from all over Chechnya, I know that for a fact."

"Have you been to the military commandant? Did you complain?"

"We've been, and he answered something like this: 'I'm under fire here myself, I can't do a thing'."

"I don't understand at all. Yes, bullets and shells are flying, but his side is doing it."

"He's not lying. No one informs him which area one of the colonels has decided to shoot at tonight. That's the kind of war we're dealing with."

"OK, agreed. But then draw up an inventory of the damage and take it to the prosecutor's office! Demand that they register your complaint. Otherwise life will never get back to normal."

Abdul Abzailov joins us. The director of Trust No 9 is a stern figure with a head of brilliant white-streaked black hair that recalls Karl Marx. With him is Magomed Vakayev, the site foreman, who is wearing a polka-dot tie and white shirt amid the piles of bricks.

"You're from Moscow. Where are we to 'take' such a paper here?! Don't make me laugh. Just look around you. Who is helping us Chechens here? The military control everything," says Abzailov. He speaks passionately but stands motionless as a rock; his gaze is unbending, as if he's gone to demand cement from the supply depot and will not leave till he gets it. "They don't waste words on us. If we weren't here everything would be just fine. We're in the way. Chechnya is like an army barracks. We just happened to be inside, and we're not needed here. If we go to the prosecutor's office to complain they'll just arrest us there: they'll call in the guards and send us off to Chernokozovo. That's happened hundreds of times. There's no freedom here, we're hostages."

While you're in Chechnya you do gradually get used to the idea that anything might happen, and that no one will be called to account. The republic is a symbol of contemporary servitude. You can't just go out into the courtyard at night and stand beneath the moon: keep to the shadows or else a sniper might pick you off. You're surrounded by bans and prohibitions and the night belongs not to lovers but to gunfire.

If I'm honest, moreover, obsessive ideas about storming off to the prosecutor's office only come when you're some distance from this reservation – only when you escape its bounds do you begin to think about the law. If the thought arises when you're in Chechnya, then it's purely from inertia.

As Vakayev, the foreman, joins our conversation we continue to wander among the ruins that show signs of recent major repair work. The plaster covering the concrete ceilings has been smashed to pieces before it has even dried out.

"We can't go on like this! Really, the authorities must decide what they want in Chechnya. Peace? For the refugees to return and cease living off the Ingush? Is that it? Then they must issue strict orders to the troops: no firing at the newly built refugee camps and construction sites. Open fire, and you face court martial. It's not even a question of our grievances and suffering. The idiocy of the situation is that the money for rebuilding – which includes those 1,300 square metres of window glass destroyed in an instant – came from the same budget that feeds the soldiers and their officers. They're just shooting at their own money!"

I go to see the military, with no particular expectations, knowing beforehand what they'll say. Sure enough, they tell me: "There were Chechen fighters there so we had to start firing."

This is the universal formula of justification here. To be applied on each and every occasion.

"Who said they were there?"

"Who can prove that they weren't?"

That's the logic of this war.

As before, no one is being punished for the unsanctioned use of weapons. Not one person. Despite all the talk in Moscow and the world's capital cities, and in spite of President Putin's assertion in his interview with CNN's Larry King that military operations have entirely halted, the soldiers continue to fire whenever and at whatever they like.

If there are "no more military operations" in Chechnya, what is going on here? The peace that follows a war? Without batting an eyelid our president, his face an impassive mask, gives the entire world something like an affirmative answer. The military are in Chechnya, he continues to lie, to maintain order. The civilian population is thankful to him, he says, for his policy.

"So what happened to the *Kursk* submarine?" King asks the President.

"It sank," he replies with a sweet smile that, evidently, is intended for those still afloat.

There was firing during the night and many heard cries. When they reached the site of this tragedy, half of the dead man's hand had already been chewed away by the thin and hungry dogs of Argun.

"I'd like to tell you, it's very difficult living here. Indescribably difficult," says Abdul Abzailov. "We constantly deceive ourselves and are willingly deceived. People have a vast longing to get back to work, to live like everyone else, like we used to do. This drives them to feats – that's what I believe – quiet, and quite unnoticed, everyday feats of determination, for the sake of the land where they were born. The rebuilding of the refugee camp here was just such a feat – and a piece of self-deception. We were living here and knew that it would certainly be destroyed. However, I'm quite sure that as soon as the opportunity arises and we hear the call 'We need you, get to work', we shall, with no thought for ourselves, do it all over again if necessary. We want to live like everybody else!"

The workers listen to us with a frown. Some nod in agreement. Some look away. The latter are in the majority. They all turn up regularly for work, although there's nothing to build. A young lad who introduces himself as Vakha decides to put across his own point of view in front of his elders.

"I don't accept this lack of punishment," he says. "If you won't punish your soldiers for their loutish behaviour then we must. Do you agree?"

"The courts must do the punishing."

"But there aren't any courts here. So we're being *forced* to fight."

"But who are you fighting against? You don't actually know who did the shooting."

"I don't know exactly. So we must fight them all. All those who carry arms."

ARGUN-MOSCOW

35

WHERE THE TRAIL LEADS . . .

The Search for the Pushkin Square Bombers

On 8 August a bomb exploded in the long and crowded underpass at Pushkin Square in the heart of Moscow. Twelve were killed outright and 97 injured.

21 September 2000

On 31 August the following people were arrested in the capital on suspicion of having organised the explosion on Pushkin Square: a 36-year-old Muscovite businessman, Turpal-Ali Djabrailov; his older brother Turpal Djabrailov, a farm-worker from the Sholkovskaya village; his cousin Alimpasha Djabrailov, who lives in Volgograd; and their distant Stavropol relative, Ahmad Djamulayev.

"Certain of those detained have already admitted their involvement and begun to give statements," the TV news calmly announced. Who believes this latest exposure of a "Chechen criminal gang"? You're right, most people believe it.

The longer this continues the further we retreat from reality. We instantly accept the myths that are fed to us, and confuse real life with these virtual worlds. So who are the Djabrailovs? Why exactly were they picked up during the latest round in the struggle against terrorism?

One Family

Turpal-Ali Djabrailov, who the investigators tried to make the chief organiser of the explosion, has lived in Moscow for the past eight years. His reasons are entirely understandable: he could not live in Chechnya because he is totally pro-Russia. He was secretary of the Sholkovskaya district committee of the Komsomol and comes from a family fiercely opposed to Dudayev, Maskhadov and the Wahhabites, not to mention Basayev. Turpal-Ali graduated from the Moscow Management Academy, then tried to set up his own business, with mixed success. On 6 August the family went on a trip to Sholkovskaya. Turpal-Ali took with him his daughters, who are four and eight, and his pregnant wife Tamara, so they could all benefit from the fresh fruits and vegetables from his parents' allotment.

They were met there, alas, by misfortune. Mariam, Turpal-Ali's elder sister, was wasting away. No one could say what the matter was. Their father decided she must be quickly taken to Moscow for examination, and he entrusted Turpal-Ali and his serious, taciturn elder brother, Turpal, to accompany her there. Their cousin Alimpasha was urgently summoned from Volgograd to go with them. (Tamara and the girls would stay for a little while longer in Chechnya.)

They were right to hurry. Mariam proved to be suffering from a rapidly developing cancer of the oesophagus and one of the clinics at the Pirogov Hospital in Moscow agreed to operate. Alimpasha and Turpal decided to remain in the capital until it was clear how successful the operation had been. On 17 August new guests arrived at Turpal-Ali's apartment on Krzhizhanovsky Street. The Djamulayevs, distant relatives from Stavropol, had come to stay: Ahmad, Angelica and their three small children. Their visit was also not a cheerful one. Ahmad and Angelica's seven-year-old daughter, Madina, had begun rapidly to lose her sight. After going to all the ophthalmologists in Stavropol it was decided that they must take her without delay for an operation at one of the eye clinics in Moscow. Ahmad rang up

Turpal-Ali. "Of course, I'll help," he replied. How could he refuse such a request?

On 26 August, Tamara and the children returned to Moscow. Five children, including one five-month-old infant, and the six adults squeezed into the small three-room apartment.

Meanwhile, they were all very busy. The Djabrailov menfolk were constantly off to the Pirogov clinic. The Djamulayevs were trying to get their daughter examined by a specialist and return with her to Stavropol for the new school term on 1 September. Often when he returned in the evening, Turpal-Ali would say: "There seems to be someone following me. There's always someone watching by the entrance to our staircase." No one in the apartment thought any more of it. If you're not guilty you have nothing to fear. To be on the safe side, however, the women sewed up the pockets on the men's clothes so that nothing could be planted on them.

On 31 August, Turpal-Ali and Tamara went to visit his sister Mariam. They parted as they were leaving the clinic: Tamara went home, Turpal-Ali went to work. The older Turpal was also out, looking for medicine for his sister. That night neither came home.

At 11.46 p.m. the doorbell rang. Some people showed Tamara a search warrant. They were all carrying bags. When Tamara asked them to leave the bags outside they at once lost almost all interest in their task. They made a pretence of examining everything, concentrating on family photographs and papers. Finally they went. They took with them all photographs of Turpal-Ali and his diaries, and they also arrested Alimpasha and Ahmad. With no idea what was going on, Tamara and Angelica stayed behind with the five small children.

Arrest

"I didn't know where they were taking me," says Ahmad Djamulayev. "It's the first time I've ever been to Moscow. I don't know a single street here, and couldn't tell where we were. They put Alimpasha in a different car. Then they took me to a cell. I wasn't questioned until the following day. The investigator asked only about Turpal-Ali: Who was he? What does he do? Why had I come to stay with him in Moscow? I told him all about our Madina's illness.

"Then I was ordered to sign a deposition which said I had insulted a policeman, used obscenities and behaved provocatively. I refused outright – nothing of the kind had happened. They threatened me, but I stood firm. Then they told me, 'Get out of here.' I asked for an official document explaining why and where I had been held for several days (I realised it was already night outside). They threatened to give me 15 days in prison for delinquency. I said, 'At least tell me which way to go. I don't know Moscow.'

"The major on duty demanded 10 roubles for the information. I gave it to him and he showed me how to get to the nearest Metro station. When I left the building I saw the sign TVERSKOE POLICE STATION [in central Moscow, not far from Pushkin Square, Tr.]. I got back to the family and discovered that neither Alimpasha nor Turpal-Ali nor Turpal had yet returned home."

Meanwhile Alimpasha was already at police headquarters on Petrovka Street. From the Tverskoe police station where he had been asked every conceivable question about Turpal-Ali, Alimpasha was taken to court. "What for? Why to court?" he asked the policemen. "Because you're a Chechen, that's why," they replied.

At the court building he was ordered to stand outside the door leading into the courtroom: "There's no need for you in there." A few minutes later they said: "That's it. You've been sentenced." And took him back to Petrovka Street, to a new cell.

"Do you know under what Article of the Criminal Code you were convicted?" I ask.

"No, they didn't say."

"Didn't they give you some document? For example, the court's decision? So that you could appeal?"

"No."

"Did they provide you with a lawyer? Did you demand one?"

"No."

Alimpasha is a very simple, straightforward fellow. He did not demand anything from anyone. When he had been detained for 72 hours he was taken to the prison gates at 2 a.m. "Get out," they told him.

When Alimpasha got back to the Djabrailovs Ahmad asked him: "At the police station did you hear the voice of that Galya who came round here a few times? I heard her outside the door."

"I even saw her there," replied Alimpasha. "I was turned to face the wall in the corridor. She couldn't see my face and was talking to the policemen, as though she was one of them, not someone they'd arrested."

The men agreed this could hardly be a coincidence. But I'll return to Galya in a moment. In the meantime someone rang up Tamara and, after introducing himself as a legal-aid lawyer, informed her that Turpal-Ali had been arrested on 31 August and found to have a grenade in his trouser pocket. He was accused of organising the explosion on Pushkin Square.

A little time later there was news of his brother, Turpal. They had also found a grenade on him, but in his case, interestingly enough, it was tucked into his waistband. Just imagine: a Chechen farm-worker, whom life has thoroughly taught to fear anyone in uniform, strides through the very centre of Moscow with a grenade bulging under his shirt while policemen stand all around.

Turpal-Ali's wife had sewn up his jacket pockets, but could not bring herself to spoil his trousers. She had sewn up every one of her brother-in-law Turpal's pockets. Hence the grenade under his shirt and conviction under Article 222:2, illegal acquisition, retention etc. of explosive substances. At best he could expect from two to four years imprisonment.

How did it happen? A simple, mundane and entirely contemporary event. Certain men, who did not introduce themselves, made the brothers face the wall with their hands behind their backs, and then put handcuffs on them. Fifteen minutes later witnesses were brought in to confirm that one had a grenade in his pocket, the other had one tucked into his waistband.

Don't imagine that the brothers were arrested together. They were in quite different places, but the same primitive and well-worn procedure was applied to both. Their arrest was the result of "active measures" and they were then labelled members of a "criminal gang". Indeed, they had been followed for several days (Turpal-Ali was right about that).

How convincing were the proofs that they had organised the explosion? Merely the grenades, and nothing else? Of course not.

Our Countrywoman

Galina Almazova is very well known among refugees in Moscow. At least, almost all those from Grozny and from Chechnya know her. She likes to hang about the office of the Civic Assistance Committee, the human rights organisation that helps those who have nowhere to stay and nothing to live on. She strolls down the queue there, making acquaintances and chatting to people. And she tells them all that she's "one of them", she herself is from Grozny.

Once acquainted, Galina Almazova frequently offers her help. She has a generous nature and appears entirely good-hearted, though, it must be admitted, a little pushy. There's another thing about her, and it's important: she never looks you in the eye. It's a noticeable trait.

This is the same Galya who Alimpasha and Ahmad saw and heard when they were each being held in different corners at the Tverskoe police station. She was in a lively discussion about something or other with the policemen, and talked to them as an equal.

It was Tamara's sister, Rosa Magomedova, who had brought Galya to their apartment. Rosa was director of the school in Chervlyonnaya village, in northern Chechnya, and taught history there. Now she

rents one room in a town just outside Moscow and sells newspapers
to earn a living since she can't return home. Her husband, Islam, used
to be a policeman in the Sholkovskaya district police department and
was twice held hostage because of his profession. The first time
was under Dudayev, before the 1994–6 war, because he was someone
who had "served Russia". The second time was in August 1996, as
soon as the army left Chechnya, because he had "been with the
federal troops".

Islam and Rosa got to know Galya in the queue at the Civic
Assistance office. On learning their story, Galya was quick to ask if
they, or anyone they knew, required weapons to defend themselves?
She could help with this, she suggested. Later it became clear that
Galya had "aided" many of her "fellow citizens from Chechnya" in
Moscow in this way. Subsequently these people found themselves
locked up for the illegal acquisition and possession of arms and
explosives.

"I saw her at the flat a couple of times," says Ahmad Djamulayev.
"She was very brazen. She came round when Turpal-Ali was not in and
introduced herself to me as his close acquaintance. She was ferreting
about the shelves all the time, and wandering from one room to
another. I even had to say to her: 'Don't take offence, but my wife
will follow you around the flat until Turpal-Ali returns from work.'
And Angelica walked behind her. I was there when Turpal-Ali told
her not to come round again."

Tamara gives a deep sigh: "How much he did to help that Galya!
I warned him, 'She's not a good person.' But he told me, 'She's one
of us, she's also having a hard time of it, and we must help.' The
investigator at the prosecutor's office was right when he said to me:
'Don't be kind to people and you won't be disappointed'."

Tamara will soon give birth. She is worn out by all these events
and is not feeling well. But when the Moscow city prosecutor's office
called her in for questioning she went immediately.

It was just as well that she did. The case against her menfolk, it turned out, was based on a denunciation provided by Galya, their acquaintance from Chechnya. In mid-August Galya was arrested in possession of a weapon. She was bringing it from Nazran to Moscow: that was her money-making business. Not for the first time, evidently, she bribed her way out of a charge by offering to provide the investigators with "information": the "entire Djabrailov family" had gathered in Moscow "to organise explosions". That was why Galya visited the apartment when Turpal-Ali was out, asking who everyone was, where they came from and why they were in Moscow.

The investigator was reassuring. He told Tamara: "We'll withdraw the explosion charge against your husband. It's clear it won't stick and that we've got the wrong person." But the grenade that was planted on him, well, that would be more difficult. If the police dismissed that charge, after all, it would be an admission of what they'd done. No one could agree to that, especially to save a Chechen. It's a simple and very contemporary tale.

Tamara has strictly forbidden her little four-year-old daughter Amina, who goes to kindergarten, to tell anyone that her father is in prison. The little girl finally gets accustomed to me, a new person in the apartment. Quietly she starts telling me what is most on her mind, how she is going to save her Daddy. The grown-ups explain that Amina talks about this almost all the time now:

"I'll take him by the hand and we'll run away."

"Where to?"

"Far, far away . . ."

The Djabrailovs are the victims of a PR campaign by the State. All the loathsome business with their "countrywoman from Grozny" is merely the result. Who would make use of Galina Almazova's "talents" if this current ethnic obsession in our attitudes had not been encouraged? She would be in prison herself. But society is hungry for "bad" Chechens.

It's a very poor game to play, because it results in a stalemate. We are already half-way to another country, to the land of "supposedly".

Supposedly there is a struggle against terrorism. It is intense, but it bears no results. Supposedly we now have strong leadership. We ourselves are responsible for that. And supposedly we are now a united nation. Supposedly.

MOSCOW

*

Two months later, Rear-Admiral German Ugryumov, deputy head of the Federal Security Service (FSB), told the Izvestiya *daily (21 December) that "as of now" there was "not a single major terrorist act for which the main perpetrators have not been identified". Not all those responsible had been detained, he admitted; search warrants had been issued for the rest.*

In late January 2001, when the FSB took over direction of the operation in Chechnya from the army, Ugryumov, who also heads the FSB's Second Section (defence of the constitutional order and anti-terrorism), was put directly in charge of the anti-terrorist campaign in the North Caucasus.

36

TWO WEEKS

A Chronicle of Violence

In October, after following the war for a year, Anna Politkovskaya decided to take time away from the North Caucasus and spent two months investigating and writing about Mafia activities at the large factories of Yekaterinburg in the Urals.

Novaya gazeta and other newspapers continued to cover the fighting in Chechnya. And, as in 1994–6, during the previous conflict, the Moscow-based "Memorial" organisation[61] *documented and made public the human rights abuses on both sides. The following reports are taken from the chronicle of events kept by Memorial. They cover 22–29 October and 15–23 November: two typical weeks in Chechnya.*[62]

---

61 Founded in 1988 by Andrei Sakharov and others, Memorial's primary purpose was to document the crimes of the Soviet regime since 1917 and to commemorate its victims. From the outset it took a very active interest in contemporary issues, and set up its own Human Rights Centre to monitor areas of conflict and ethnic tension in the "trouble spots" of the Soviet Union.

62 Those incidents recorded by staff at Memorial's office in Nazran, opened in March 2000, are indicated by the annotation (MN). All other reports cited during these two weeks came from Interfax, Russia's major

October–November 2000

October

22 SATURDAY

Valerik village in the Achkhoi-Martan district came under fire from the nearby 245th motorised rifle regiment. One shell landed in the courtyard of a private house and four people suffered concussion (MN).

At 10 a.m. the burned corpse of a 17/18-year-old girl was found by shepherds in a wooded area not far from the side-road to the "Northern" collective farm in Naurskaya district (MN).

> Only the soles of her feet, still wearing black shoes, and the underwear around her ankles had not been burned. Not far from the murder site were tracks left by an armoured vehicle that had turned off the main road and then driven back there.

Three inhabitants of Ternovoz village were killed by mines and land-mines.

A home-made explosive device, found near the points on the railway line between Ishchorskaya and Staderevskaya stations, was defused. A similar device was defused 100 metres away from the Terek Station on the North Caucasus railway.

Federal agencies carried out raids in 36 locations throughout Chechnya including Grozny, Gudermes, Achkhoi-Martan, Bachi-Yurt, Vedeno, Germenchuk, Goragorsk, Goryachi Istochnik and Itum-Kale. They conducted identity checks on more than 36,000 citizens and examined more than 16,000 vehicles. Almost 500 violations were uncovered, including 168 infringements of passport regulations.

independent news agency (see www.memo.ru/hr/hotspots/Ncaucus/hronics). In December 2000 the Memorial Human Rights Centre was able to open an office in Grozny itself.

Five radio-controlled explosive devices were discovered on the road near Novye Atagi and destroyed.

Two federal soldiers were killed this day and ten wounded.

23 SUNDAY

Six corpses bearing signs of bullet wounds were found on the outskirts of Pobedinskoe village. Their identity is unknown.

Federal forces directed artillery fire at suspected Chechen armed groups to the north of Tsa-Vedeno village, Vedeno district. Three Chechen fighters died in a clash with federal forces near Alkhan-Khutor village.

A landmine was defused near Lugovo village in the Sholkovskaya district.

Chechen armed groups fired six times at checkpoints, five times at army and police posts and twice at administrative buildings.

Federal agencies detained 31 people during "cleansing" operations intended to catch those suspected of belonging to Chechen armed groups.

Lecha Yeshurkayev, head of the Kurchaloi district, was killed near Khegi-Khutor village.

> Yeshurkayev (b.1948) was head of the district administration in 1995–97 and again since 1999. A *Volga* car signalled to Yeshurkayev's vehicle to halt and its occupants then tried to kidnap him. Yeshurkayev's driver intervened and the armed men shot Yeshurkayev in the head, but did not touch his driver or a woman passenger travelling with them. A note was found at the scene of the crime threatening all who co-operated with the federal authorities.

Federal soldiers opened fired on civilians near the apartment block at 27 Mozdok Street in Grozny. One person was killed and another wounded (MN).

At about 10 p.m. Movsar Ismailov and Aslan Matayev left their five-storey residential building (near Hospital No 9) for a smoke. Probably aiming at their lighted cigarettes, federal soldiers in the nearby bushes opened fire with automatic weapons. Aslan died immediately from wounds to the head and heart. Movsar was not killed and called out to his friend, provoking another round of shots in his direction.

The soldiers threw a grenade towards the two young men and Aslan's body was covered with shrapnel wounds. Doctors later removed twelve bullets from Movsar's body.

24 MONDAY

At 00.20 a.m. an APC carrying federal paratroopers detonated a land-mine near Akhtury village, Shali district. One soldier was wounded.

A local inhabitant, Apti Vaganov, was seriously wounded during identity checks in Sernovodsk (MN).

At dawn federal forces closed all routes into Sernovodsk. Around 10 a.m. that morning, Vaganov (b.1978) from 19 Vysokovoltnaya Street, walked towards the town's outskirts, where the soldiers were now dug in, to fetch his calf. A shot from a sniper's rifle hit him in the head. Vaganov is now in the intensive care unit at the Sunzhensk district hospital (Ingushetia) and his condition, following an operation, is serious.

Since November 1999 he and his family had been living in a tent at a refugee camp in Ingushetia. Only in September 2000 had the Vaganov family returned home to Sernovodsk.

During the last ten months four guards have been killed and twenty wounded on the Chechen section of the Russia-Georgia border, according to Lieutenant-General Alexander Manilov of the Federal Border Service.

25 TUESDAY

A tractor was blown up by a home-made device in Argun. The driver was taken to hospital in a critical condition.

One soldier died and three were wounded after an explosion at the military commandant's office in Shali.

At 2 p.m. a boy aged 14–15 was shot dead opposite the "Oil-worker" shop by soldiers carrying out a "cleansing operation" along the main road in Grozny's Staropromyslovsky district (MN).

Federal troops shelled and bombed suspected Chechen armed groups in the Terkhkort mountain district (Ingushetia) who were making their way across the border from Georgia.

Ministry of Interior troops, together with units of soldiers and policemen, carried out "cleansing" operations in the October district of Grozny, and in Mesker-Yurt, Novaya Zhizn, Sernovodsk and Yukerchu-Gonkha.

> During these operations 20 illegal mini oil-refineries, three large oil-tanks, four landmines, three shells and about 20 hand grenades were destroyed. The following were seized: one hand-held anti-tank grenade-launcher, ten automatic weapons, about a thousand rounds of ammunition for automatic weapons, a motorised mini-glider, and a store of medicine. Twenty-six people were detained on suspicion of belonging to armed Chechen groups.

A radio-controlled landmine was defused, and two wire-controlled mines destroyed, near Mesker-Yurt. A radio-controlled landmine was defused in Grozny.

A 22-year-old Chechen died in Kurchaloi village after a booby-trapped video cassette exploded.

26 WEDNESDAY

The body of Zelimkhan Soltamuradov (b.1982) was found by the hoist on the rubbish dump outside Argun (MN).

> He had left his home in Argun on the morning of 19 October and never returned. A shepherd who was herding his flock

nearby found the corpse and reported it to the local police station. After the standard investigations, the law enforcement agencies handed over the body to the mosque where he was identified by relatives.

According to the forensic examination he had died on 25 October as the result of bullet wounds to neck and head. There were several other wounds. His cousin said that both earlobes had been cut off, his right eyelid had been slashed and his skull crushed. The shots to the head and neck were probably to make sure he was dead.

Federal artillery bombarded forested areas in the Vedeno district near Kharachoi, Makhkety, Khatuni and Benoi.

27 THURSDAY

Persons unknown killed an OMON man in Grozny by the railway bridge over the River Sunzha.

At the army post on the entry to Sernovodsk from Samashki federal soldiers detained Musa Labazanov, an 18-year-old inhabitant of Davydenko village, and beat him. He was handed over to relatives several days later when they paid for his release from the preliminary detention centre in Achkhoi-Martan (MN).

Labazanov attends the driving school in Sernovodsk and had regularly passed this post before. The soldiers put a bag over his head and began to beat him. According to his relatives Labazanov repeatedly lost consciousness as he was beaten and subjected to electric-shock treatment. He was forced to sign a deposition that the soldiers had confiscated two packets of hashish from him. He was then transferred to the detention centre in Achkhoi-Martan.

Four Interior Ministry officials died in the Tarumov district of Daghestan, near the administrative boundary with Chechnya, when their car came under fire.

Three teenagers were blown up by a mine in Grozny. Two of them died without recovering consciousness, the other was taken to hospital and doctors consider his condition to be serious.

A unit of Interior Ministry forces clashed with armed Chechen groups near Ersena village.

28 FRIDAY

Federal soldiers detained 18 men at the wholesale market in Grozny. They were beaten and released the same day (MN).

> At 11 a.m. Russian soldiers drove up to the wholesale market at the intersection of Tukhachevsky and Ionesiani Streets in a *Ural* truck, an armoured vehicle and an APC. Within minutes they sealed off the market and began to detain and beat the men, without asking to see their papers or offering any explanation. They set off several smoke sticks to deter the women from coming any closer.
>
> The soldiers piled the 18 men they detained, one on top of another, in the truck and drove off to an unknown destination. Among those seized was a 16-year-old boy. The women managed to write down the numbers of the vehicles used in the operation and immediately lodged a complaint at the temporary police station of the Lenin district. By that evening the detainees were released, but many of them had been beaten.

2.5 kilograms of TNT was discovered in a car at one of the checkpoints in Grozny.

Persons unknown shot dead four civilians near Hospital No 9 in Grozny (MN).

> Ramzan Bagiev (*b.*1959), father of three, was shot dead in the courtyard of the apartment block at 13 Oleg Koshevoi Street, where he was temporarily living with his family. He was finishing repairs to his own house on Academician Pavlov Street, said witnesses, and intended to move back there in a few days.
>
> Malika Gashayeva, a neighbour of the Bagiev family, said that the dead bodies of two acquaintances with whom Bagiev

was seen talking the previous night were found the following morning. Bags full of tools were lying next to them. The same night Usman Muzhedov (b.1959) was murdered on Sedov Street. Since the death of his wife in August 1996 he had been bringing up their three children single-handed. Muzhedov had died from a shot to the head but there were six other bullet wounds on his body.

In none of these cases had anyone heard gunshots.

29 SATURDAY

Federal soldiers arrested Ramzan Magomadov at his home in Nagornoe village and took him to the police station where he was tortured and beaten. His relatives paid money to secure his release from the preliminary detention centre in Achkhoi-Martan (MN).

Masked soldiers burst into Magomadov's home at the dairy farm in Nagornoe and searched every room, smashing crockery and breaking furniture as they went. A gold chain, a ring and 1,000 roubles were later found to be missing.

Guns were trained on Magomadov, his mother and sister. After the search the soldiers demanded to see their papers and told Ramzan he must go with them. When his mother tried to prevent them taking away her son, a soldier hit her with his rifle butt. Ramzan attempted to intervene but was immediately knocked down. His hands and legs were tied with wire and he was taken in an armoured vehicle to the Rapid Response Unit's base at the grain store in Samashki.

That day he was continually beaten and subjected to electric-shock treatment and told to confess to various crimes. They tried to force him to sign certain documents. All this time Ramzan was blindfold. When he refused to sign he was hit across the head with a rifle butt and started bleeding.

On 30 October they took him to the preliminary detention centre in Achkhoi-Martan. Relatives secured his release by paying 20,000 roubles and surrendering an automatic weapon and two grenades that, they said, they had bought from other Russian soldiers.

Seven people died in an explosion at the Elita café in Chiri-Yurt. Two café workers, seven federal soldiers and four others were wounded.

Federal soldiers and policemen carried out mass arrests in Samashki. Members of the Rapid Response Unit based at the town's grain store arrested and beat up eight young men (MN).

> The eight detained – Shama Gechiev (35), Ismail Sharipov (33), Ibragim Sharimov (25), Balaudi Vukiev (29), Said-Selim Vukiev (28), Zhalaudi Vukiev (44), Magomed-Emin Vukiev (32) and Shakhrudi Askhabov (35) – all live on Ordjonikidzevskaya Street. Balaudi Vukiev described what happened:
>
> The street was sealed off by armoured vehicles and people in military uniform. About ten soldiers came into our courtyard. They demanded to see our papers. Not one of them said who he was. We showed them our documents: they were all in order, and there was nothing they could pick on. We four brothers were asked to get into the vehicle and ride with them to their unit in order to clear up certain matters. We protested and demanded to see someone in authority. One of them said: "We're you're authorities, we're the law for you."
>
> My mother and sister tried to dissuade them and grabbed hold of us and wouldn't let go. But the soldiers pushed them aside and warned them that they were making things worse. I wanted to defend my mother but only took one step in their direction. They got ready to shoot and several grabbed me. They pushed us with their rifle butts into the armoured vehicle and put bags over our heads. When we arrived they hit us and threw us down on the floor. We were not allowed to stand; we could only kneel. They kicked us and hit us with their rifle butts. There were a lot of them and it was hard to guess where the next blow was coming from. They kept asking, "Have you been fighting?"
>
> "No."
>
> "Why not?" And they hit me again.
>
> "Do you have a gun?"
>
> "No."
>
> "Why not?" Again they hit me.
>
> "Do you have any dollars or gold?"

"No, where would I get gold?" Again they hit me.

"We know you Chechens, you've all got gold, dollars and weapons."

Then they took it in turns to put their feet on my neck. I could hear a camera running. Evidently they were making a video film. One of them put the muzzle of his pistol against the back of my head and said: "That's your lot. Pray to your Allah." I mentally recited a prayer. I heard a click but there was no shot. He gave an obscene curse: "There won't be any more cock-ups. Grey, give me your shooter." I heard a shot next to my ear.

"That's fine, just the way we like it," he said. "Tell me where the gold is and I'll let you live. If you won't, I'll shoot you and no one will find out where your body lies rotting." That was how they ridiculed me.

They also used psychological pressure. They said they raped Chechen girls and women. "If you like I'll rape your sister in front of you." Another said: "She's not good-looking, a real fright. Better cover her with rags while we do it."

On 30 October the detainees were delivered to the preliminary detention centre in Achkhoi-Martan and three days later, on payment of 3,000 roubles for each of them, they were released to their relatives.

A radio-controlled landmine exploded next to an army post in the Staropromyslovsky district in Grozny. Three people were injured. An anti-tank mine was discovered next to the railway station in Gudermes and defused. Sappers defused eight powerful explosive devices laid on both roads and railway lines, next to the Daghestan border and in the Naurskaya district.

Four federal soldiers died and three were wounded. Federal units came under fire 17 times.

On the night of 29–30 October Kheda Serbieva suffered gunshot wounds in her apartment at a five-storey block next to Grozny railway station (MN).

Their building had several times come under fire from the unfinished hotel nearby which the Russian soldiers often used to organise ambushes. Kheda was afraid to leave her little son alone, and that night they were sleeping in the same bed.

She was woken by an excruciating pain. The bed was covered in blood and she discovered she had been wounded in her left arm and stomach. At first it was thought that a stray fragment of a shell had entered the room. The doctor at the hospital, however, found a bullet in her pelvic region. Evidently the shot had been fired from the roof of the nearest multi-storey building.

November

15 WEDNESDAY

At 4.30 a.m. Shamil Yashuyev (*b.*1974) was detained in Mesker-Yurt village, Shali district. Nothing is known of his fate (MN).

Masked soldiers burst into Yashuyev's house, entered every room and began to beat the men there, breaking furniture and crockery. After some time it became clear that it was Shamil Yashuyev the soldiers were looking for and he was taken away without even being allowed to get dressed.

The soldiers demanded the documentation and keys of the *Zhiguli* car parked outside, but then, without waiting, they broke the car windows and set fire to it from inside. Soon the barn was also alight. The soldiers would not allow anyone to put it out. They took away documentation for the *Kamaz* truck also belonging to the Yashuyev family. The soldiers suggested that Yashuyev's mother should go to the military commandant in Argun if she had any complaints about their actions.

That morning the soldiers seized three other men from the village. By mid-January 2001 nothing further was known about them.

Federal forces carried out a routine operation in Urus-Martan to catch those participating in armed Chechen groups.

Identity papers were checked in a "cleansing" operation in seven towns and villages across the republic. Thirty-two people were detained on suspicion of belonging to armed Chechen groups.

There were 19 attacks on army posts and other locations of federal forces.

Federal aviation and artillery bombed suspected positions of armed Chechen groups in the wooded mountain areas of south-east Chechnya.

On the verge of the road, one and a half kilometres south-east of Bachi-Yurt village, a trip-wire anti-personnel mine was discovered and defused.

16 THURSDAY

During the night persons unknown killed Sharani Dudagov (b.1948), head of the Mesker-Yurt village administration, Shali district, and his deputy Khasmagomed Tsumtsayev (b.1958) (MN).

The former head of Bachi-Yurt village administration (Kurchaloi district), Lecha Aliyev, was seriously wounded. His attackers were not identified.

The local administration building in Novogroznensky village was blown up. There were no fatalities or casualties.

A vehicle carrying seven people came under fire by persons unknown. The driver, a federal soldier, and five passengers who live in Akhkinchu-Borzoi village, Kurchaloi district, all died (MN).

> The five villagers had gone to gather firewood for heating the local school in a truck lent to them by the nearby army unit. At the time of the attack, Nazhmudi Borziyev (b.1959), his brother Zamrudi, Suleiman Askhabov (b.1970), Suleiman Djanbekov (b.1969) and Bisarbek Djanbekov (b.1970) were in the back of the truck. The soldiers had several times helped the locals in this

way and provided an armoured vehicle to protect them. Apart from the soldier sitting next to the driver, there was no additional protection on this ocassion.

In the woods the vehicle came under fire from unknown armed people equipped with automatic weapons. All seven in the truck were killed. The military took no action in response to this event.

Twenty-seven firearm attacks on federal positions were registered.

Twenty-three explosive devices were defused in Chechnya.

17 FRIDAY

During a "cleansing" operation in Selmentauzen village, Vedeno district, Russian soldiers blew up the first floor of the local school by tossing grenades into the building. They also blew up a house belonging to Vakha Tesayev, currently taking refuge in Ingushetia (MN).

Abdul-Kasim Zarubekov, a crane operator for the October district police department in Grozny, disappeared. Nothing is known of his whereabouts (MN).

> Zarubekov (*b.*1951) came to the department that morning to collect his paycheque, leaving his son outside in the car. Having waited until 7 p.m., the son went to find out what was keeping him so long. No one in the police department could give Zarubekov's son a clear answer, but he noticed that Abdul-Kasim was registered in the visitors' log as having arrived at 11 a.m. By mid-January 2001 nothing more was known of his fate.

Two St Petersburg policemen, Vladimir Yeremenko (30) and Dmitry Krivenko (26) were killed in Goity village, Urus-Martan district.

An explosive device disguised as a crankshaft from a *Zhiguli* car was discovered next to the railway station in Gudermes.

18 SATURDAY

Six federal operations in the republic (including the town of Shali) resulted in the detention of eight people suspected of belonging to armed Chechen groups.

Fourteen landmines of various types were defused in Chechnya. Among them were mines on the Rostov-Baku Highway, in the Vedeno district, near Starye Atagi village, and close to Petropavlovskoe village and Argun.

19 SUNDAY

A "cleansing" operation took place near the Karpinsky Hill district and Trust No 12 in Grozny. Those detained were held in the nearest military unit and beaten. Eight people from the Karpinsky district were released the same day; those picked up by the soldiers near Trust No 12 were allowed to go on Monday (MN).

Five local residents were detained by federal soldiers and driven to an unknown destination during a "cleansing" operation in Mairtup village, Kurchaloi district. Other villagers were beaten and, as of mid-January 2001, the fate of the missing five remained unknown (MN).

> One of the soldiers fired at close range at Aslanbek Masayev, and others beat him over the head with rifle butts. Nevertheless he remained alive and was left behind. His 60-year-old father Danilbek Masayev was also beaten and there was an attempt to take him away, but at the last moment he was not taken.
>
> Twenty-six year-old Yusup, who is mentally handicapped, was taken by the military and found that evening not far from Argun. He said he had been held in Khankala. There he had seen three fellow villagers, Elsi Edilkhanov (b.1951) his son Ahmed (b.1973), and Minkail Murtazov (b.1956). Two months later nothing was known of their fate, or that of Hozha Islamkhanov (b.1959) and Ramzan Masayev (b.1959, son of Aslanbek) who were also arrested that day in Mairtup.

A Russian army officer was killed in Kalinovskaya village, Naurskaya district, by unknown persons.

Unidentified attackers wounded Hasan Adayev, the imam of the Gudermes mosque.

Two soldiers died and one was wounded in a café in Urus-Martan when it came under fire.

After their papers were checked, 49 people were detained on suspicion of belonging to armed Chechen groups.

There were 16 attacks on federal units. One soldier died, one was wounded and another went missing.

20 MONDAY

Persons unknown destroyed the traders' stalls on Mir Street, near the Central Market in Grozny during the night of 19–20 November (MN).

Military helicopters carried out missile attacks in the Vedeno and Urus-Martan districts of Chechnya, and the Khasavyurt district in Daghestan.

A Chechen cameraman, Adam Tepsurgayev, who worked for Reuters and other TV companies, was killed in Alkhan-Yurt.

21 TUESDAY

A *Ural* truck with a mounted anti-aircraft gun was blown up by a landmine on the Samashki–Achkhoi-Martan road, near the turning to Davydenko village. One soldier died, two were wounded. This was the pretext for detaining Husein Gaziev, from Davydenko, whose corpse was found on 24 November near the village (MN).

> Gaziev (*b*.1955) got off the Samashki bus at the turning to his village. Federal soldiers were at the bus stop and other passengers saw them approach Gaziev, put a bag over his head, shove him into an armoured vehicle and drive off to an unknown destination.
>
> Gaziev's relatives began to search for him. They applied to the preliminary detention centre in Achkhoi-Martan, the district

prosecutor's office, and to the commanders of the military units based nearby. However, for two days they could not locate him.

On 24 November, Gaziev's disfigured body was found on the outskirts of Davydenko. Witnesses said that the dead man's nose had been cut off and his eyes put out. A deep knife wound was visible in his neck. The head was a pulp of flesh and bone. The jaw was broken in two places and his teeth were missing. His fingers and wrist-bones had also been broken.

A 24-year-old inhabitant of Ilaskhan-Yurt village was arrested in Gudermes on suspicion of being involved in kidnapping activities.

Two soldiers died and four were wounded as a result of military operations in Grozny.

On the outskirts of Roshni-Chu village, Urus-Martan district, two local inhabitants were killed by an explosive device on the roadside. An explosion in a private house in Shali killed the owner. A local resident was killed by a landmine on a road in the Kurchaloi district.

One Interior Ministry soldier was killed and two others wounded when a landmine exploded in Samashki village.

Thirty search-and-disarm operations were carried out by Interior Ministry detachments in Grozny, Gudermes, Argun, Alpiiskoe, Vedeno, Achkhoi-Martan, Naurskaya, Pervomayskoe and certain other population centres. They checked the papers of some 16,000 citizens, and examined more than 11,000 vehicles. 228 violations were uncovered, including 31 infringements of regulations governing passports and residence permits.

Seventeen people were detained on suspicion of belonging to armed Chechen groups.

Russian soldiers and federal positions came under fire 18 times.

Twelve explosive devices were defused, some in the centre of Grozny.

22 WEDNESDAY

An attempt was made on the life of Ibragim Yasuev, head of the Zavodskoi district administration in Grozny, during the night.

A *Ural* truck carrying Russian troops hit a mine in the capital's Lenin district. Several soldiers suffered wounds of varying severity.

Persons unknown fired on the *Niva* automobile of the Lenin district administration, killing the driver.

Federal artillery shelled suspected concentrations of armed Chechen groups six times in the Khasavyurt district (Daghestan) and Urus-Martan district.

A group thought to be part of an armed Chechen unit were injured by a landmine not far from Khatuni village, Vedeno district.

Two residents of the Karpinsky Hill district, Grozny, were killed in the evening by persons unknown (MN).

> Ruslan Verigov and Djambulat Chaadayev were found dead not far from their homes on Volodarsky and Copernicus Streets, respectively. There were eight knife wounds on Chaadayev's body and four on Verigov's. Both had been shot in the forehead to make certain they were dead.

Federal positions, army posts, border guards and administrative buildings came under fire more than 20 times by armed Chechen groups.

Nine explosive devices left on roads and six planted in towns and villages were defused.

23 THURSDAY

The corpse of a middle-aged man, resident in the Karpinsky Hill district, was brought to the capital's Hospital No 9 (MN).

> He had gathered a large sum of money and was on his way to relatives in Volgograd. His family thought he had already arrived there.

His body was brought to the hospital by soldiers who did not identify themselves. Cigarette burns were visible on the dead man's right hand. Doctors noted a broken jaw and other closed fractures. He had been shot once in the head. There was no sign of the money.

The car of Malika Gezimiyeva, head of the Gudermes district administration, came under attack from firearms and a grenade-launcher. Her bodyguard and son were injured; she herself was not in the vehicle.

During the "Chechen campaign" total casualties among paratroopers were 839, of whom 257 were killed, announced Colonel-General Georgy Shpak, commanding officer of the federation's paratroop regiments.

Fifteen explosive devices on the roads, two on the railways and eight mines and landmines planted in towns and villages were found and defused.

During "cleansing" operations and checks on identity documents and residence permits 34 people, including two wounded individuals, were detained on suspicion of belonging to armed Chechen groups.

Federal forces came under fire 26 times.

On the night of 23–24 November Grozny's 1st suburb came under fire from federal soldiers. Many houses were damaged, but there were no human casualties (MN).

37

TREATMENT DEFERRED

Until after a Political Settlement

21 December 2000

As the second winter under siege sets in, Grozny today is a living hell. It is another world, some dreadful Hades you can only reach through the Looking Glass. There are no signs of civilisation among the ruins, apart from the people themselves. More important are the ideas and expectations that rule here. For some, laying mines has become a more familiar activity than cleaning their teeth. Going out into the streets of Grozny increasingly resembles a step towards the abyss. Going back to your apartment can be like a trip to the next world.

Grozny City Hospital No 9, the only hospital still continuing to admit the city's wounded, is the most accurate mirror of all that is going on in this blockaded city at the end of the twentieth century.

An Apartment-Minefield

Like a small hunted animal, Isa Shashayev peers out from under the blanket drawn up to his chin. All he does is shift his suffering gaze from the hospital wall on the right to the wall on the left. He maintains an expressive silence. The doomed look in his eyes is that of someone who's decided to drown himself. Isa is 25.

"When they brought him in there were splinters dangling from his calf. They looked like a fan. His legs were torn and shattered, one foot had gone and the other was barely attached," explains traumatologist Hasan Khadjiev.

In half-empty Grozny this winter there are hardly any doctors. Anyone who is able has got as far away as they can from these heart-rending horrors. Hasan stayed behind, though, and his motives were deeply ideological. He offers such a clear and simple explanation that it's awkward to press for any clarification:

"Who if not me? Knowing my skills as a surgeon and having taken the Hippocratic oath, I was obliged to remain. From a surgical point of view, I mean."

Naturally. Today Hasan is one of three traumatologists on whom all Grozny depends – this appalling contemporary Stalingrad where every day the mines take their cruel and merciless toll.

Yet what happened to Isa is not at all straightforward. It isn't the usual story of one of the city's inhabitants who went out to find bread and water and was crippled when he accidentally stepped in the wrong place. The way Isa lost his leg is a particularly cynical story, which, alas, is growing more typical of life in the Chechen capital.

During the daytime on 6 December he came home to check on his half-destroyed apartment, which had not been repaired for use this winter. (Isa's family are living scattered among relatives and acquaintances, while the men try to patch up the shattered walls.) Isa had just lifted a board from the floor when there was an explosion. Some visitor had packed away an anti-personnel mine there, as a present for the owners.

Such atrocious cruelty did not occur the previous winter in Grozny, nor this summer or autumn. Mined apartments typify the present winter. There may be some logic behind it, but it is the thinking of humans who have lost all normal decency.

"Who benefits? Who's doing such a thing? Why put mines in apartments and people's homes?" I ask.

"So that they don't return," Isa answers with difficulty, not wanting to say a word. He prefers not to speak and the words are as hard to drag out of him as the fragments embedded in his legs. "So that people go anywhere but back to their homes. So that Grozny closes down."

A grim-looking nurse who has come into the ward joins in:

"Usually the mines are planted by those who want to take over the apartment. Neighbours. They want to improve their own living conditions. Actually, Isa was lucky. My aunt died from the mine left in her flat. She was killed outright."

The nurse has come in to fix up a drip for Isa's fellow patient, Musa Shapayev, a 30-year-old from Alkhan-Yurt, not far from Grozny. Musa was caught in crossfire on the same day, 6 December, when he was driving through Argun in his car. No one knows who was firing at whom. He was hit in the head but managed, barely conscious, to get away from the shooting. He then crashed his car into a telegraph post.

"Our motto is: Be extremely careful when entering your apartment – it's a minefield," Musa tries to make a joke of it.

His lips even curve to form a smile. But not for long.

Doctor Hasan asks me to come into the next ward. There Asya Khasuyeva, a smiling fair-haired beauty, is trying for the first time to get back on her feet. Asya and her family had returned home from the refugee camp in Ingushetia, to Okruzhnaya Street in Grozny's October district. She was walking in front, the children a little way behind, so she took the full impact of the explosion. She is only now learning to stand: it will take a great deal longer for her to walk again. The doctors performed three operations, trying to reconstruct her legs from what remained and restore some feeling. Even so she now has only half of her left leg which is covered in scars, while the right has no foot.

"Where are the children?"

"My husband took them back to Ingushetia. They're waiting in a tent there, hungry and cold, and they don't go to school. But they're alive. People don't lay mines for each other there."

Salman's Band

There are as many different Salmans as there are Ivans. Some make it hard to live, others help people survive. Judging by appearances Salman Raduyev,[63] who was formerly thought to be mentally ill, is now quite cured and lives far more comfortably in Lefortovo prison than the patients in Grozny Hospital No 9. There is another Salman, though, who is today probably the most popular doctor in Chechnya. Salman Yandarov heads the traumatology and orthopaedics department at the hospital and is already a legendary figure.

Yandarov is 62. He had everything in St Petersburg – a career, a professorial chair, a clinic and research facilities, students and admirers, medical congresses, published articles, and all the brandy and receptions that go with the job. He lacked for nothing. When it became clear, however, that there were no surgeons left in Chechnya and that more and more people were being crippled and injured by mines, Professor Yandarov renounced all the pleasures and temptations of civilised medicine and returned to the city he had left 40 years before. What does he possess today?

Nothing. To begin with, he has no home. Between operations and his tours of duty he moves from one friend to another, and they give him shelter and food. He is also without money. A short while back doctors were given a month's salary for the first time in half a year.

But that is not the most important thing, Salman and Hasan Khadjiev assure me. The hospital is crammed with the most seriously injured patients: amputees suffering from gangrene and sepsis, to which are added the penniless soldiers who urgently need operations.

But Hospital No 9 has absolutely nothing with which to get people back on their feet, let alone equip them with artificial limbs.

63 Jokhar Dudayev's nephew, Salman Raduyev, who led the January 1996 raid on Kizlyar (see Chapter 3), is today in the FSB prison in Moscow, awaiting trial on charges of terrorism.

There are no reagents for the X-rays, no medicines, no serums to combat gangrene, no Ilizarov appliances,[64] nor even anaesthetics. "It's absolutely surreal," says Salman Yandarov in the sad, slow, deliberate tones one adopts when speaking at a funeral. "Call it what you will, but one thing it's not is medicine in the late twentieth century. We're dragging people back from death with our bare hands. We have none of the things that are usually considered the achievements of traumatology in the last 50 years. We've returned to the 1950s as far as our methods of work are concerned."

Hamsat Elmurzayev, a 58-year-old traumatologist joins the discussion: "Tell them the most important thing, Salman! Methods? What methods? We're analysing urine samples here by taste and appearance. Just like in Ancient Greece. We don't even have reagents for analyses. It's inconceivable!" Hamsat is the third doctor on whom all depend in today's mine-ridden city. Every morning, as soon as the curfew ends, he goes out to the road leading from Starye Atagi to Grozny and tries to get a lift into the city. The distance is 24 kilometres. He used to have a house in the very centre, next to Minutka Square, but it was struck by a penetration bomb and now Hamsat has to pass several army posts where, like everyone else, he receives a daily portion of humiliation.

"I am a doctor," he tells the soldiers, who with deliberate slowness flip through his passport in search of rouble notes inserted between the pages. "I am in a hurry to get to my patients. Let me through."

The reply ("Stop!") is rude and categorical. So Hamsat stands there waiting, because there is no 50-rouble note in his passport. How could there be? Long ago it was reported to Moscow that the money to pay medical salaries had been transferred, yet the heroic doctors at Hospital No 9 have not had a sight of any for months. The only ones who remain, therefore, are the idealists. The rest have long since disappeared in search of a better future.

64 In the 1960s Professor Ilizarov devised innovative appliances for enabling
   damaged limbs to recover.

"Do you know how to carry out an operation, when you don't have the essential range of anaesthetics that any accident and emergency hospital like ours should have?" asks Dr Elmurzayev.

I don't know. They tell me the kinds of things that happen: the doctors are forced to break the law (according to the letter of our Criminal Code) rather than violate the Hippocratic oath.

Let me describe one of these crimes of salvation. It's obvious that no other narcotic substances, apart from those officially licensed, should enter the republic. Chechnya is a restricted area surrounded on all sides by checkpoints and army posts where a body search has replaced the morning shower. A private trader who tried smuggling drugs in those circumstances would be buying a one-way ticket to jail.

Official statements by Russia's Ministry of Health indicate that the Ministry of Health in Chechnya is receiving more or less the quantity of anaesthetics it requires. They're just not reaching the hospitals. Having legally passed all army posts and borders, accompanied by Health Ministry documentation, the narcotics immediately become a commodity for private dealers. You need an operation? Pay them. Who? Naturally they are front-men for someone else, these private chemists. Although neither doctors nor relatives of the wounded have the right to do so (it's a criminal offence!), they buy narcotics from under the counter. What choice do they have? Someone is already on the operating table; he's bleeding and at that moment the chemist appears, while the cost of every passing second could be the life of your patient.

Incidentally, this also applies to the seriously wounded soldier who has been brought to Hospital No 9 from one of the surrounding posts because there is no time to get him to the military hospital at Khankala. The doctors all chip in and then someone runs off to buy the necessary anaesthetics.

Why, you ask, does the health system force Drs Salman, Hamsat and Hasan to work in such conditions? Who's making a profit here? Where is Uvais Magomadov, the Minister of Health for Chechnya?

What can be taking up all of his time and energy?

Like everyone else in government, Magomadov prefers to keep well away from the hell that is Grozny and is sitting things out in Gudermes. Only when important officials from Moscow pay a visit to Chechnya does Magomadov return to Grozny. Then he is always with them, listening resignedly to the outraged cries of the patients and doctors who demand that he "do anything, but do something". After which he returns to his other affairs.

Next, a consignment of humanitarian aid is sent to Gudermes, to Mr Magomadov, thanks to the generosity of those same important officials: medicine, Ilizarov appliances, bandages, disinfectant, plaster of Paris . . . Many thanks. Above all from the members of Magomadov's family, because they lack nothing in this world. The reason is that these precious gifts can only be obtained hereafter from private chemists. Their prices are astronomical and people are forced to mortgage their apartments and houses so that one of their relatives can have an operation.

Why doesn't the prosecutor's office in the republic do something? It is also based in Gudermes, like Magomadov. The revolting and shameless behaviour of local officialdom, which now has its hands on the money and the goods, is as typical of Chechnya today as the ubiquitous anti-personnel mines and the ceaseless gunfire. The war has thrown up its Salman Raduyevs, its Salman Yandarovs and also its Uvais Mogamadovs. The only remaining question is which of them will win?

The patients in the wards are always better informed than the doctors. They begged me to expose this lawless and shameful situation so that people in Moscow finally understand: Hospital No 9 is the only place where operations are carried out today in Grozny and so medical supplies should be sent there directly, by-passing the warehouses of the Chechen Ministry of Health. They should be handed over directly to the doctors; otherwise everything they need to save people will only be available outside, in the market place.

There is one other reason for the very difficult situation now affecting Hospital No 9 and the health system in Chechnya as a whole. As is our custom, it is ideological in nature. At the federal Ministry of Health in Moscow it is hardly a secret that an unspoken principle reigns in every official's office. Why should any of them get upset and make efforts to send something down to Hospital No 9 if it is only going to help wounded Chechen fighters? This attitude has such a hold on our officials that it paralyses any attempt at control or supervision: the medicine was sent, and that's an end to it. There wasn't very much of it? Well, perhaps not. The military also add their arguments: "The Chechens are the ones laying mines and explosives, and they're the ones who get blown up. Serves them right."

"Nonsense," retorts Dr Yandarov, "I should know. If there are a great many fragmentation wounds then it means the victims are civilians. You'll find that in any textbook. In this hospital 95 per cent of the patients are suffering from shrapnel wounds, the rest from bullet wounds. As concerns wounded Chechen fighters I don't believe these fairy tales about hundreds of them crossing the mountains into Georgia and Azerbaijan, and then going on to Turkey. That's rubbish. You couldn't carry the seriously wounded across our mountains; they'd die before you got over them. That means that most of the fighters would surely be brought to us. Yet nothing of the kind is happening. So this war is being fought against civilians. I should know."

"But they say the fighting is over."

"The fighting continues. If there's no fighting then who are my patients?"

Everyone is tired of this war. Even of talking about it. At least, in my native Moscow. When you tell even very close friends and relatives on your return about that other world you are met with disbelief. A shadow of doubt crosses their faces and they think to themselves: "There she goes again, making up these hellish stories. Don't bother us. You'd do better to start thinking about the New Year celebrations."

All right, I'll give it some thought. But what will Isa Shashayev do now with the rest of his life? A 25-year-old Chechen, he stepped on a mine in his own apartment. For the last ten years he has faced the uncertainties, unemployment and the lack of a future that is life in Chechnya since 1991. Now, to crown it all, he is permanently disabled.

"What am I going to do, you ask?" says Isa. He retreats into his thoughts, sinking ever deeper beneath the blanket. "I'll play the bandit, of course. You lot don't expect anything else of us, do you . . . ?"

GROZNY

38

MURDER OR EXECUTION?

One Year On and Still No Investigation

22 January 2001

For the civilian population the tragedy in Novye Aldy was the most terrible incident of the second Chechen war. Yet there has never been a court case or even an investigation. The prosecutor-general's office is doing everything it can to make sure that no one is charged with the war crimes committed there.

Malika Labazanova comes from Novye Aldy on the outskirts of Grozny. She has worked at a bakery all her life and early each and every morning, with no break for holidays or weekends, she journeys into the city centre to work. That is the only joy she now has in life.

Only once has she ever had to stop work for a time and that interval split her life in two – before and after 5 February 2000. For during the taking of Grozny by federal forces that winter, Malika stayed at home and witnessed the brutal massacre the soldiers carried out in Novye Aldy on 5 February.

From 6 February onwards Malika herself was laying out the corpses in the basement. It was she who protected them from the hungry dogs and crows, and she who then buried the bodies. After which, she washed down the basement tiles.

That was not the end of the nightmare, however. A tragedy that claimed more than 100 victims was followed by another that drags on to this day. As a result Malika, who has never been involved in any kind of public activity, is today chairwoman of the Aldy committee, set up last autumn by the relatives of the victims. The committee's main goal is to make the authorities reply to one question, and one alone: who was responsible for the terrible death of their loved ones?

October 1999 to February 2000

In September and October 1999, after military operations began and Grozny came under fire, many inhabitants of Novye Aldy left for Ingushetia. Others remained behind and families were separated. The old people and those who looked after them decided to guard their homes from looters of every description, whether the newly arrived federal forces or their fellow citizens.

Those who stayed protected their houses and their village from the Chechen fighters. When the federal forces first moved into Grozny in early December the nearest positions held by Chechen armed groups were only two kilometres away (in the 20th precinct, another district of Grozny). There were no fighters in the village itself. Nevertheless throughout December 1999 and January 2000 Novye Aldy was mercilessly bombed and shelled every day.

People hid in their basements and only once in a while did they come out to draw water from the spring. As a result of these trips, 75 of the basement-dwellers died in two months. They were shot dead, or, lacking medical aid, they died from their wounds. Some were old people who simply could not take the stress, or withstand the hunger and the cold.

On 30 January, as we all know, a special military operation began to lure Chechen fighters out of Grozny – Shamanov's little trick. The Chechen field commanders were deliberately misinformed that, if they were prepared to pay, then the Feds were ready to create a corridor for their organised retreat from the city. The money was handed over, but the fighters soon found they had been led into a minefield. Meanwhile, federal artillery and aviation mercilessly struck at the surrounding villages through which lay the corridor that the General Staff had designated. Novye Aldy took its full share of the punishment.

On 3 February, when it became clear that federal troops were gradually taking over the positions of the Chechen fighters in the 20th precinct, a delegation from Novye Aldy, for the most part old men, set out under a white flag to talk to the commanding officers of the 15th motorised infantry regiment. The soldiers opened fire on the delegation and one of the Russians living in Novye Aldy was killed outright. Nevertheless the old men managed to persuade the soldiers to stop shelling the village and on the afternoon of 4 February it became quiet again in Novye Aldy.

Soon the first checks on people's ID documents and residence permits were carried out. The soldiers thumbed through the passports of those who had now emerged from the basements and said something strange to them: "Get out now. Those coming after us are animals. Their order is to kill." The old men did not believe this, however, and even decided that it was a trick to get them out of their houses so they could be looted.

On 5 February, from early morning, a second "cleansing" operation began in the village. It proved to be an irrational and bloody settling of scores with anyone who got in the way.

The Cleansing

Aza Bisultanova is a young schoolteacher. It's hard to understand what she's teaching the children today. How can she give any lessons now? She is still in a state of shock following what happened, though eleven months have passed. On 5 February her 68-year-old father, Akhmet Abulkhanov, died. "If only they'd just shot him . . ." she mutters.

It was Abulkhanov, a respected figure in Novye Aldy, who walked through the village on the morning of that Day of Judgement and persuaded people to leave their basements. It was he who chivvied the doubters: "Why do we need to hide any longer? Things will only get better from now on. If we stay in the basement the soldiers will think we're guilty of something. But we've done nothing wrong." It was Abulkhanov who took the hand of the smiling soldier who entered their courtyard and said, "Thank you, my boy. We were waiting for you. I'm glad to see you come at last."

"Take out your teeth, old man," said the soldier, "and bring some money as well, or I'll kill you."

Abulkhanov did not understand and continued to stroke the soldier's hand. But Malika Labazanova, who was standing nearby and would witness the reprisal that followed, quickly took off her earrings, handed over her wedding ring, and explained that the fillings in her teeth were not pure gold but simply plated. They allowed her to go to the neighbours and get some money. Malika came back and held out all that could be found: 300 roubles. The soldier took the notes and roared with laughter: "You call that money . . . ?"

They shot the old man, turning his execution into target practice that took off the top of his head. Next they killed three others. One had been disabled since childhood and tried desperately to make them listen: he was disabled, he had papers to prove it.

For some reason Malika was spared. She was ordered to drag the bodies into the basement and she obeyed. The soldiers decided to burn the cow alive in the barn. And also all of the sheep. The cow was already locked in when one of the young privates suddenly took pity on the beast and tried to help it escape the fire. His senior officer warned him to stop or he would kill him too. The blazing, terrified sheep ran from the fold, their mouths gaping, gasping for air, and dropped dead.

People too were burnt alive. Zina Abdulmejidova, Husein Abdulmejidov, Gula Khaidayev, Kaipa Yusupova, Yelena Kuznetsova and Victor Cheptura were so disfigured that one could no longer tell their age.

The only term for what happened is *hell on earth*.

To begin with, those villagers who by some miracle survived were convinced the soldiers were simply out of their minds. Perhaps insanity had led them to carry out this massacre or perhaps they'd been taking drugs. Someone in his right mind would never permit himself to do such a thing. All subsequent events, however, demonstrated that the motives behind the 5 February events were quite different.

For several weeks, contrary to all their traditions, the families did not bury their dead. They were waiting for staff from the prosecutor's office to take statements, begin an official inquiry, and carry out the necessary investigative procedures. When they could wait no longer, they buried their loved ones. Then they waited for death certificates to be issued. Only a few received them. However, soon the man from the Grozny prosecutor's office who had issued these documents specifying that knife wounds, bullet wounds and so on had been the cause of death was hurriedly transferred somewhere else. All to whom he had given such certificates were called in to the Zavodskoi district administration and ordered to hand them back in exchange for "death certificates on the new forms" (that was the explanation offered). These, it turned out, did not even contain an entry for the cause of death.

January 2001: One Year On

Soon a year will have passed since the atrocity in Novye Aldy, the Khatyn massacre of modern-day Russia.[65] There has been no investigation. During the entire eleven months since it happened, the witnesses have not once been questioned. No one has presumed to create photofit pictures of the criminals, though many of the killers did not hide their faces.

Photofit descriptions, indeed! The majority of the affected families have not even received death certificates. They have almost nothing to present in court, in order to assert their constitutional right to justice.

65 All the inhabitants of the Belorussian village of Khatyn, several hundred people, were massacred or burned alive by German soldiers in 1942.

Today it is quite obvious that the investigation by the Prosecutor-General's office has been successfully halted. Officially the office fobs off any interested parties from Novye Aldy with the assertion that they are monitoring the situation. To everyone else involved they offer the shameless lie that the Chechens, faithful to their customs, refuse to allow the bodies to be exhumed and therefore the investigation is prevented from going ahead.

This lie is logical and understandable if, of course, you look at things from the point of view of those shielding the killers. Hardly any civilians have the chance to check anything since Grozny is almost constantly closed for outside visitors. *Novaya gazeta* has managed to discover a little, however.

The inhabitants of Novye Aldy, it turns out, no matter how terrible they may find it, are begging, pleading and demanding that all the necessary exhumation procedures be completed. They insist that the chief material evidence in this investigation, the bullets that were fired, finally be removed from the bodies and then it will be possible to establish who were the monsters in military uniform that carried out the massacre. The response to all these persistent demands was an outrageous insult. A brigade of forensic experts from the military roared into the village and demanded that people add their signatures to already completed forms stating that the relatives refused to permit exhumation.

The Prosecutor-General's office – which has proved so responsive when the oligarchs are under discussion[66] – begins to wriggle and make excuses in this case. Lower-ranking staff at the office who have had something to do with the Novye Aldy case will agree to "speak out" only if they are given complete anonymity. It is as though they were being asked to reveal the State's most highly guarded nuclear secrets. They say there is pressure from the very highest authority and orders

66 Since Putin's election as President the two most prominent media magnates in Russia Boris Berezovsky and Vladimir Gusinsky have been pursued by the prosecutor's office on a variety of charges and have both taken refuge abroad.

have been given to halt the investigation, codenamed "5 February".
Under no circumstances does Putin want to quarrel with the country's
leading military figures.

Our sources in the Prosecutor-General's office tell us that if the
Novye Aldy nightmare were exhaustively investigated and led to
charges against individual officers, then other similar cases would
follow. The staff we talked to also referred to their own fears, since
the officers who risk being prosecuted for these atrocities have
supposedly been threatening them as well.

That's a little hard to believe, of course. Only time will tell.
Meanwhile we must accept the fact that among the majors, colonels
and generals that the country is praising, defending and decorating
with awards there are also war criminals. Among the heroes are a
percentage of unspeakable scum. And we all live together, side by side.

Not long ago, on 23 November, Hasan Musaev was buried in
Novye Aldy. On 5 February 2000 this old man had watched as four of
his relatives were shot dead. He fell to the ground and a soldier held
a gun to his head when he heard a voice say: "You can live. And
suffer because we didn't shoot you."

Old Hasan certainly suffered and he died from his third heart
attack. Surely no one in Russia feels any relief at that?

CHECHNYA—MOSCOW

POSTSCRIPT

In January 2001 the Parliamentary Assembly of the Council of Europe (PACE) gathered for its quarterly session to consider whether to restore voting rights to the Russian Federation. When this sanction was imposed in protest against the war in Chechnya there had been talk of expelling Russia altogether from the Council of Europe.

Three days before the vote, President Putin confirmed that the size of the armed forces contingent in Chechnya (by then 80,000 strong) would be reduced. Henceforth the "anti-terrorist" campaign in the North Caucasus would be headed not by the Minister of Defence but by the director of the Federal Security Service (FSB). The fighting was over, in other words; all that remained was to track down and eliminate the remaining terrorists. The Assembly noted some "encouraging if limited developments" in Chechnya and on 26 January 2001 Russian voting rights in PACE were restored.

On 18 February Anna Politkovskaya finally reached the mountainous southern area of Chechnya. Until then her reports had come from the republic's central plain and the foothills south of Grozny. Now, in response to an extraordinary demand for resettlement sent to *Novaya gazeta* by 90 families in the Vedeno district, she travelled south to investigate stories of conditions so unbearable that the villagers wished to leave their homes and Chechnya itself.[67]

After hearing first-hand accounts of torture and mistreatment, talking to the paratroopers based outside Khatuni village, and seeing the deep pits where Chechen suspects and detainees were kept, Politkovskaya herself was arrested by local FSB officers on 20 February. For a night and day she was verbally abused, intimidated, and threatened with rape and "execution" before being released on 22 February. She submitted a written complaint to the chief military prosecutor and in an interview with NTV she said: "After seeing how they treated me, a journalist, I am convinced that all the complaints of local residents about how they are mistreated are true."

To join the Council of Europe in February 1996, Russia had signed both the European Convention on Human Rights and the Convention Against Torture and Other Cruel, Inhuman or Degrading Treatment or Punishment. Its most public reservation concerned abolition of the death penalty, but even here it imposed and, for the most part, observed a moratorium (leaving some 700 on death row). There was no outside agency, however, that could make the Russian government respect and honour the provisions of these and other international treaties. It was not a Bosnia or a Somalia, a "weak" or "failed" state where any national or international force might intervene. It was up to pressure groups within Russia to monitor and attempt to restrain Putin and his administration.

Several million people across the country continued each week to read critical reports about the Chechen war in a handful of outspoken periodicals. Many more had access to the sceptical accounts of the daily press ("That's the sixth time since spring that the military have won 'the decisive battle'," *Izvestiya* dryly observed in September 2000). Yet national TV stations were tamed and generally obedient.

---

67 The letter had already been sent to all the relevant military and civil authorities in Moscow and Chechnya with little result. Politkovskaya travelled to Khatuni with the knowledge and permission of the new Chechnya government.

Long before NTV was taken over by pro-government management in April 2001, the country's only independent television channel had been noticeably muted in its coverage of the second Chechen campaign. In this stifling media climate, public outrage and objection were slow to accumulate in Russia's vast hinterland (it is, after all, the largest country in the world).

Opinion polls did reveal a shift in mood against the fighting. In early 2000, 68 per cent supported a war to the finish. By January 2001 the total was down to 45 per cent. The sheer speed and ruthlessness of the Russian campaign had taken its Chechen opponents by surprise, and public opinion in the rest of the country was similarly wrong-footed. Sympathy for the Chechen cause among more liberal Russians had been ebbing for some time, however, well before the bombings in Moscow provoked a wave of fear and revulsion.

Chechnya's fate in 1994–6 became a matter of central concern for Russia's intelligentsia, well aware of the injustice of wartime deportation that the Chechens shared with the Crimean Tatars, the Ingush, Kalmyks and Volga Germans. Opposition to the first war in Chechnya was, for many, motivated by a consciousness of this historical wrong and by the threat the fighting posed to Russia's fragile new democracy. By 1999 the mood had changed. The intelligentsia, liberal political opinion and the human rights agenda were less prominent and influential. The mass mobilisation of the reforming years could not be maintained. A certain fatigue and the apparent achievement of so many of the sought-for political and economic freedoms had led to a lessening of interest in politics and popular activism.

There was also disappointment with what had been happening in Chechnya between 1996 and 1999. Russian reports from the republic were not just media manipulation: stories of hostage-taking, corruption, mistreatment of the remaining Russian population, and the introduction of public executions and punishments repelled opinion in the rest of the country. When, in the wake of the Daghestan events and the Moscow bombings, the government assured everyone that these problems would at last be rapidly and decisively tackled[68] there was an almost palpable sense of relief. It took many weeks for doubts and concerns about the effectiveness (not to mention legality) of the "anti-terrorist" campaign to catch up with events. By then the political landscape in Russia had critically altered.

The West also seemed ready to suspend judgement if this "more authoritarian" approach to an internal matter proved successful. Putin's parliamentary gains in late 1999 won guarded international approval: he could now resume reform of the economy, and prominent economic liberals in Russia assured the rest of the world that he would. Past experience justified caution. The International Monetary Fund had indirectly helped to finance the first Chechen war by continuing to hand over funds intended to support economic reforms. In November 2000, an IMF team returned from Moscow after failing to reach agreement with the Russian authorities on any new loans. Yet with world oil prices at a record high, Russia, the world's fourth largest exporter, for the time being had ample additional resources to finance its campaign. Meanwhile, the hitherto oppositionist parliament, which attempted to impeach Yeltsin in 1998 over his waging of the last Chechen war, had been largely neutralised. A curious incident highlighted this change.

In late September 1999, watchful residents in the provincial town of Ryazan spotted men moving suspicious objects into the basement of their apartment block. The local police evacuated the building and their bomb-disposal expert identified and defused a powerful explosive device. Two days later, however, the FSB in Moscow announced that this had been merely a training exercise by the Service and the sacks actually contained sugar. Despite official displeasure, *Novaya*

---

68 A symptomatic change in attitude was expressed by Alexander Solzhenitsyn, the great proponent of Russian isolationism and "self-limitation". In 1992, he said, he had advised Yeltsin not to use force on Chechnya, but cordon off the country south of the Terek; now he saw military intervention as the only answer.

gazeta returned repeatedly to this subject and in spring 2000 liberal opposition deputies tried to ensure a full and detailed parliamentary investigation. The motion was blocked by an alliance of Communist deputies and Putin's supporters in the Duma.

All were agreed that without the restoration of genuine law and order in Chechnya there could be no way out of the present impasse. It was critically important for the courts to give an open, honest and fair assessment of all the criminal acts committed since August 1999. Only this could begin to restore some of the damage done to Chechen-Russian relations – and to Russia's democratic institutions. In spring 2001 two trials offered an uncertain contribution of this kind.

In Makhachkala on 19 March, sentence was passed on those accused of the Buinaksk explosion on 4 September 1999. The Daghestan Supreme Court condemned the organisers, local Wahhabites Isa Zainutdinov and Alisultan Salikhov, to life imprisonment and two other accomplices to nine years each. And in Rostov-on-Don, 37-year-old Colonel Yury Budanov of the 160th tank regiment was put on trial. The first federal officer to be charged with committing a crime in Chechnya in either war, Budanov was initially accused of torturing, raping and murdering a young Chechen woman. The case was unprecedented.

The civil prosecutor-general's office had shown no enthusiasm for investigating the numerous allegations and appeals concerning abuses in Chechnya; the body with direct responsibility for the military was even less forthcoming. In December 2000, presidential aide Sergei Yastrzhembsky released details of the activities of the chief military prosecutor's office in 1999 and 2000: of the 748 crimes by servicemen it had investigated, most concerned minor offences and internal discipline and those convicted were very junior (248 privates, 10 corporals and a single officer). Only 37 of the military prosecutor's current investigations referred to events in Chechnya.

Yet in June 2000, Vladimir Kalamanov, the President's recently-appointed Special Representative for Human Rights in Chechnya, reported that in three months he and his staff had received complaints and appeals from 5,689 individuals. The tank commander's case, however, had been personally taken up by Anatoly Kvashnin, head of the General Staff. Apparently with the support of Putin, Kvashnin insisted on Budanov's immediate arrest.

Perhaps Budanov was a scapegoat, but his actions, and those of his subordinates, were particularly horrifying. They were committed off-duty, not in the heat of battle or under the pressure of "active operations". After voting in the presidential elections on 25 March 2000, Colonel Budanov and his colleagues celebrated his three-year-old daughter's birthday by getting drunk, and then went out that night and abducted Elza Kungayeva. On returning to the unit they tortured, raped and strangled the 18-year-old, on the pretext of interrogating her for information about the Chechen fighters. Then they tried to conceal the body.

"There is no adult in Russia who has not heard of this trial," remarked the *Segodnya* daily on 17 March 2001, as the case continued its slow progress through the courts. Budanov stood accused of abduction and murder. His superior officer, General Shamanov, now governor of the Ulyanov Region, and General Troshev, head of the North Caucasus Military District, spoke out in his defence. As the trial began in Rostov, a picket of extreme Russian nationalists outside the court harassed the family of the dead woman and even the judge Major Kostin.

Society was divided. Many assumed that if Kungayeva were proved to have been a sniper then Budanov should be absolved. The president's Special Representative, Kalamanov, was robust in denouncing such attitudes: "People who think like that are not just juridically but morally illiterate," he told a Moscow newspaper. Budanov's conviction did not seem in doubt. The charges and the duration of his likely sentence were. His subordinates had already been amnestied, and the charge of posthumous rape shifted to them; if Budanov's lawyer was successful in his plea of temporary insanity and his client received the lighter three-year sentence the chances were that he would also be amnestied and out of prison in little more than a year (just like the coup-plotters of 1991 and the Supreme Soviet leaders in 1993).

Faced with such limited protection from the Russian courts, and their complete absence in Chechnya, the victims of the conflict in the North Caucasus began to use their right of appeal to the Court of Human Rights in Strasburg. Sixteen such applications, prepared with the aid of Memorial, had been submitted by November 2000 and, grouped together as three cases, were then receiving the Court's active consideration: the 29 October 1999 bombing of a column of refugees; the murder of inhabitants of Grozny's Staropromyslovsky district during a "cleansing" operation in January 2000; and the deaths of civilians in Katyr-Yurt caught in a trap set for Chechen fighters on 4 February 2000. By March 2001, almost 100 individual applications had been made to the Court. Yet the fate of Russia was not to be decided in Strasburg.

The first anniversary of President Putin's inauguration in May would coincide with the continuing examination of the repellent Budanov in Rostov. There were no signs that the collective and apparently systematic acts of brutality against civilians during the campaign were also to be publicly investigated. The military prosecutor's office offered the extraordinary suggestion that Ukrainian mercenaries had been responsible for the killings in Alkhan-Yurt and Novye Aldy. Official reactions to the discovery in early March 2001 of a mass grave near the army base of Khankala were not encouraging. Up to 50 bodies showing clear signs of extra-judicial execution were exhumed, but serious forensic investigation was obstructed. Called on to support international investigation of this and other alleged atrocities, Vladimir Kalamanov rhetorically demanded in Geneva, where he was attending the session of the UN Human Rights Committee, "Who is more independent than the President's special representative?"

Foreign reaction seemed a mixture of unfounded trust in the Russian President's assurances and tacit acknowledgement of international impotence. "Russia's seat on the UN Security Council must not allow it to evade scrutiny of its human rights record," asserted Amnesty International. If other countries could do little to change the situation, however, perhaps it was best to keep quiet about it?

"Many European politicians do not want to see what is really going on in Chechnya", a Memorial report regretfully concluded in January 2001, "and are prepared to take the desire for reality."

Yet as Anna Politkovskaya argues repeatedly in her reports, the longer it takes for the lawlessness and abuses in Chechnya to end, the greater the danger to Russia itself. The suspension of the constitution in that small republic puts democracy and free speech throughout Russia at risk. And that is a danger that no one can ignore.

JOHN CROWFOOT

25 April 2001

CHRONOLOGY

Russia and Chechnya

1991 *January*: Soviet tanks in Lithuania met by strong local resistance and international outcry. *February*: Yeltsin visits Estonia and condemns attacks on the Baltic States. *June*: Yeltsin defeats Communist Ryzhkov in elections to become first President of RSFSR (Soviet Russia). *August*: Attempted coup d'etat against USSR President Gorbachev. Three die in Moscow. *6 September*: In Chechnya, Dudayev's supporters storm parliament building in Grozny. Later this date became Independence Day. *December*: End of Soviet Union. All 15 of its constituent republics become sovereign and independent states; eight join to form the new Commonwealth of Independent States.

1992 *January*: Beginning of economic shock therapy in Russia. Prices freed and rise 8–20 times. Free street trading allowed. Gamsakhurdia, President of Georgia, overthrown. Dudayev gives him refuge. *July*: Russia joins International Monetary Fund (IMF) and gets $1 billion loan. *October*: Privatisation of the economy begins.

1993 *January*: Fears of hyperinflation in Russia as monthly inflation runs at 30 per cent. Moscow supports Abkhazians in their struggle against the Georgian government. Basayev gains battle experience at head of Abkhaz battalion. *June*: Abulfaz Elchibei, President of Azerbaijan, overthrown in coup. *4 October*: Storm of Supreme Soviet building in Moscow. Hardcore supporters of parliament refuse to accept dissolution. 100–200 defenders die. *December*: Voters approve new Russian Constitution but in elections to new parliament, the Duma, choose a majority of Communist and nationalist deputies.

1994 *15 February*: Tatarstan reaches separate agreement on its status with Moscow leaving Chechnya isolated as the only non-signatory of the new Federation Treaty. *11 December*: Federal forces enter Chechnya to "restore constitutional order".

1995 By *March* rouble begins to stabilise, monthly inflation 10 per cent. *17 December*: New Duma elections give Communists strong showing and make their leader prime contender in coming presidential elections.

1996 With one-figure rating in polls, Yeltsin says he will run for President. IMF conditionally agrees $10.2 billion loan. *21 April*: Dudayev killed by Russian rocket. *July*: Yeltsin wins second round in presidential elections, gaining 54 per cent to Communist Zyuganov's

40 per cent. *August*: Peace brokered with Chechnya at Khasavyurt by Alexander Lebed.

1997   *January*: Maskhadov elected President of Chechnya in election monitored by the Organisation for Security and Co-operation in Europe (OSCE). *July*: Yeltsin announces that industrial depression has ended.

1998   *January*: Symbolic end to inflation. 1,000 rouble note becomes a rouble, kopecks reappear. *17 August*: Russia defaults on $40 billion in short-term debts and devalues the rouble by 200 per cent. *December*: Four Western engineers beheaded in Chechnya.

1999   Early in year Maskhadov reluctantly establishes Sharia law in Chechnya. *March*: Bombing of Kosovo. *May*: Russian forces dash to Pristina. Oil prices reach 30-year high. *August*: Third successive Russian Prime Minister with a background in the security services appointed. Vladimir Putin succeeds Sergei Stepashin.

Second Chechen War

1999
August

7   Self-styled Wahhabites from Chechnya, led by Shamil Basayev and the Saudi warrior Khattab, stage an armed rebellion in neighbouring Daghestan. They take over seven villages near the border.

9   Vladimir Putin, Head of the Federal Security Service (FSB), is nominated Prime Minister by Yeltsin. (The Duma later confirms the appointment in the first vote.)

13   Moscow warns that Islamist bases will be attacked, "even in Chechnya".

15   Chechen President Aslan Maskhadov declares a state of emergency.

25   Federal forces take back the Daghestan villages of Tando and Rakhata.

31   Bomb explodes in Moscow's Manege shopping centre: five seriously injured. Two separatist Islamic villages in northern Daghestan (Karamakhi and Chabanmakhi) are captured by federal forces.

September

4   Federal planes bomb Chechen villages next to the Daghestan border. 62 Russian soldiers and members of their families die in an explosion in Buinaksk (Daghestan).

8   93 die in Moscow apartment block bombing.

13   116 die in second Moscow apartment block bombing. Yeltsin announces a nationwide "anti-terrorist campaign".

14–20   15,000 are expelled from Moscow and 69,200 made to re-register in "Operation Foreigner". "Unity" Party backing Putin formed to contest parliamentary elections in two months' time.

Federal armed forces (20,000–30,000 strong) mass along the frontiers of Chechnya.

16 17 die in Volgodonsk bombing in southern Russia.
23 Grozny is bombarded by the Russian air force for first time since 1994–5. Police in Ryazan find and defuse explosives in an apartment block.

October
1 Russian troops enter Chechnya. Prime Minister Putin announces that he no longer recognises the legitimacy of Maskhadov's government.
5 Maskhadov imposes martial law in Chechnya.
6–10 Chechen forces withdraw from the north of the republic, retreating behind the Terek River.
18 Russian army enters the suburbs of Grozny.
21 Ground-to-ground missiles hit Grozny. Chechen side announces 137 dead.
27 Second missile attack, leaving reported 112 dead (Chechen sources).
29 Refugee column fleeing towards Ingushetia is bombed by federal forces.

November
12 Russian army enters Gudermes, second largest town in republic.
17 Capture of Bamut. Missile bombardment of Grozny and Urus-Martan.
18 OSCE summit meeting in Istanbul demands that Russia seek a "political solution" to the conflict (Organisation for Security and Cooperation in Europe).
end Nov As a result of two months fighting around a quarter of a million refugees from Chechnya flee to neighbouring Ingushetia.

December
2 Federal forces enter Argun.
6 Russians take Urus-Martan. Civilians in Grozny are given an ultimatum: they must leave Grozny by 11 December.
10 European Union threatens Moscow with sanctions. Moscow repeats its ultimatum.
12–20 Federal troops penetrate several areas of Grozny and announce the capture of the city's civilian and military airports.
19 Elections to Duma, the lower house of parliament. The new Unity Party, built around the figure of Putin, gets almost as many votes as the Communists.
20–21 Violent battles near Serzhen-Yurt, 25 miles south-east of Grozny.
25 Attack on Grozny. About 2,000 Chechen fighters prepare for house-to-house fighting.
27 Maskhadov declares that Grozny will be defended to the last.
31 President Yeltsin resigns and Putin takes over as acting president.

2000

January

3–6   Chechen fighters recapture Alkhan-Kala and Alkhan-Yurt, but are forced to withdraw after three days.

7   Moscow announces the suspension of operations in Grozny, in order to protect civilians and avoid an ecological catastrophe. Shamanov and Troshev are replaced by new military commanders.

10   Moscow revokes the truce in response to Chechen attacks in different localities.

12   Federal troops retake Argun, Shali and Gudermes following their temporary occupation by Chechen fighters.

16   Federal troops launch a new offensive to capture Grozny.

18   Committees of Soldiers' Mothers dispute official figures: they claim that 3,000 have already been killed and 5,000 wounded in the present campaign.

29   The defenders of Grozny begin to surrender. By 1 February, 216 have laid down their arms.

31   Minutka Square captured in centre of Grozny.

February

1   Chechen fighters withdraw from the capital.

3–4   Russian army proceeds to "cleanse" Grozny. Chechens confirm that most of their armed men have left the city.
Main army spokesman Manilov says there are 93,000 federal troops in Chechnya.

6   Putin announces on television that "the operation to liberate Grozny is over".
Fighting continues in mountainous south of country where the Chechen fighters have regrouped, notably in and around the encircled settlements of Shatoi and Komsomolskoe.

29   Released Radio Liberty journalist Andrei Babitsky describes abuse of detainees at the Chernokozovo filtration centre near Grozny.

March

3   During the capture of Shatoi, federal troops free two Polish scientists being held as hostages by a Chechen band.

5   Heavy fighting around Komsomolskoe where the fighters have regrouped (according to Russians, there are 2,000 of them).
Putin visits Grozny and announces there will be a reduction to 23,000 of a permanent garrison stationed in the country.

21–22   Komsomolskoe taken by federal forces.

26   Russian presidential elections: Putin wins in first round, taking 52.9 per cent of the vote.

29   Chechen ambush of a Russian armoured column near Argun (fighters claim 60 dead). Despite assertion of Russian General Staff, Chechen fighters continue to move freely.

April

1–4   Mary Robinson, high commissioner for UN, visits Chechnya. She denounces human rights infringements by Russian troops.

6   Parliamentary Assembly of the Council of Europe suspends the voting rights of the Russian delegation and demands that the Council of Ministers begins procedure to expel Russia.

10   In interview with biggest circulation Russian daily news-paper, Chechen president Maskhadov declares himself ready to enter a dialogue without prior conditions.

13   Kremlin indicates it is ready to enter discussion with Chechen representatives.

May

7   Putin inaugurated as Russian president.

11   11 soldiers die in Chechnya after rocket-propelled grenade attack.

13   Seven presidential plenipotentiaries appointed to rein in the Russian regions; General Kazantsev is put in charge of the Southern Area, administered from Rostov.

17   2,500 Chechen "policemen" (led by Gantamirov) disbanded.
Sergei Zverev, deputy to Koshman, the Russian-appointed administrator of Chechnya, is killed in an ambush.

30   Koshman dismisses Gantamirov for absenteeism.

June

8   "Temporary" presidential rule established. The Mufti of Chechnya Kadyrov replaces Koshman.

25   Troshev, now military commander for the North Caucasus Military District, claims that the war is over.

July

2–3   Five suicide-bombing attacks. Total of 42 soldiers die at Argun, Gudermes, Urus-Martan and two other localities.

9   Bombs in Vladikavkaz and Rostov kill eight.

13   Gantamirov is appointed Kadyrov's deputy and mayor of Grozny, but almost immediately has armed confrontation with Gudermes leader.

August

8   Bomb in central Moscow underpass kills 12 and injures 97.

12   *Kursk* submarine sinks.

18   In defiance of the authorities, newspapers publish a list of servicemen aboard the *Kursk*.

20   By-election for Duma seat in Chechnya. Retired Interior Ministry general Aslanbek Aslakhanov beats 11 other candidates, gets 31 per cent of the votes.

September

9 *Moscow Times* claims up to 1.3 million "dead souls" voted for Putin in presidential elections. Half a million votes cast for him in Daghestan were doubtful.

October

6 Largest oil discovery in world for last 30 years claimed after preliminary exploration of Kashagan deposit in Caspian Sea.
Three explosions in Stavropol Region; two in Nevinnomysk and one at Pyatigorsk rail station.

12 Seven killed in explosion outside police station in Grozny.

26 Report by Human Rights Watch denounces "indiscriminate and disproportionate" federal bombing, and documents widespread arbitrary detention, torture and extortion.

29 Seven federal soldiers and two local waitresses killed in café blast. Trial begins of three former paratroopers accused of murdering journalist Dmitry Kholodov in October 1994.

November

9 Russia's Security Council declares intention to reduce the armed forces by 600,000 (or 20 per cent of total) by the year 2005.

13–15 Media magnates Berezovsky and Gusinsky fail to appear at the prosecutor's office, on charges of fraud and embezzlement. Arrest warrants are subsequently issued.

22 IMF mission leaves Moscow without reaching new agreement. Almost certain that Russia cannot now restructure its debt of $3.9 billion to the Paris Club.

December

3 Federal aviation bombed suspected concentrations of Chechen armed groups in Shali district and Vedeno Gorge.

9 A *Moskvich* automobile packed with explosive blew up next to the mosque in Alkhan-Yurt, killing 22.

12 Two Russian army privates kidnapped in Vladikavkaz on 4 December were freed in Sernovodsk.

20 Five students of the Grozny teacher-training college were killed, and four others wounded, in a mortar attack.

28 Residential buildings belonging to the Akhmadov brothers in the centre of Urus Martan were blown up by the security services.

2001
January

22 Putin announces cuts in armed presence in Chechnya and transfer of anti-terrorist operation to FSB.

25 PACE restores voting rights of Russian delegation, claiming a change in heart by the federal administration.

BIOGRAPHICAL NOTES

Aushev, Ruslan
(*b.*1954) Major-General, in Soviet Army since 1971, veteran of Afghan campaign (1980–87). President of Ingushetia since March 1993.

Basayev, Shamil
(*b.*1965) Most famous Chechen field commander, anathemised by Russian authorities as a terrorist. Studied in Moscow in 1980s and lived by trading computers. In November 1991 hijacked plane to Turkey; in 1992–3 led Chechen battalion fighting for Abkhazian separatists against Georgians; a leader of the defence of Grozny, 1994–5; led June 1995 raid on Budyonnovsk; in 1997 lost presidential elections to Maskhadov and briefly entered his government.

Berezovsky, Boris
(*b.*1946) Media magnate and politician. Research associate at Academy of Sciences institute who moved from car dealership, into finance and gained influence over various media outlets, above all Channel One TV (ORT). Out of favour following Yeltsin's resignation.

Dudayev, Jokhar
(1944–96) First President of Chechnya (1991–6). In Soviet air force and away from Chechnya since 1962 (with Russian wife Alla). Service in Afghanistan, based in Estonia 1987–90; in 1990 returned home, and led Chechen revolution. Killed in April 1996 when rocket tracked his satellite phone signal.

Gantamirov, Beslan
(*b.*1963) Policeman turned businessman. Organiser of National Guard that helped Dudayev to power. Mayor of Grozny 1991–3, then went into opposition. Arrested and imprisoned in Moscow on fraud charges, May 1996. Returned to Chechnya in support of federal forces, October 1999. Again Mayor of Grozny from June 2000.

Kadyrov, Ahmad-Hadji
(*b.*1951) Chief Mufti of Chechnya 1995–9; from June 2000 head of provisional administration appointed by Moscow (see Chapter 23).

Kazantsev, Victor
General. Overall commander of combined forces in Chechnya. Head of North Caucasus Military District; in May 2000 appointed presidential "super-governor" for the Southern Area.

Khattab
Alias of Saudi-born citizen fighting in Chechnya since February 1995. Veteran of Afghanistan, he brought with him mujahedin, self-professed Wahhabis, of Saudi and North African origin.

Kovalyov, Sergei
(*b.*1930) Veteran human rights activist. In prison camps and internal exile from 1974 to 1984; member of every

Russian parliament since 1990. He stood down in 1999. Presidential human rights commissioner 1993–6 and most prominent critic of first war; spent winter of 1994–5 in Grozny as federal aviation bombed the Chechen capital.

Lebed, Alexander   (*b.*1950) Lieutenant-General turned politician. Served in Afghanistan and "hot spots" of former Soviet Union, especially Moldova (1992–5). Ran for president in June 1996; in Yeltsin's admin-istration until his dismissal in October 1996, signed peace accords with Chechnya. In May 1998 elected governor of Krasnoyarsk Region, Siberia.

Maskhadov, Aslan   (*b.*1951) Colonel. Soviet army officer, 1969–91. Served in Baltic States and took part in January 1991 action by Soviet forces against Lithuanian independence activists. Chief of Staff of Chechen forces 1993–7; elected president of Chechnya in 1997.

Putin, Vladimir   (*b.*1952) President of Russia, elected March 2000. KGB officer for 15 years (7 spent in Dresden), moved to Petersburg city administration, 1990–6 becoming deputy mayor; 1996 joined presidential staff, 1998 headed FSB (KGB successor), August 1999 appointed prime minister. Acting president in January 2000.

Shamanov, Anatoly   (*b.*1957) Major-General served in both Chechen wars. Elected governor of Ulyanovsk Region in December 2000 (see Chapter 22).

Shoigu, Sergei   (*b.*1955) Builder. RF Minister for Emergency Situations, 1991–9, led column of humanitarian aid to Serbia in spring 1999; made leader of Unity Party backing Putin.

Starovoitova, Galina   (1946–98) Ethnographer who became Russia's most prominent woman politician. Yeltsin adviser on nation-alities and ethnic policy 1990–2; from 1989 deputy of each successive Soviet and Russian legislative body. Led rump of "Democratic Russia" movement that supported Yeltsin in 1989–92. Shot dead in Petersburg.

Yeltsin, Boris   (*b.*1931) Communist Party leader in Urals from 1968, transferred to Moscow in 1985, became a figurehead of radical opposition in Soviet Union, 1987–91. Elected President of Russia in June 1991; re-elected in July 1996. Started both wars in Chechnya. Resigned on New Year's Eve 2000.

INDEX

(Biog) indicates a reference in the Biographical Notes